Scoops and Swindles

By the same author

SCOOPS AND SWINDLES

MEMOIRS OF A FLEET STREET JOURNALIST

Alfred Draper

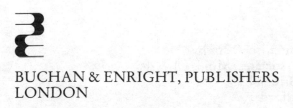

BUCHAN & ENRIGHT, PUBLISHERS
LONDON

First published in 1988 by
Buchan & Enright, Publishers,
(Fountain Press Ltd)
45 The Broadway
Tolworth
Surrey KT6 7DW

British Library Cataloguing in Publication Data
Draper, Alfred
    Scoops and swindles : memoirs of a Fleet
    Street journalist
    1. Journalism – England – London –
    History – 20th century
    I. Title
    070'.92'4   PN5129.L6

ISBN 0-907675-73-5

To those old Fleet Street friends who
helped to dust off the cobwebs of my memory

Photoset in Garamond 11/12pt by
Derek Doyle & Associates, Mold, Clwyd
Printed in Great Britain by
Biddles Ltd, Guildford

Contents

ILLUSTRATIONS

1

THE FAREWELL PARTY

I paused at the Ludgate Circus end of Fleet Street to take a last look at the wall plaque which bore the elegantly chiselled profile of Edgar Wallace and his rather Kiplingesque epitaph:

HE KNEW WEALTH & POVERTY, YET HAD
WALKED WITH KINGS & KEPT HIS BEARING.
OF HIS TALENTS HE GAVE LAVISHLY
TO AUTHORSHIP – BUT TO FLEET STREET
HE GAVE HIS HEART.

Although he died in Hollywood rich and famous, his love for The Street had never deserted him, whereas my own affair, in the words of the popular song, had been too hot not to cool down.

I reckoned that I would need a calculator to work out how many times I had passed the plaque on the way up the slight incline to the black glass building which housed the *Daily Express* and which was known to the journalists employed there as the 'paper palace' or the 'glass house', depending on whether they were on a peak or in a trough.

On that evening in mid-August the words on the plaque were rather blurred, for I was leaving The Street where I had spent so much of my working life. It would be nice to record that it was tears that made the reading difficult, but that would be a travesty of the truth. There was no sorrow, sweet or sour, in my parting. If my eyes were glazed and my speech slurred it was because I had just left my farewell party.

I had spent thirteen years on the *Express*, and had also worked on the *Mail* and the now defunct *Daily Herald*, and as I waited for the traffic light to change so that I could negotiate the road into the City – no one was ever arrested there for being drunk; if you were the worse for wear a kindly bobby escorted you back into the Met area: the City did not want to acquire that kind of reputation – I reflected on the hours I had spent waking and sleeping, dreaming of the day when I would get to Fleet Street. Now I was departing, and although the future looked distinctly bleak I did not have the slightest regret. I had a cheque for £5,000 in my pocket, eight golf balls distributed around the various pockets of my suit and raincoat (there should have been a dozen but someone had pinched four), and an envelope containing what was left of a parting whip-round from my colleagues. But I had no job to go to and no intention of ever taking another in The Street. I had left once before and had returned, and I was determined there would be no repeat performance. It had been a topsy-turvy marriage, and now the divorce was final. I was rather like the man who wakes up one morning, looks across the pillow towards the person to whom he has sworn undying love and wonders what the attraction had been. I find it difficult to remember when the dream began to fade and the tinsel to lose its glitter. Beaverbrook claimed that the *Express* stood 'on the sunny side of the street'; for me there had been a total eclipse. I don't know what brought about the change because I was reasonably highly regarded on the *Express* and my by-line regularly appeared above my work. But something had occurred and Fleet Street no longer held my interest, certainly it had not claimed my heart. I had changed, but so too had The Street.

The accountants had moved in, and the newspaper world had lost its brash glamour. A shadow was beginning to settle over the golden days. Days could pass without you ever leaving the office. The bedside telephone seldom rang in the middle of the night with a voice at the other end telling you to pack a bag and head for London Airport where a ticket to some faraway place was waiting to be collected along with some cash and a folder of travellers cheques. Even those murders which used to keep you out of town for weeks at a time were now seldom more than one-off stories. The end of capital punishment may have been enlightened but it had knocked the drama out of murder. And I had begun to notice that young reporters looked upon old hands such as myself as rather rare birds, a species now endangered. They seldom went out of town, and dreamed in vain of their first foreign assignment. The writing on the wall was clearly decipherable.

I had witnessed the demise of many famous titles, including the *Daily Herald* and the *News Chronicle*, circulations everywhere were plummeting, and the future of many more newspapers was threatened as a money crisis developed; and when economies were made it was always the editorial department which suffered the brunt. Foreign bureaux were closed, and a penny-pinching policy adopted towards news-gathering, apparently with no one realising the one salient fact – that it was news which sold papers. Yet old-fashioned production techniques were adhered to and the print unions were able to continue their restrictive practices and get away with things that no sensible management should have tolerated.

In addition, a powerful new challenger had emerged which threatened to topple newspapers from their previously unquestioned pedestal as sources of information, entertainment and the moulders of public opinion – television. Those proprietors with any foresight invested in the medium, accepting that the day might not be far off when the written word was overshadowed by the spoken word, and still photographs replaced by on-the-spot moving pictures of world-shattering events, to be viewed in the privacy of the home. What's more, television threatened to drain newspapers of their life blood, advertising. Already a number of bright and extremely talented journalists had seen the light and forsaken the typewriter for the microphone. Desmond Wilcox, Peter Woods, Michael Parkinson, Tom Mangold, Alan Whicker were some of those who achieved a star status no newspaper could offer.

Some older journalists believed that survival would depend to a large extent on a new style of journalism, a more descriptive and probing approach to news. But there were no radical changes. All owners could come up with was the tabloid to replace the old broadsheets, which reduced stories to such an extent that descriptive reporting, at which the *Express* excelled, virtually ceased to exist.

Those who advocated change were lone voices in a wilderness of complacency, and today newspapers have a depressing likeness, while the challenge of television has been met with boobs and bingo and endless stories about the stars of The Street – alas not the 'street of adventure' but the longest running soap opera in history. Front-page splashes report what the Prime Minister said on a certain channel the night before. They are feeding the mouth that is devouring them. Newspapers which in my time cost 1½d now sell for 25p and they still can't make ends meet.

Now The Street is in danger of existing in name only. More and more printing plants are moving to London's dockland, and one can't imagine a wall plaque to anyone who gave his heart to Wapping.

When I stood gazing at the memorial to Edgar Wallace I knew changes were in the offing but I certainly never envisaged such a drastic transformation. Not only has the legendary street disappeared to an area where towering cranes once dominated the landscape, but a new breed of proprietors has emerged – men who do not capture the imagination as Beaverbrook, Northcliffe and the old Press barons did. Nor have they a firm hold on the reins; newspapers which for years told other industries how to run their businesses now fill the columns with their own industrial disputes.

The decision to leave had not been taken light-heartedly, and I had experienced as many sleepless nights thinking about it as I had spent thinking of making The Street. But, after much heart-searching, I had applied for voluntary redundancy, a scheme which had been introduced in an effort to try and cut costs.

I was earning a pretty good wage for those days, plus a generous expense allowance which too often showed a flair for pure fiction. Yet I was throwing it all up for an uncertain future. I had saved nothing, I had two young boys at school, a mortgage to pay and an overdraft. But I was undismayed. I had two novels to my credit and my ambitions now lay in that direction.

The Editor of the *Express* had urged me to change my mind, but I had put in my application and was simply waiting for it to be confirmed. One morning soon afterwards, I went into the office, expecting to work as normal, when the News Editor told me not to leave the office but to make myself available at any time for an interview with Sir Max Aitken, who had been running the paper since the death of his father, Lord Beaverbrook. The form I had filled in requesting voluntary redundancy was solemnly torn up in front of me by a senior executive – Sir Max had intimated that he did not want me to leave, and such was his authority that my own feelings were of no consequence. I waited for the summons from above; literally, for his office was high in the building. Eventually it came and I was escorted to the lift by the Editor, presumably to make sure I did not make a bunk for it. It was the first time I had set foot in Sir Max's eyrie and I waited outside like a patient with a raging toothache preparing to meet his dentist, uncertain whether or not he wanted to be put out of his agony. It was only my second meeting with him.

Sir Max was very patient and generous with his praise for my work, but gradually his mood hardened as I showed no sign of changing my mind. He wanted to know who had bought me, which made me feel like a piece of prime beef up for auction, though I was too scared to say so.

'What are you going to do?' he asked.

'I'm going to write, sir.'

'You will write for me,' he replied, giving his desk a thump.

I explained that I was going home to write, not to another paper, whereupon he suggested that I returned to the Big Room and write him a letter saying just what I would like to do in order to stay on. So, when I had made my escape, I sat down at a typewriter and wrote a polite letter which contained some impossible suggestions. I got no reply, and shortly afterwards the executive who had torn up my original application handed me a fresh one. This time it was accepted without comment. No one was indispensable on the *Express*, and far greater talents than mine had departed without causing the slightest ripple.

Derek Marks, a former Editor who had reverted to writing about his first love, politics, and a man whose friendship I valued highly, came up to me and asked if there was anything that would make me reconsider my decision. Tall and enormously built, his physical presence was quite over-whelming (I had often wondered how he had managed to fit into the cockpit of a fighter aircraft until his son Patrick explained that a special seat had been built into his Mosquito). 'I would like,' I answered, 'to be Editor of the *Falmouth Packet*.' This was a small local newspaper the firm owned which covered shipping news and local events and was used as a training ground for new recruits.

Derek peered at me through his thick lenses and growled, 'Over my dead body. That's the job I want.'

Architecturally there is nothing particularly attractive about the street which runs from the Royal Courts of Justice in the Strand to Ludgate Circus, but it has lured ambitious young men and women from all corners of the world. For many it never lost its magic. And anyone who doubts that has only to enter Wren's beautiful church of St Bride's which lies, hidden by newer buildings, in a serene oasis opposite the *Daily Express*. There, the pews and walls bear the names of many famous journalists who spanned its history – to a jounalist it means far more to be remembered there than in St Paul's Cathedral or Westminster Abbey's Poets' Corner.

Backing on to St Bride's is The Bell, or Ding-Dong, another annex to the *Express* office where, it was said – I have never been able to verify it – Wren had had a special tunnel excavated which connected the pub, or hostelry as it was then, with his masterpiece, so that craftsmen could nip through for a drink. It was, apparently, considered unseemly for workmen engaged on such edifying work to be seen entering a boozer. Reporters on the *Express* suffered no such inhibitions and a near-visible furrow has been ploughed by countless feet in the road from the office to the pub.

It was there that my farewell party had begun, before it transferred (dictated by the paper's shift system) to Poppins, the tiny smoke-clogged pub in the narrow alley adjoining the *Express* building, where you needed the services of a sherpa to negotiate the winding staircase that led to the gents way up at the top. (It was also the ladies and it was not unusual to come out and see a distinguished woman journalist patiently sitting cross-legged on one of the bare wooden stairs.) Actually it was called the Red Lion, but no one ever referred to it as that. It had always been Poppins because of the gaudy bird which adorned an alcove above the entrance to the arched lane. It was the emblem of the Abbots of Cirencester and had been carved from a solid block of Red Mansfield stone quarried in Nottingham, and the entrance to their court had originally been known as Popyngaye Alley. (Reporters, like diaries, are mines of useless information.)

There was nothing unusual about the pub never being referred to by its proper name because it was almost tradition that the 'watering hole' most favoured by a particular office should have a nickname, so that the White Swan, used by the *Daily Mail*, was invariably The Mucky Duck, and the *Daily Mirror*'s The Stab in the Back because it was there that so many reporters were fired. (I once heard it referred to as The Stab in the Chest during one period of furious pruning.) There were also Winnie's and Auntie's and Barney Finnegans, and if they did have proper names I never got to know them.

My farewell binge was a do-you-remember evening which was attended by a lot of the 'enemy'. It was only on such occasions that people from rival newspapers ventured into someone else's pub, otherwise the rumour would speed along the grapevine that So-and-So was touting for a job or had been sent there with instructions to keep his ears to the ground in the hope of finding out what a rival was up to. I was moved by their presence because Fleet Street departures were so frequent they often passed unnoticed, and I was only too happy to make a big hole in the cash that had been collected. It was only our bosses who believed that we were always bitter foes; in fact our rivalry did not extend beyond our working hours. Then we did everything, not always in a gentlemanly fashion, to scoop each other, get an exclusive interview or a new angle to a story. Off-duty, there was a remarkable camaraderie, and once the first editions were away there was a regular pooling of material so that everyone would end up happy and there was no danger of the sack for missing out. Survival was our key word. Close co-operation existed more on out-of-town assignments than on any others, for we usually booked in to the same hotel and sat up drinking until the first editions dropped on our various Night News Desks. Then the hotel phones would start ringing. The *Mail*'s Night News Editor would want to know, for instance: 'Why has the *Mirror* got that bit about the murdered man's dog and we haven't?' The *Mirror* always loved an animal touch. (A dog that had survived by eating hunks of his murdered owner was invariably described as the loyal pet who would not leave his master's side.) And so the queries would go on, and the reporters would be told to catch up on the opposition and put things right. Knocking someone up in the middle of the night never bothered Night News Editors, who did not have to leave the comfort of their chairs to face the wrath of someone awakened from a deep sleep to be asked some banal question. Sometimes you were threatened with grievous bodily harm. It was not uncommon for a reporter to telephone the Night News Editor back and say, 'A big bastard built like a brick latrine threatened to knock my teeth through my arse,' only to get the reply, 'Go back and tell him he can't frighten me.'

Memory Lane was well and truly trampled at my farewell binge and the ears of many a Night News Editor must have been as red as a baboon's backside. They were hard men who had hides that made a rhino's seem baby-soft, but it was the nature of their job that made them that way; off-duty they could be charming. Mellowed by beer, we generously conceded that you had to have a touch of tungsten to ask a man to track down a woman called Jones in a street of several hundred houses all divided into flats. And it was invariably at night and pouring with rain, but you pressed on knowing full well that the opposition had received the same instructions. If you happened to bump into a couple of pals you could trust not to do the dirty on you, an agreement was reached whereby the street was divided into sections and information was pooled. Next night you would do it all again, quite indifferent to the rain and rebuffs and the knowledge that a few hours later your efforts would be keeping someone's cod and chips warm.

There was a lot to account for the irascible behaviour of the average Night News Editor, for they led a totally unnatural existence. When most people were fast asleep, their adrenalin was flowing. They ate their meals at the desk, and rare were the occasions when they were not interrupted. They were buried under an avalanche of copy – from PA (the Press Association), Exchange Telegraph, from Staff men and Local Correspondents, while a battery of telephones in front of them, each with a different light attached, seldom stopped ringing or flashing. There were informants with tip-offs, reporters ringing in to report progress or lack of it. One eye was constantly on the clock, for the Night Desk was harassed and badgered by the Back Bench – the men who wanted immediate results otherwise an edition would be missed. 'Hold the front page' was strictly for the silver screen – editions *had* to get away on time otherwise they missed the train. The night staff was always depleted by the Day News Editor so that the Night News Editor never had enough men to cope with the flood of work.

Ben Voss, the *Express*'s Night News Editor at the time, came in to wish me luck. He enjoyed the stories as much as anyone. And, as the beer flowed, famous stories were retold that improved with each fresh telling. Inevitably the conversation was entirely shop. We raised our glasses to absent and departed friends, and remembered only the good times, like looking back into one's childhood and recalling only summers that were long and hot and the skies cloudless.

Some friends from the *Mirror* were there, and it was inevitable that the name of Hugh Saker should crop up. Hugh, who died tragically young, was one of the *Mirror*'s finest 'trouble shooters', and there is a plaque to him in St Bride's. It bears the simple inscription 'Reporter'; it was all he wanted. Millions of *Mirror* readers had seen his by-line, but it is doubtful if any remembered him. To us he was a much-loved man who had not let the harsh and seamier side of life which he had witnessed at close quarters blunt his warmth and generosity. He was sadly missed. But an outsider hearing some of our stories could have been forgiven for thinking that we had a strange way of showing our affection.

Hugh had lost an eye during the war, and someone recalled the occasion on an 'out-of-towner' when a reporter sharing a room with him woke up in the middle of the night dying for a glass of water. He filled a glass standing by the hand basin –

and swallowed Hugh's glass eye. We doubled up as the long vigil to reclaim it was recounted in all its anatomical detail.

No one, however, could cap the story of the night Hugh got drunk and his car keys were, wisely, removed from his pocket. His wife, Viv, who worked on the *Evening Standard*, was telephoned at home and told to pick him up. She had decided to have an early night and, wearing only a nightie and dressing gown, was just about to sit down to a meal of steak and chips. Dutifully she put her supper in the oven and drove to Fleet Street, still in her nightie. On the way home Hugh fell asleep, and, as they passed Wimbledon Common, Viv decided she wanted to spend a penny, so she stopped the car and nipped into some bushes. At that point Hugh woke up, wondered how the heck he had got there, slipped across to the driver's seat and drove home. There, he locked the door, ate the meal in the oven, and went to bed, leaving a note protesting that his dinner had been burnt.

Viv, stranded there in her nightclothes, with no money, eventually found a call box from where she made a reverse-charge call to her sister-in-law – nothing could rouse Hugh from a deep slumber – and asked to be picked up.

Many Fleet Street marriages failed to survive because so many journalists put the paper first, but it was astonishing the number that lasted. I had often deputised as Night News Editor on the *Herald* and on the *Express*, and I knew at first hand the tremendous pressures that wives endured with unruffled calm. There was one close friend present who was renowned for his extra-marital involvements, and I reminded him of the night he phoned in and said, 'Alf, do me a favour, ring my wife and tell her I've been sent out of town on a big story and won't be home.' I did as he asked and made suitably apologetic noises, explaining that it was one of the hazards of the job. Some time later he rang me from his home and demanded, 'What the hell do you mean phoning my wife and telling her I'm out of town?' It transpired that on the way to his tryst he had stopped for a jar and got caught up in a big school, with the result that when he turned up at the young lady's flat he had the door slammed in his face.

It hadn't bothered me at the time, for as far as his wife was concerned I was a faceless voice. But some months later I met her at an office party where she rounded on me and said, 'You're the bastard who's always sending him out of town when he should be due home.'

I recounted the story of the pretty young girl reporter who wrote a theatre review: when her phoned-over copy dropped in front of me, I couldn't understand a word of it and put it on the spike. When she came back on to see if there were any queries, I rather pompously told her it didn't make a lot of sense and was too high-falutin' for our readers and would she please rewrite it. She hung up, and a few minutes later one of the top executives on the Back Bench came up and asked me what the hell I was up to. The piece was brilliant and would go in as written. The spiked story was retrieved and it appeared next morning word for word.

It had, I said, taught me an invaluable lesson: always keep abreast of office romances.

We talked and drank late into the night, and there were moments when I began to doubt the wisdom of my decision to leave The Street. But when I ventured out into the cool fresh air I knew there was no turning back. I no longer had the burning ambition that blunts the cutting edge of the biting winds, while the fat by-line that banishes the memory of snow, rain, rebuffs and the frustrations of trying to find a telephone had lost its magic. Instead, the passage of time had made me acutely aware of the foul weather and I'd long begun to wonder whether it was worth the candle. Once that zeal and enthusiasm had gone there was no point in staying. Fleet Street had no room for anyone who was not prepared to give their all, and there was little compassion for those who fell down on the job. You were fired on the spot, and I preferred to avoid that indignity. There had been good times and I had had the privilege of working with many of the legendary giants, whose pyrotechnic talent had seemed undimmable. Yet many had departed into anonymous obscurity. Others, even when they had retired, could not keep away; they had given their hearts to the place and had nowhere else to go. But they were unwelcome intruders.

As I sat in the swaying carriage of the last train home, my battered portable Olivetti – the one which had accompanied me to many remote places and on which I had pounded out so many famous stories that no one would remember – resting between my feet, I was content with my *nunc dimmitis*. I had vowed that I would leave The Street when I was forty-five. It was a young man's game, and I did not want to end up as a has-been touting for drinks and boring young people with stories of faded triumphs. Hilde Marchant, whom the late Arthur Christiansen – considered by many the greatest editor in living memory – had called 'the best woman reporter that ever worked in Fleet Street', was a typical casualty. She rocketed to fame and plummeted to self-destruction. Bernard Hall, one of the *Express*'s longest-serving reporters, with a heart that had been touched by Midas, used to nip out and give her the occasional fiver. She was picked up dying on the pavement, alone and destitute, the lovely features that had turned many a reporter's heart ravaged by the demon that stalked The Street. Bernard made all the funeral arrangements without telling a soul.

I had not achieved my deadline, but I hadn't missed it by much. I was forty-seven.

2

JACOB'S LADDER

When I was demobbed from the Royal Navy several months after two of Japan's major cities had disappeared beneath the mushroom-clouds that ended the war in the Far East, I possessed a smart Moss Bros doeskin suit of Number Ones with the wavy-navy stripe of an RNVR sub-lieutenant on each sleeve, a blue pin-stripe suit and a green pork-pie trilby. I must have been one of the very few who did not dance in the street when the war ended. Not because I liked war, but because I just did not have the courage to face the future. For years I had had little or no say in the conduct of my life; every decision had more or less been made for me: what I did, where I went, what time I woke up and what time I ate. The bosun's pipe or a bugle had dictated my life. And I had enjoyed it. Apart from being sunk on D-Day and later forced to abandon ship in a freak storm in the Atlantic, it had not been a particularly perilous war for me. What action I had seen had not scarred me, and I was too young to have been scared.

When my time came for demob I did my utmost to postpone it, even volunteering to stay on. Among the various chores I was given was a stint with the vice-squad in Hong Kong which turned out to be one of the softest and most lucrative I ever had. I was given a jeep, a petty officer and some ratings for the job of touring the out-of-bounds brothels to make sure no British sailors were there. The petty officer would burst in without too much ceremony and demand to see the proprietor, who when he appeared invariably produced a bottle of whisky which the petty officer would hand to me. At the next port of call it was his perk. By the end of the patrol we had done very well for ourselves.

It was all most improper and contrary to King's Regulations and Admiralty Instructions. But we had no qualms.

The routine never varied. Having been assured that there were no matelots patronising the place, the PO would put his foot against the side of the first cubicle in a row of similar ones and give it a hefty kick. The whole lot would topple like a house of cards. Men would emerge, hauling up their pants and cursing at the *coitus interruptus*, and make a beeline for the nearest window. The PO would say, 'No one here, sir,' and off we would go.

But my evil day could not be put off for ever and the time arrived when I had to sail home to an uncertain future. My problem was that I knew what I wanted to do, but had not the foggiest idea of how to set about achieving it. Long before, I had decided I wanted to be a journalist, but I had no qualifications whatsoever. All I had acquired was a portable typewriter in exchange for a tin of fifty duty-free Passing Cloud.

When I got home I applied for jobs with newspapers all over the country; all my approaches were greeted with the same response: 'Apply again when you have some experience'. It was the classic chicken-and-egg situation: how could I get the experience if no one would give me the opportunity? I even wrote to 'Cassandra' of the *Daily Mirror* saying how much I wanted to be a journalist and seeking his advice. His reply was far from encouraging. Having read my letter, he suggested I give up the idea, I did not have what it needed. (Many years later, when I had made something of a name, I mentioned this to Bill Connor, who wrote the 'Cassandra' column, and he replied that nothing had happened to make him change his original opinion.)

Although I had my demob suit, I continued to wear my uniform; it was a carapace into which I could escape, my armour against reality. The letters of rejection dropped through the letter box with the monotony of rain in a wet week in Manchester. When my gratuity ran out I applied for a job with a well-known travel agency. 'What experience have you had of travel?' asked my interviewer, and I listed the places I had visited until I saw his face disappearing behind an enormous yawn. India, Singapore, the Philippines, Borneo, Burma ... were obviously places of no interest. People did not go there for holidays.

Nevertheless, I got the job and was given a small desk in a basement room where I sat day after day ordering pencils and envelopes from the reps who called, desperate unhappy men who had lost their dignity and would have crawled across the floor to get an order for a dozen HB pencils.

Eventually I was given the opportunity of rewriting old brochures, and I did my utmost to inject some colour into the description of places I had never seen and, as things were going, had little hope of ever doing so. But no one was really interested in fresh descriptions of the various resorts; the pre-war ones were perfectly adequate. What was of importance was the change in prices.

I continued to send off my stereotyped letters, and the time was rapidly approaching when I would have no more newspapers to write to. Then one morning I received a letter from the Editor of a small weekly newspaper inviting me for an interview. The office was on the ground floor of an old butcher's shop, and the hooks which once supported carcasses still adorned the walls. The basement was occupied by an elderly man who looked like the old carpenter in Walt Disney's *Pinnochio* and who hand-set all the headlines. The copy was set by an outside printer, and the 'matter' was collected by taxi the day before the paper went to press.

It was not what I had visualised, but it was a newspaper. The Editor was an attractive young woman who asked about my previous experience but did not register dismay when I said I hadn't any but was busy doing a correspondence course. Did I do shorthand? she asked. 'Yes,' I lied, 'but not verbatim.' The lie, was, I felt, a white one; my shorthand was in fact non-existent, but I had enrolled with Duttons, who did a postal course and promised, if one worked hard, results that would be surprisingly quick. On the strength of that I was given a trial assignment. It was a political meeting addressed by the local Member of Parliament. I arrived at a grave-cold school hall and sat down at the Press table where I laid out my freshly sharpened pencils and opened an unblemished notebook. I cannot recall the name of the MP, but I will never forget the speed with which he spoke; he made a Vickers gun sound faltering. He gave promises and pledges in sweeping emotional terms, full of rolling defiant phrases, but my pencil was rigid in a palsied hand and I only got down the odd word. When the rapturous applause ended I accepted that my career as a reporter might make the *Guinness Book of Records* for its brevity, and as the hall was emptying and the MP was being escorted to his car, I went on to the platform and pleaded with one of the party officials to tell me what he had said. He patiently nutshelled all that the Member had said, and I rushed to the nearest pub to elaborate on my notes before my memory deserted me. Then I went home to make bricks without much clay, let alone straw.

I must have rewritten it a dozen times, and when I had finished I realised it was long on colour but extremely short on quotes. It was also full of praise for the speaker and audience, but it was a safe seat and no one present had really cared what he had said. They would have voted for him if he had announced the repeal of the Corn Laws. They were only there to wave the flag.

I dropped it in on my way to the travel firm the next morning, and could not wait until the Friday to buy a copy of the newspaper. There on the front page was my story, improved no end by the professional touch of the Editor. Since then I have had a great many scoops, but few have given me as much pleasure as that first story to appear in print.

I forget what I was paid, a matter of shillings, but I did not care, I would have worked every night for nothing.

Soon afterwards I was asked to do another job. I must have done it to the Editor's satisfaction, because I was offered a permanent job. My foot was on the bottom rung of Jacob's ladder and although I could not see the top I knew I was on my way to heaven.

It was hard work on a weekly as you were expected to work during the evening as well as the day. But I could not have got a better grounding. I not only wrote for the paper, I also collected the type, delivered to the newsagents and collected the money. I pirated film reviews from the daily and evening newspapers, covered Magistrates Courts, sat through seemingly endless council meetings and rewrote the sports news sent in by local clubs. We had a darts competition sponsored by the paper which was always won by the White Hart pub, yet the man who sent in the report always began it, 'Those dark horses, the White Hart ... ' In addition, there were features to write, a gossip column and a letters page to fill. The latter was often plagued by a dirth of material and I became something of a dab hand at writing letters to the Editor. It was not without its dangers, and even 'name and address supplied' did not offer protection. I remember strolling past the statue of Mrs Siddons on Paddington Green and noting that it had been vandalised. I wrote an irate letter, signed 'Siddons Lover', in which I expressed dismay that the monument to one of the borough's most famous figures had been allowed to fall into a state of neglect. To my amazement and embarrassment I received a letter from America containing a cheque, asking for it to be contributed towards a restoration fund. I could hardly pocket the cash, so I handed it in at the Town Hall.

Baby shows were a regular source of copy, and one in particular provided me with the idea of writing a strongly worded letter of protest, which sadly boomeranged. I had attended a baby show at a church bazaar where a smiling vicar handed out the prize to the beaming mother of the 'bonniest baby'. I wrote a letter which I signed 'Outraged Mother', and added authenticity with the customary 'name and address supplied'. In it I berated the vicar for being so heartless, and urged him to call a halt to any further shows. Did he not realise the heartache they caused? Every mother entered her baby in the sure confidence that it was the prettiest, bonniest, bounciest child in the world. Imagine, therefore, her feelings when another infant was chosen. To my dismay the vicar turned up at the office looking very penitent and carrying a huge cuddly toy. Would the paper present it to the aggrieved mother with his compliments and apologies? He would certainly heed her advice. I cannot remember what I did with the toy, but I do know I gave a lot more thought to my ghost writing in the future.

Another of my many jobs was to take photographs for the paper, something for which I was totally unqualified, but I was given a crash course with a Rolleiflex and a series of lessons in a makeshift dark-room in the basement on how to develop and print the negatives. Aside from the extra money, I quite enjoyed it, and regularly gave up my Saturdays to do weddings. I became quite adept and slipped into an unalterable routine. 'Head and shoulders of the bride and groom, please ... now a full length one.' This would be followed by one of the newly-weds with the best man and bridesmaids, then a family group, and finally one with all the guests. I would then dash into the dark-room and produce contact prints which I rushed to the reception, as people were an easier touch immediately after the ceremony. At one wedding, as I was in a hurry, I thought I would speed up the developing by warming everything up. The result was disastrous, the negatives came out like frosted glass. When I confessed that there were no pictures to commemorate the happiest day in their lives, the groom had to be forcibly restrained from knocking my teeth out. I was given another chance, however, but was warned that my career as a budding Baron would end abruptly if there was another mistake. My demise came much quicker than even I anticipated.

A woman called in and wanted a photograph taken of her baby. It was something quite new to me, so I consulted a professional photographer and asked if there was any special equipment I would need for indoor work. He said a flash, but when I told him that I did not have one he suggested some floods. I found some in the dark-room, and set off, full of confidence and burdened down with enough powerful lights to illuminate Blackpool.

The woman lived in a very select block of mansion flats in an apartment furnished with the kind of items I associated with Hampstead antique shops. A table was covered with a spotless white shawl and the baby as naked and as beautiful as a Botticelli cherub was placed on it. I arranged the lights around the subject; some on a stand, others draped over the top of the door, and was snapping away merrily when I smelt burning. 'Have you left something on the stove?' I called out. 'You bloody fool, you've set fire to the door!' came a furious

cry. I looked round to see the paint bubbling and flames
spreading from two deeply charred holes. I hurriedly
unplugged, but by then the door was burning like a
well-fanned fire. As the woman snatched up her child, I threw
a bucket of water over the door: it put the fire out but did not
improve the appearance of the carpet. I was ordered out
before I did any more damage. Back at the office I was
relieved of the camera and the key to the dark room.

Not long after, I was approached by a rival newspaper and
asked if I was interested in joining them. In fact, there were
two sister papers, the *Kilburn Times* and the *Willesden
Chronicle*, which circulated in adjoining areas of north-west
London. They had much larger circulations than the newspaper I was on and covered a wider area, which offered much
more scope. And so I crossed over the Edgware Road.

The offices were in a disused laundry and the papers
actually printed on the premises. The work was very similar
to what I had been doing, but it was there that I acquired a
lifelong loathing of Gilbert and Sullivan, for seldom a week
seemed to pass without my having to listen to *The Mikado,
The Gondoliers* or *The Pirates of Penzance*. I recall my first
visit to a local hall for a performance of *The Gondoliers*. I
rather fancied my chances as a drama critic, and during the
performance feverishly scribbled notes on the programme
and jotted down the occasional remark which would scorch
the page and put me in the same class as those celebrated
butchers who could make or break a show with their dazzling
wit.

The Editor read my review with what was clearly mounting
dismay, and handed it back to me saying, 'This will not do,
Alfred.' Patiently, he explained that drama criticism consisted
of getting in as many names as possible: the more you
mentioned the more copies you sold. Suitably chastened, I
rewrote it, racking my brains for superlatives and adjectives.
It was harder to write than the original piece, which had
flowed like liquid gold, as it was extremely difficult to write
admiringly of someone sitting in the box office or selling
programmes, and even harder to wax lyrical about some
unseen name working the lights, or about each individual
member of the chorus. But with time and familiarity I became

quite adept at never offending anyone, although the price was high – contempt for the two men who had given so much pleasure to millions and caused agony to one.

They were good times, but no more than a rung on that tempting ladder. On the paper I was introduced to what had hitherto been a mystery to me, namely lineage. From time to time one came across a story that had a wider interest and was therefore saleable to the evening papers or the dailies. Then, you telephoned the various News Desks and said you had an interesting story, and an uninterested voice would reply, 'Put it over. We'll have a look at it.' In time your name became known and your reliability accepted, and you were put on the books as a local correspondent. It was hard work in those days when there were so many more major newspapers than there are now, which meant phoning over the same story several times – but the cheques that came at the end of the month made it all worth while. At least I got to know what the inside of a decent restaurant looked like. Until I discovered lineage I used to contemplate whether I would have half a bitter and a sandwich, or two halves of bitter and no food, before setting off for an evening assignment, or both and walk there.

One story comes vividly to mind, for it resulted in my becoming friendly with a man I would otherwise never have met, Sir Thomas Beecham. Willesden Council was among the first in London to set up an Arts Council, and one of its most ambitious projects was a concert at the State Cinema, Kilburn, given by Sir Thomas and the Royal Philharmonic Orchestra. I was due to write it up and went along with my wife, Barbara, whom I had married a few months before. I seldom took her on jobs, but she had a genuine love for music and played the piano and cello extremely well, whereas I didn't know the difference between a semi-colon and a semi-quaver and could just about distinguish a piano from a piccolo. So Barbara was there to make sure I didn't make a fool of myself.

When the concert ended I was asked to escort Sir Thomas to his Rolls-Royce, but when we stepped out of the theatre you literally couldn't see your hand in front of you. An old-fashioned London pea-souper had descended like a wet

brown blanket, and it was impossible for Sir Thomas's driver
to think of going to the Ritz, where the conductor had a suite.
Although Sir Thomas lived in nearby St John's Wood, he was
adamant that he wanted to go to the Ritz. As there were no
buses running, I suggested the only way was by
Underground, and Sir Thomas was thrilled at the thought –
'I've never been on the Tube,' he said. So Barbara and I and
'Bomber' Harris, the Borough's Entertainments Manager, got
some old paraffin torches – I can't for the life of me remember
where from – lit them and marched down Kilburn High Road
like torch-bearers escorting some returning Caesar. Behind us
was a crowd of cheering fans.

When we reached the nearest station, a disembodied voice
was announcing that, owing to the fog, trains were liable to
delay, and I took the opportunity to ring three morning
newspapers to tell them that a good picture story was
available if their reporters and photographers intercepted the
train at one of the stations along the line. I would let them
know which carriage to get into by waving from the open
doors.

Sir Thomas loved every minute of the journey. When he
wasn't puffing at his enormous cigar he was using it as a baton
and singing snatches from Beethoven's Choral Symphony;
naturally, the other occupants of the carriage joined in the
impromptu sing-song. I can't recall at which station it was
that the Fleet Street corps piled aboard, but Sir Thomas
wasn't at all perturbed by the sudden barrage of exploding
flashbulbs and he happily posed, answered questions and
submitted to the repeated demands of the insatiable
photographers for 'Just one more, Sir Thomas.'

When we got to the Ritz – it was the first time I had ever set
foot there, and neither Barbara nor I was dressed for the place
– Sir Thomas gave us a drink and then asked how we planned
to get home at that late hour. I said that he shouldn't worry,
we'd find a way somehow, but he wouldn't listen and insisted
that we should be his guests for the night, and promptly rang
down to the reception and booked a room for us. The suite
we were ushered into was palatial, with an enormous brass
bed and a bath that wasn't much smaller than an Olympic-
sized pool.

Sir Thomas had said we were to call on him before we left, but we were so overwhelmed by the unaccustomed opulence that we departed immediately after I had written a note of thanks on a sheet of hotel notepaper and asked for it to be delivered to his suite. Soon afterwards, however, to my surprise, I received an invitation to visit him at his St John's Wood home. I remember we chatted about the trip on the Tube and how much he had enjoyed it, and I took the opportunity to interview him and do a profile of the famous local resident for the paper. It must have met with his approval because I received further invitations from Sir Thomas.

Our rival newspaper was the *Willesden Citizen*, which I recall was written almost single-handed by a thin Welsh lad who lived alone in digs and hadn't had too much of an easy passage. Orphaned very young, he had been brought up at Barnado's and learned very early how to fend for himself. At lunchtimes we used to play cricket in the nets at Paddington Recreation Ground, and we frequently met in the Magistrates Court and sometimes socially at local dances. I never imagined that one day he would become one of the world's most celebrated authors. It was not long before he left to join the *Evening News*, and while there he wrote a hilarious yet moving story about his National Service days in Malaya titled *Virgin Soldiers*, the first of a string of bestsellers. His name was Leslie Thomas.

3

FRONT-HALL CALLERS

They were happy carefree days, but I was aware of a sense of growing discontent; there was only one place for me, The Street, but that seemed as remote as ever. Then, out of the blue, I was asked if I would consider taking a holiday relief job with the *Daily Herald*, the TUC-controlled voice of the Labour Party. If I made the grade I stood a reasonable chance of being taken on the staff. It was a risk, but an opportunity too good to miss.

Strictly speaking, the *Daily Herald* wasn't in Fleet Street; geographically, it was a couple of miles away, in Endell Street, in the heart of Covent Garden market. But very few newspapers were in Fleet Street itself then – as now, once again – and the name was used to encompass all the national dailies and London evening papers.

I walked into the imposing edifice for the first time, filled with apprehension and misgivings. I need not have worried, however; I was greeted warmly by the News Editor and introduced to the members of the editorial staff. Most of them had up till then only been names to me. There was Victor Thompson, who remains for me one of the wittiest columnists The Street ever produced. London's buses carried huge banners between the top and bottom decks warning the public of what they were missing if they did not read him. Unfortunately, Victor had a drink problem, though he usually managed to discipline it, and even when he couldn't he remained the perfect professional. He was once sent to write a story about Jack Solomon's gym in Windmill Street where boxers trained, but got a trifle confused and ended up in the Windmill Theatre, then considered very risqué because statuesque girls appeared topless on the stage – they were not allowed to move, though, and as soon as they dropped their ostrich fans the stage lights went out. They were about as sexy as the Venus de Milo, and it was all very tame when you consider what can be seen in hundreds of Soho strip clubs now. Even so, a visit was an experience not to be missed. The show was almost continuous, and as soon as one house finished there was a mad stampede to fill the vacated front stalls, with men in grubby raincoats leaping over the backs of seats like jumpers in the Grand National. When Victor returned to the office there was a mild altercation about him having got his venues mixed, but he shrugged it off and said it did not matter – both places were concerned with big chests. Whereupon he sat down and wrote a brilliant piece in which he used the phrase 'We never clothed', a parody of the theatre's famous wartime slogan which boasted that even Hitler's bombs had not been able to close it.

For a long time his editor was Percy Cudlipp, one of the famous trio of brothers who left their mark on Fleet Street. Percy was an extremely talented man, but vain and a trifle snobbish for a Labour paper, which led Victor to say of him, 'The trouble with him is he's Perce-proud.'

Sadly, Victor went on the binge once too often. He was sent to San Marino, then the smallest and oldest state, to cover an election – the type of story tailor-made for his deft touch. But on the aircraft he was tempted to have a brandy, then another … By the time the plane touched down at San Marino he was in a sorry state, and he was put back aboard. He died when it reached Heathrow. His death was a blow to all of us.

Alan Dick, another *Herald* star, was a gentle giant of a man with a touch as light as a soufflé. I was disconcerted when, the first time I met him, he proffered his advice for survival in Fleet Street: 'It's just one big barrel of shit, so make sure you remain at the bottom. *They* never roll their sleeves up far enough to scrape the bottom.' *They*, I discovered, were the mysterious, faceless persons who ruled our destiny. To look at him one could never imagine that during the war his health was so bad he was written off, but he replied with a brilliantly witty book completely devoid of self-pity which he called

The Walking Miracle, and which was an inspiration to others similarly afflicted.

If there is one thing a reporter needs it is luck. Without it he will never make it to the top, but you have to be able to spot it when it comes and grab it. I had more than my fair share of luck on my first assignment. It obviously wasn't considered much of a story otherwise someone much more accomplished would have been sent. All I can remember is that it was a convention of private investigators, which was extremely boring, and did not look like providing a word of copy. They were all rather dully dressed men who it seemed did nothing more exciting than serve writs or provide evidence for divorce. There wasn't a Marlowe or Sam Spade in sight. In the bar during the lunch break I got into conversation with an attractive woman who wore a hat that would not have been out of place at Ascot. To my surprise she too was a private eye. When she told me this, I asked if she wasn't scared of being beaten up: she was more than capable of looking after herself in a rough house, she assured me, and removed the pin from her hat and demonstrated how such an innocent-looking item could become a lethal weapon. So I wrote about her and got a by-line.

Any worries I might have had about my future were ended when the News Editor told me I would be taken on the staff at £14 a week plus expenses. The latter was almost as important as the salary, for during my first day Alf Richman, later to become Harold Wilson's Personal Assistant, took me aside and explained the mysteries and importance of an expenses form. I had to get my priorities right. He also introduced me to the cash advance – the system on which reporters depended for survival. You borrowed the money and then claimed it back on expenses.

Then I was escorted to the office pubs, the Cross Keys, almost opposite, and The Enterprise, the walls of which were plastered with photographs of past and present stars of the *Daily Herald*; its importance lay in the fact that it was a market porters' pub, which meant you could get a drink there at four o'clock in the morning.

Knowing the political complexion of the paper I was

naturally anxious to know if one was expected to slant a story, but Alf assured me that no such pressure was ever brought to bear and he gave me an example of how to be impartial. 'If Clem Attlee drives through a town and is given a rough time, you write, "To tumultuous cheers and some good-natured heckling, etc." If it's Churchill you just turn it round.'

When Labour swept to power on the serviceman's vote, Alf was masterminding the compilation of results as they poured in. The Night News Desk phone rang and Alf picked it up to hear a growly voice announce, 'Winston Churchill here. Can you read me the *Herald*'s leader?' Alf replied, 'And this is Jesus Christ here. Stop fucking me about'; and hung up. Of course, it was Churchill, who rang back demanding to speak to the Editor to complain about the rudeness of his staff.

Since then I have heard of many reporters who claimed to have told Churchill to ' —— off' when he unexpectedly telephoned. It says a lot for their fertile imagination, and even more for Churchill's resilience.

Being a new boy, I was often given the Saturday morning stint which the established reporters considered below their dignity. That was understandable because there was no one else on duty in the office as there was no paper the following day, and all I had to do was open the mail, most of which was Government handouts in triplicate and which ended up in the waste bin, or invitations to Press conferences which were left for the News Editor to peruse. Occasionally there were theatre tickets which I knew the critic would not bother with; those I pocketed, along with any invitations to the opening of a new restaurant. They were the perks of the job. If the telephone rang with someone wanting to pass on a news item, I transferred him to the Sunday paper, *The People*, which occupied a separate part of the building, but if it was a good story that would hold Sunday-for-Monday, I sat on it and made a note in the log, with the caller's name and address for credit purposes. I enjoyed it. I could sit in the News Editor's chair imagining myself in that exalted position one day, and issuing orders to an invisible staff. But what I most looked forward to were the explosive visits of Hannen Swaffer.

Swaff, as everybody called him, had been a legend when I

was still in nappies, and he was then in the twilight of his career, still working for the *Herald* and producing a lively column for *The People*. He loved a captive audience, and in my case that was literally true; he would trap me behind the desk to ensure I did not escape. He was extremely skilful at cutting off any line of retreat, for he had plenty of experience with those who had heard his stories so often they could not bear the thought of listening to them again. He claimed to write a million words a year, and I am sure that was nowhere near his verbal output. But his stories were all new to me, and I was quite content to be regaled with yarns about the Golden Age of journalism, never for a moment thinking that one day I would myself be lamenting their passing.

He was a tall, cadaverously thin man with a mane of flowing white hair, a bulbous nose, and a weakness for the kind of battered black hat one usually associated with arty Bohemians. He was also addicted to floppy bow ties, and invariably wore spotless white gloves, not for sartorial effect but to ease the discomfort of the eczema that plagued him. An incurable chain-smoker, he never removed the cigarette from his lips, just keeping it in his mouth, letting the ash drop like snowflakes onto his grey waistcoat. (The late comedian Danny Kaye, who became a great friend, once remarked when they met, 'I see you're wearing Players today, Swaff.') I used to watch in readiness for the cry that would be emitted when the quarter-inch-long butt eventually burnt into his flesh, but it never did. He simply lit another cigarette from the dog-end, then curled his lip and with unnerring accuracy spat it out, and he wasn't at all particular if you happened to be in the line of fire.

He was known as The Pope of Fleet Street, but I don't know whether that was in deference to his age and reputation, or whether it was a reference to his deep-rooted belief in his own infallibility. I remember he once told me that he was the only man who could report the death of the King and begin it with 'I'. Modesty was not his weak point.

Hannen was a total enigma. He was a dedicated socialist who had turned to spiritualism, yet still lived in a flat overlooking Trafalgar Square so that he would have a pigeon's-eye view of the Revolution when it came. His wife

had a soft spot for 'fallen women', and there were plenty of
them, soliciting in the grimy streets in nearby Soho. Any tart
who felt like renouncing the error of her ways was welcome
to the flat and given a cup of tea and a pound note to help her
along the first steps of her new-chosen path. In rainy weather,
when the gutters ran with water and business was slack, a
great deal of tea flowed and a considerable amount of money
changed hands. Sadly, the realisation of the error of their
ways was of short duration; as soon as the weather improved
the primrose path lured them back. But Mrs Swaffer, like
Gladstone, was a trier when it came to reclamation.

I don't know what Swaff thought about her mission in life,
he never discussed it. He may have thought the tea was
wasted, but I'm sure he did not give a damn about the cash;
money was something that never occupied much of his
thoughts. I suppose materialism and spiritualism were
incompatible. Yet he told me that the wonderful thing about
journalism was that it enabled you to live like a millionaire
even if you weren't paid like one. He had joined the *Herald*
many years previously because its politics were more in
keeping with his own, but that did not mean he renounced the
pleasures of life. Certainly, the *Herald* did not expect its staff
to live the life of the proletariat. We stayed in the best hotels,
and the editorial cars were splendid-looking limousines
driven by chauffeurs, who wore peaked caps, not flat ones.

I knew that in his younger days he had been a celebrated
theatre critic, but, although I had not read any of his reviews,
I developed strong doubts about his judgement. One
afternoon he was recalling his friendship with Bernard Shaw.
'G.B.S. told me he had written a new play,' he began in his
quavering voice, 'and was going to call it *Saint Joan*. "What a
bloody silly title," I said to him, and when he outlined the
story I replied, "It'll never go. It'll never go." And of course I
was right.'

Whenever I did the Saturday stint my lunch consisted of a
pint of bitter and a sandwich in the Cross Keys, a habit of
which Swaff strongly disapproved and did his utmost to
discourage. Like many a reformed drunk he had gone over
the top and sounded like Aggie Weston urging everyone to
take the pledge. Nevertheless, there was a certain pride and

bravado in the way in which he used to describe his own drinking, as if to suggest that as no one else could possibly emulate his prodigious feats they might as well give up. 'I was terrible. Many a time I had to be dragged from under the hooves of the horses as I lay in a Fleet Street gutter.'

One of the stories, I recall, was of an occasion during the days that Swaff was editing the *Daily Mail*, then under the proprietorship of Lord Northcliffe. Swaff had been drinking heavily and was returning to the office very much the worse for wear. 'I was crawling up the stairs on all fours when I found myself staring at a pair of pin-striped trousers. I looked up and there was His Lordship. "Swaffer," he said, "there's too much drinking going on here." I said, "I quite agree, and if you step aside I'll go upstairs and sack a few of the bastards."'

Hannen negotiated the stairs with some difficulty and entered the Big Room, with Northcliffe close behind. Most of the sub-editors were asleep at their desks. 'For God's sake, do something about it!' shouted the Press Baron. 'No, let lying dogs sleep,' replied Swaff.

It is difficult to imagine two more dissimilar men than Swaffer and Lord Beaverbrook, the dynamic gnome-like Canadian newspaper tycoon I was later to work for. The Beaver was the apostle of capitalism, Swaff the champion of the masses, but although they preached different gospels they remained close friends.

When Beaverbrook died, Swaffer interviewed him on the other side for a spiritualist publication. Beaverbrook seemed to have had second thoughts about his own way of life and adopted views more compatible with the writer's. It was a Swaffer exclusive which no one was in a position to refute – and certainly not one that anybody wanted to check out the hard way. Beaverbrook would have chuckled – he was an admirer of enterprise and initiative.

The doyen of what were called the general reporters – a rough-and-ready description for any non-specialist – was Maurice Fagence, a stocky rumple-suited man with a magnificent leonine head. He was likened to America's Ernie Pyle for his reporting from the Western Desert, Italy, and later Korea. Unlike the younger reporters, he was excused

night shifts, as were others of the best men; the most
hackneyed phrase in newspapers is 'news is made at night',
but the truth is that nights provide very little copy, for the
obvious reason that most people are in bed, which greatly
reduces the chances of anything happening. It is a glib
soporific dished out by senior editors to young men who are
sick and tired of late shifts, and who bitch about never seeing
the light of day. Every night, they are assured, could provide
the opportunity of a lifetime, for then the old hands are not
available and the younger men therefore have a chance to
prove their ability. (In time you found yourself repeating the
same old hoary chestnut to newcomers.)

Maurice had a fatal weakness: he was simply incapable of
punctuality, and this used to send the News Editor into
hair-raising rages as he sat glowering behind his desk waiting
for Maurice to arrive and offer his latest excuse. These were
priceless and imaginative, and he never repeated himself,
neither was he ever in a hurry to offer them. He followed an
unruffled procedure which did not vary: he would come in,
hang up his coat, comb his hair with his hands, then stroll
over and perch his bottom on a corner of the News Desk and
rifle through the incoming copy. 'Anything worth while?'

Then the News Editor would explode and demand to know
the reason for his lateness. No man could ever have endured
and survived so many hazards on his short journey to the
office. I used to hover in the vicinity of the desk lapping up
his alibis, until I was told in the most forceful and inelegant
language to make myself scarce. From time to time the News
Editor tried to punish Maurice by sending him out on jobs
that were an insult to a man of his talent, but he soon
abandoned any thought of retribution as Maurice would
return with a first-rate story. In any case, nothing would
make him mend his ways.

There was an occasion when the News Editor became so
irate he sent Maurice to cover a pigeon competition, confident
that not a line of copy would emerge and Maurice would
return suitably chastened. When Maurice got back he went
through his usual laborious ritual of hanging up his coat and
smoothing his hair before sitting down at his typewriter.
'Good yarn,' he declared to no one in particular, and

produced a gem of a piece which appeared under the headline
'Who put the cat among the pigeons'. It told in a semi-serious
manner of the chaos that had ensued when a cat disrupted
the judging and feathers began to fly.

Over a drink I asked him how the cat had got in. Without
batting an eyelid he replied, 'Under my coat.'

Maurice had been one of Northcliffe's original bright
young men and, considering that he had had quite a rapport
with the Press Lord, I wondered how he had come to leave
Northcliffe and join the *Herald*; he gave the following
explanation:

One day he was sent down to the front hall to interview
someone who had called in with a story. All newspapers
suffer from what are known as 'front-hall cranks', men who
have irrefutable proof that they are the rightful heir to the
throne, or are the victims of Government persecution. The
News Desk's attitude was: 'See him; then get rid of him as
quick as you can.' Maurice listened to the caller who told him
that he had a new invention which enabled a picture of a
person in one room to be transmitted to a screen in another; it
was called television.

A regular ruse to get rid of unwanted callers was to say,
'It's a good story, but it's not quite up our street. Why don't
you try the *Mirror* or the *Express*?' And that is what he did.
The next morning a newspaper – I can't recall which one –
carried an exclusive story about the historic invention by
James Logie Baird.

As a penance, Maurice was detailed to see all front-hall
callers. Everything went well until a man called who claimed
to have built a machine that was capable of foretelling the
future. It was not, he insisted, mumbo-jumbo, but science.
Determined not to be caught out again, Maurice agreed to see
it demonstrated, whereupon the inventor arranged for the
contraption to be manhandled into the front hall. All he
needed was a socket to plug it into.

Maurice, who had visions of knowing the Derby winner in
advance, duly obliged. But when it was plugged in it blew out
the entire switchboard and plunged the building into
darkness.

'That's how I came to join the *Herald*,' he said.

There was a lovable streak of eccentricity about the man which I found irresistible. He told me that when he got home from the office his routine never varied. He went into his garage and urinated into an old kettle. It was, he said, a scientific fact that urine was good for roses. 'My wife disagrees. She thinks it's a filthy habit.'

And when he made a pot of tea he meticulously measured out how many cups were required before he filled the kettle. Not, of course, the one reserved for horticultural purposes. Then he would tinker with the gas until the jets covered a precise area of the bottom on the kettle. Experiments, he told me, had shown him at which height there was the least heat loss. Over the years, he reckoned, he had saved pounds. Although he was obsessed by thrift, he was the softest touch in The Street.

Over the years I did my fair share of seeing front-hall 'nutters', but only one sticks in my mind. I was sent down into the *Express* foyer to interview a man who wanted to talk about his role in the IRA. In those days the IRA were not in the news, they had lain dormant for years and it was to be a long time before the violence which still exists today erupted. They were seen as idealists in shabby raincoats, tragi-comic characters in the O'Casey mould. My task was made slightly less onerous by the News Editor's bribe that I could nip into Poppins as soon as I had got rid of him. Sitting in the hall was a nondescript character hugging a shoe box; he immediately began to regale me with stories of his clandestine work, which he coupled with a willingness to disclose all ... for a suitable sum. I listened politely before telling him the paper was not interested. Quite apart from it sounding old hat, I did not believe a word he said. Perhaps he sensed my disbelief because he became extremely angry and said, 'You don't believe me, do you?' Whereupon he opened the box and took out a very real revolver which he aimed at my head. I could see a good story in the offing, but not one I would be writing. 'Hang on, I'll have a word with the Editor,' I said, and got into the lift, got out at the first floor, nipped out the back and ran round to the front of the building where a patrolling policeman was always on duty.

I grabbed hold of his tunic and said, 'We've got a crazy bastard inside with a gun.'

'Is it loaded?' he asked.

'How the hell do I know? I wasn't going to find out the hard way.'

With that the constable turned his back on me and began walking up Fleet Street at a speed which was considerably faster than the regulation pace.

I went back and, with a certain amount of trepidation, renewed my conversation, explaining that the Editor wanted more information before he would consider buying. I then asked him if the gun was loaded. 'What kind of prick do you take me for? I'm not daft enough to go round with a loaded gun.'

I got into the lift again, repeated my little subterfuge and caught up with the constable near Chancery Lane. 'It's all right, the thing's not loaded.'

His shoulders stiffened visibly and he came back with me, walked into the front hall, grabbed the man and marched him off.

On a cold afternoon in September 1961, I was one of a group of newsmen standing on the wind-swept Denton Marshes near Gravesend while police frogmen dived into a narrow but deep ditch. We all knew what they would recover, for among the reporters was Hugh Saker of the *Daily Mirror* who had told us the strangest story. Soon afterwards the police found the body of Malcolm Johnson, a local lad, still wearing his Boys' Brigade uniform. Earlier they had recovered the body of his sweetheart Lillian Edmeads.

It was the front-hall story to crown them all.

It began at 10.30 in the morning when Tom Tullett, the Chief Crime Reporter of the *Mirror* was in his office working out the seating arrangements for a lunch he was giving to a visiting senior detective from abroad. Tom, an ex-detective himself, had covered some of the most hideous killings in his time and had become acclimatised to violence, if not immune to it. But what was to happen in the next half-hour was to shake even him. Like many younger reporters I owed much to Tom's wisdom and experience which he was never loath to share, and our friendship has extended over many years. He recalled the story in detail for me, standing in his favourite corner near the door at El Vino.

A very young secretary had knocked on his door and announced that he had a front-hall caller who had filled in the customary form, but had listed the purpose of his visit as 'confidential'. He gave his name as E.D. Sims and an address in Gravesend.

Tom agreed to see him, and was confronted by a tall, well-built man of about thirty, wearing hornrimmed glasses and carrying a parcel wrapped in newspaper.

The surprisingly conventional conversation – in view of what was to emerge – went:

'What can I do for you?'

'I want to confess to a double murder.'

'Who have you killed?'

'A man and a woman on the marshes at Gravesend.'

Tom, who was writing it all down, must have been reminded of his days as a policeman. Then the visitor produced a woman's handbag, a wallet, and two wrist-watches, one a woman's, the other a man's. Tom then asked him how he had killed them, and the man replied that he had gone there with a shotgun and two knives but had strangled them, then thrown the weapons away.

Tom decided that this was the appropriate moment to have an urgent call put through to the police, and whilst this was being done he continued his interrogation, eliciting from the man that he wanted to 'get it off his chest'.

Tom's pencil moved at speed across the paper as the man described how he had seen two teenagers on Denton Marshes, and attacked them at a spot not far from the Isolation Hospital. He gestured towards the paper parcel and said calmly, 'That contains parts of their bodies.' He then produced the names of the dead couple which he had scribbled on a scrap of paper. Having strangled them, he had mutilated them and thrown the bodies into a ditch.

Shortly afterwards, the police arrived, and opened the parcel, which contained two female breasts and other grisly portions of human anatomy.

By then my own office had been tipped off and I was

already on my way to Gravesend.

That same day I was in the Magistrates Court when the man accused of the double murder was remanded in custody. The *Mirror* was the only paper to carry a picture; it had been 'snatched' in the office by an astute photographer.

Tom went ahead and acted as host at his luncheon party, but admitted he had not eaten much.

At his trial, the man was described as a sexual psychopath suffering from diminished responsibility. He was jailed for twenty-one years.

That is too grim a note on which to end a chapter. Maurice should have the last word which is in much lighter vein.

He was sent down to see a particularly recalcitrant caller who insisted that he was the sole possessor of the story to end all stories. When Maurice asked him what it was, he confided that the world would end the next morning; it would be swept by a terrible pestilence and he would be the sole survivor. But, he said, brightening, as Maurice had been so attentive he would share the secret of survival with him so that together they would escape the holocaust. With that assurance he opened his suitcase and produced a pistol with two bullets in it. 'I will shoot you, then I will fire the other bullet into my brain, and together we will escape.'

Maurice thought quickly. 'We have a strict rule that before a reporter leaves the office he must seek the News Editor's permission.' To his surprise the caller agreed to his request, and Maurice was allowed to go upstairs where he called the police who promptly overpowered the poor wretch.

'Nothing untoward happened next day,' Maurice remarked.

4

OUT-OF-TOWNERS

I had no ambition to be anything other than a general reporter, although I knew many whose ultimate in life was to become a specialist, for that carried with it an aura of expertise which put them above the foot-in-the-door men, and their often suspect methods of news gathering. But it was a limited field, while the general reporter did everything, and never knew from one shift to the next what he would be doing, or where he would be going. One day he could be interviewing the Prime Minister, a famous film star, a millionaire, standing in a cemetery watching an exhumation, or talking to a gangster or to a down-and-out under Hungerford Bridge.

When the telephone rang at home in the middle of the night you awoke with a pounding heart; sometimes it was to change your shift, on the other hand it could be a call from the Foreign Desk, sending you half-way across the world.

It was great fun and unforgivably vain to name-drop in your local when you were asked what you had been doing. 'Oh, yesterday I interviewed the PM', or 'I was with J.B. Priestley.' Seldom did you reveal the fact that it had been an acutely embarrassing occasion.

(Name-dropping is, of course, not a weakness confined to journalists. I remember being at a party when a woman, learning that I was with the *Express*, came up and asked, 'How's Bill?' I had no idea to whom she was referring, and said so. 'William Hickey, of course. He's a great pal. Give him my regards.' I did not have the nerve to tell her that William Hickey was an eighteenth-century gossip and writer, who spent a long time in India, and most of his leisure hours

in brothels. The William Hickey column in the *Express* –
recently replaced by the Ross Benson column – was written
by a team of men and women supervised by an Editor, who
changed with great frequency.)

I did in fact interview the Prime Minister, Edward Heath,
in his Albany apartment. Although I can't remember a word
of what he said, I vividly recall that I split my trousers right
down the back as I was getting out of the taxi. Mr Heath was
a charming host, but could not understand why I insisted on
keeping my overcoat on in his warmly heated flat. When I got
back to the office I had to sit in the gents while one of the
secretaries went out and bought a needle and some thread.

And I did interview J.B. Priestley, who also lived in
Albany. When I arrived at the flat of the great novelist and
playwright, a cocktail party was in progress and an
impressive-looking gentleman stood at the open door
introducing guests in a booming voice. 'Mr Alfred Draper,'
he declaimed, making me sound like a contender for a boxing
title.

The great man, a portly figure with a pronounced
Yorkshire accent, grasped me firmly by the hand and asked
me what I would like to drink. 'A Scotch please, sir,' I said,
and an enormous tot was thrust into my hand. 'Where have
we met?' he enquired. 'We haven't. I'm from the *Daily
Express*.' He took the glass from my hand and uttered two
words which he would never have dreamed of using in one of
his books, and the man who had announced my arrival with
such gusto chucked me out.

It was, however, to be some time before I joined the
Express. I covered all kinds of stories on the *Herald* and
although I got my share of by-lines I had yet to break into
what was called the big time. Often that happened by pure
luck, but as I have said you had to have the ability to spot it
when it came and grab it, like a well-thrown pass. Fumble it
and the ball doesn't come your way again.

My first real break was on a story that came to be known as
the Houseboat Twins Case. It began with the story of the
discovery of the bodies of two small babies in a burned-out
houseboat in Benfleet on Canvey Island on the Thames
Estuary. Looking back, I'm surprised at the tremendous

interest it aroused, but the story ran for weeks and nearby Southend became my home from home, until two women were committed for trial at the Old Bailey. During that time I got several exclusives which brought commendations from the Editor. It also came close to bringing about my demise as a reporter. I had phoned over an exclusive story which made the front page, and I was cock-a-hoop with myself. Then I was summoned to the telephone and told by the News Editor that a colleague had been assured by a police contact that there was not a word of truth in it, and that it would be pulled out of the paper. If I agree it would be tantamount to saying I had made it up – which I hadn't – and face the sack. So I stuck to my guns and refused to agree to it being withdrawn. One of my close friends, Bill Tadd, a reporter with the Press Association, was sleeping in the hotel room adjoining mine and I knocked him up and handed him my copy. 'I've got an exclusive in the first edition. I don't want you dragged out of bed to chase it up. So I'm happy to let you have it.'

He gratefully accepted the story and soon afterwards I was called to the telephone again. The Night News Editor said, 'Sleep tight. PA have confirmed your story.'

To survive one had to be prepared to think fast and act quickly. As the story was true I did not think I had used Bill unfairly. But I must admit I was mightily relieved when, by courtesy of PA, my exclusive appeared in the next edition of every other paper.

Soon afterwards the entire Press contingent covering the story came perilously close to the sack. At the end of the committal proceedings, which were reported in full in those days, the solicitor acting for one of the women stood up and began a lengthy submission on the grounds that there was no case to answer. That may have been true, but we knew from past experience that magistrates usually disliked making such a decision, preferring to leave it to a jury. So we closed our notebooks and headed for the nearest pub, planning to return in time to hear the committal for trial. As we sipped our beers the local reporter dashed in and told us that the magistrates had agreed there was no case to answer, and the woman had been discharged. We left our drinks unfinished and raced back, knowing damn well that our offices would want an

interview with the woman in which she spoke of her undying
faith in British justice. Unfortunately, she had been taken off
to an unknown address, and all rivalry was forgotten as we
pooled our energies to try to find out where she was. The
police too had been caught napping and became as busy as we
were. Eventually they came up with an answer – they applied
for a Voluntary Bill of Indictment, a most unusual step,
which meant her immediate re-arrest. Our interest was one of
pure self-preservation; the rights and wrongs of the
magistrates' decision did not concern us in the least. If we had
not got an interview we would have been sacked *en masse*, so
when the police threw us the ball in the form of her re-arrest
we caught it and ran like hell – for the phone, to explain that
an interview was out of the question as the matter was now
sub judice.

I'm happy to record that a jury at the Old Bailey took the
same view as the magistrates and the woman was acquitted.
But I had been taught a lesson I was never to forget.

Those out-of-towners were great fun, for we usually stayed
in the best hotels, ate marvellous food and concealed the
amount drunk by getting the receptionist to provide 'moody'
bills which doubled the price of the room, and made us
appear commendably abstemious. I am sure that many hotels
were grateful for the unexpected revenue, but not at all sorry
to see the back of us. When a big story broke, Fleet Street
descended like a plague of locusts on a town, which often
wondered what had hit it. Whenever possible we booked in at
the same hotel in order to keep an eye on each other, and
when the day's work was over we would indulge in the most
schoolboyish pranks. This made us unpopular with the other
guests, although I never heard a night porter complain – they
were kept busy dispensing drinks until the early hours, but
they were well-tipped.

I recall one rather stuffy and rambling seaside hotel where a
group of elderly people, who enjoyed a rubber or two after
dinner, were casting disgusted glances in our direction as our
boisterous conversation destroyed their concentration.
Eventually they got up and departed in a cold and chilling
silence. As they entered the lift, all wrought-iron and velvet
wallpaper, they were confronted by the sight of a diminutive

photographer lying fast asleep on a mattress wearing his winceyette pyjamas and his trilby. A couple of reporters had crept into his room and carried him, mattress and all, into the lift without waking him.

If reporters seemed over-exuberant, even childish, one has to realise that normality did not exist for us. The commonplace did not make news, but events which ordinary people seldom encountered were everyday occurrences to us. We saw charred and unrecognisable bodies being retrieved from crashed aircraft and trains. (On a Yugoslav mountainside in broiling heat, I saw men with fly-killer kits strapped to their backs spraying the bodies of British holidaymakers killed in an aircrash so that they could be identified.) And we wrote about monsters such as Haigh and Christie, and about tragedies like the one that struck the small Welsh mining village of Aberfan and wiped out all the children. We had to be case-hardened to continue.

The number of hours we worked was unlimited – you could start in the morning and still be at it when the last edition went to bed. Overtime was unheard of, and you stayed with a story until it was finished. Sometimes a considerate News Editor would observe at the end of a story, 'We must owe you some time off.' Their deeds seldom matched their words; when you totted up the days owing you were lucky to be told, 'Take tomorrow off.' But no reporter ever complained, and if the suggestion was made that a relief should be sent, all hell was raised. It was *your* story.

But some kind of safety valve was needed to counteract the tremendous strain under which we worked, and this often took the form of high spirits. Only those who have worked on a daily paper can appreciate that. The celluloid image of the reporter sitting at a typewriter hammering out his story, with an editor peering anxiously over his shoulder, seldom happened in real life. Stories were written on the bonnets of cars, in phone booths, roadside cafés and pubs. All too often they were dictated off the cuff.

Looking through my long-forgotten and dust-gathering files I came across this letter from my boss Keith Howard, News Editor of the *Express*:

What a wonderful story we had this morning on the Diana Dors situation. The opposition looked quite sick with their rather anaemic accounts of what happened at London Airport. Most of them failed completely to capture the rather bizarre humour of this situation. This morning, I have heard nothing but the most enthusiastic and glowing comments round the office on the fine piece which you turned in for us.

It was a long day – but a most successful one, and I am very grateful for the tremendous effort which you made and which produced such a good story.

It was that kind of pat on the back we lived for and were prepared, as we often did, to risk our lives for. But I can say in all honesty that I cannot even recall what the Dors story was about.

I was on the *Herald* when I first met Brendan Behan, the tearaway Irish poet and playwright who had in his youth been an IRA man. He first came to prominence with his book *Borstal Boy*, and had by the time I met him become a famous literary figure, lionised wherever he went. He had a comic genius and was a wonderful raconteur, but already he was showing signs of that fatal Celtic flaw for self-destruction which has ruined so many great talents. He was drinking too much and was seldom out of scrapes. A stocky, unkempt chap with a bent beak of a nose, his suits were always rumpled and creased as if he had slept in them, which in many instances was the case. He was invariably tieless, and I got the impression that his appearance was not entirely due to indifference, but also to a belief that he had to live up to his image. At the time, he was writing a regular column for the *People*, and although he was often drunk he was a true professional who never failed to produce his copy on time. On this particular occasion he had had a mid-air row aboard a transatlantic aircraft when he suddenly decided he wanted to get off. If it had not been for the other passengers I'm sure the pilot would have happily obliged. When he arrived at London Airport he was sporting a prune-coloured black eye and I was sent to find out what had happened. But when he came through customs he refused to talk; he was, he said, in no fit state to grant interviews, he wanted to clean up and change first. However, he would meet me in the Cross Keys opposite the *Herald* in a couple of hours' time. I was resigned to his not turning up, but I went there and waited. To my surprise he arrived at the appointed time and gave me a long interview. Contrary to what many people said he did not revel in his misbehaviour and was quite penitent. As a pressman, he explained, he felt he should be exposed. Unfortunately, his conscience was very elastic, especially after he had downed a few Guinnesses.

I met him again in Dublin where he invited me to his home and introduced me to the dubious delights of poteen, illegally stilled potato whisky. I found it vile-tasting and more suited to be a paint remover, for it hit the stomach like a ball of molten metal. A glass of water in the morning was enough to revive its lethal qualities. I can't believe that anyone seriously enjoyed drinking it, and I suspect it was sheer bravado on his part; it was as Irish as a peat bog and that was reason enough for Brendan.

In the early summer of 1959, Brendan's play *The Hostage* opened at Wyndham's Theatre to rapturous applause and rave reviews; it is a wildy rambling play but hilariously funny, poking irreverent fun at the Irish, the IRA, the British, Royalty, religion, and the author himself. But Brendan was not there to witness his triumph. He was reported to be seriously ill in a Dublin hospital and drinking only lemonade instead of stout and Irish whiskey chasers. 'I haven't had a jar for over a week,' he said. 'I'm getting what I really want – plenty of rest and sleep.'

His friends kept their fingers crossed, but their hopes were short-lived. He discharged himself and decided to visit London and see his play. By this time I had joined the *Daily Express*. Brian Park, one of the paper's most versatile reporters, who knew Brendan well, was telephoned by anxious friends and asked if he would meet the writer at London Airport. He was again drinking heavily and causing a great deal of concern to those close to him, especially his wife Beatrice. Unfortunately, neither she nor any of his friends were able to fly with him to ensure he reached the theatre without any mishaps.

Brian, who was off duty, promised to do his best and waited at the arrival point for the Dublin passengers to come through. 'I knew,' he told me, 'that Brendan had arrived as soon as I heard the racket erupting from the Customs Hall. The playwright eventually appeared, escorted by an airline official and a policeman, trying not very successfully to tuck in his shirt which was open to the waist. His fellow passengers looked deeply shocked and gave him a wide berth. Brendan dragged his escorts to where I was waiting and said it was a hell of a time since he'd had a drink and it was my round.'

The airline official, however, said that a drink was the last thing Brendan needed as he had been at it throughout the flight, and the policeman warned Brian to get him out of the place before he was forced to arrest him.

From then on it became a saga of disasters for Brian. As he tried to lead Brendan to his car, he found himself being tugged towards the nearest bar. 'I was upset to see the state of the man since our last meeting. Then he had seemed merely uproarious with the apparent ability to shrug it off with a stream of chatter that was brilliant. But now the clothes, the face, and the man inside looked none too good.'

Brian managed to get him into his car, but, a short distance from Heathrow, Brendan grabbed the wheel and said that he was determined to have a drink and if Brian did not believe him he would crash the car and they would meet an even queerer fellow. After a hair-raising drive, they stopped at a pub where Brendan gave a beery rendering of 'The Red Flag' and was showered with pennies before being thrown out. Eventually Brian managed to get him to the flat of the friend he was due to stay with, and there he was put to bed, with Brian promising to pick him up later and drive him to Wyndham's. This he did, but before he could hand Brendan his suit, which was in the boot of the car, he disappeared. It was at this point that I was brought into the story, sent by the Night News Editor to give Brian a hand in finding the wayward genius. After touring various pubs, I found Behan in one which was renowned for its theatrical association, holding court before a mesmerised audience who, stupidly, were encouraging him to drink even more. His shirt was wet with spilt brandy and he could only get the glass to his lips with the aid of a tie which was tied to his wrist and passed round his neck and used like a pulley. It was a tragic sight to see such a great talent being rapidly destroyed.

By then he was beyond listening to reason, and insisted that he was going to see his play. He burst into the foyer, pounded on the box-office counter and demanded two seats; one of the management staff uttered a forlorn 'Oh, Lord, no', but Brendan was adamant. Before taking his seat, though, he decided to go outside and perform to the waiting queue of galleryites. They were already being entertained by a group of buskers, but Brendan bellowed, 'Shut up! I'm here now.' Grabbing one of their bowler hats, he sang three Gaelic songs, passed the hat round and handed over its contents to the buskers. We observed it all with growing apprehension.

Eventually a dishevelled Brendan took his seat in the stalls, where most of the audience were wearing dinner jackets. He greeted them with a shout of 'Idiots!', before his companion pulled him down into his seat. But he rose unsteadily and sang an Irish rebel song, then roared, 'Up the rebels! Up the Chinese!' During the playing of the National Anthem he was the only person who remained seated.

He was certainly playing to the gallery, but, even worse – or better, depending on how you viewed his antics – was to come, as he continually interrupted the cast – forcing the actor who was playing an IRA man to introduce an improvised line: 'I'll have *you* shot.'

At the first interval, Brendan headed for the nearest pub, with Brian and me close on his heels. 'If my wife is expecting me back in Dublin tonight she is wrong. I'll be back when I feel like it,' he stormed. 'I had to get away for a few days. I'm fed up with milk and lemonade. They're all right for children and weaklings.'

After the interval, there were further interruptions, which some of the audience found more entertaining than the play, and which others found inexcusable and tiresome. At one stage he stopped an actor in the middle of a speech, announcing, 'I've altered it for you.'

When the curtain came down he went onto the stage, started to make a speech, abandoned it and danced a jig instead.

Next day Brendan got the headlines he hoped for.

The jag continued, however. His wife Beatrice and his father-in-law sent urgent pleas from Dublin: 'Please stop him drinking – it could kill him.' But nothing short of a humane killer could have done that.

I did not share Brendan's view of his own drinking; he thought he could see everyone else under the table, but he could not. Very little made him extremely ill. The image of a riproaring genius who could hold his booze existed only in his own mind. Mercifully, this bender was halted by the arm of the law in the form of a very concerned constable, who spotted the familiar figure weaving a precarious and unsteady course past the Astor Club and the fashionable boutiques and florists of Mayfair. The playwright was escorted to a nearby telephone booth, and a few minutes later a black maria arrived and took him to West End Central police station. It was the best thing that could have happened to him. He was charged with being drunk and put into a cell where he promptly fell asleep. When he had sobered up he was released on a ten-shilling bail, to appear at Bow Street Magistrates Court the following day.

He pleaded guilty, and when asked if he wished to say anything replied, 'Yes, sir. I want you to know I didn't get the black eye from the cops. They were very nice and civil to me.' He was fined five shillings, and ordered to pay £1 for the doctor who had been called out.

A crowd of about sixty people lined the pavement outside the court and saw him whisked away in a waiting car. Brian and I heaved a heartfelt sigh of relief at his departure. But, on the way to the airport, he insisted on stopping at a pub where he downed a quick Scotch followed by a beer. That was enough to trigger off another bout. At the airport he cheerfully signed autographs and continued drinking. And it carried on in Dublin. Commenting on the trail of havoc, he had left behind, he said, 'It was worth it. It has done my play a world of good. I wanted to get away and collect some money. I got an advance from the theatre and I had a good time.'

The boasting and braggadocio were veneer-thin, and he knew it; he was heading for skid row and could not halt the slide, and so hid his concern by pretending he was living as he wished to. But, in a moment of lucidity, he confided that he dreaded what he was doing to his talent.

Brian never saw him after that disastrous night at Wyndham's. 'He died five years later. Our last meeting was a pathetic dress-rehearsal for the inevitable,' he said.

But I bumped into Brendan occasionally, and, quite by chance, happened to be in Dublin on the day of his funeral. It had been a tragic end for a man who could have risen to even greater literary heights. I did not attend the funeral, but I remember going into a public house where some people who claimed to have known him were holding a wake. A tourist came in, and the talk centred around the dead author. When the stranger tried to sit in a chair below one of the windows he was stopped. 'You wouldn't be after sitting in Brendan's favourite chair, now, would you?' he was warned. The chair, he was told, was where the writer had sat and pondered over his best work. The tourist ended up buying it.

I was convinced that Brendan had never sat in it – just as I'm convinced that it was only one of many chairs sold that day. He would have appreciated it.

5

THE SUNNY SIDE OF
THE STREET

I enjoyed my time on the *Herald*, which would have been an extremely good paper if it had not been hampered by the TUC, which had a controlling interest, and tended to concentrate on Labour Party and Trades Union news, and there were those among us who resented the belief among some politicians that they could dictate to the Editor and the writers. Tragically, there always seemed to be a self-destructive element in the Labour Party which managed to throw a spanner in the works at the most crucial times. A typical example occurred during the visit to Britain of the Russian leaders Bulganin and Kruschev. Although Anthony Eden was Prime Minister, it was the view of the Labour Party that only they were capable of establishing the rapport that would take the chill out of the Cold War, and that belief was reflected in the *Herald*. Every move of the two visitors was followed and dutifully reported, which was understandable as it attracted phenomenal interest in a people who were sick and tired of living on the brink of war. Security was on an unprecedented scale, and it was the first time I saw police marksmen concealed behind the chimney pots of buildings overlooking the places the Russians visited. I never envisaged the day when such scenes would be commonplace.

One of the highlights of the visit was a dinner, given in the visitors' honour by the Labour Party, in the House of Commons. It was a private affair from which the Press was excluded, but it was soon leaked that the volatile George Brown had lost his temper, thumped the table and said some harsh things to the guests of honour. George Brown was renowned as a tippler, and it occurred to every newsman that he had dined too well and let his tongue get the better of him, but he was a figure of importance and his words and actions were newsworthy. The *Herald had* to report the row, but did so in no great detail; the damage had been done, however, because the right-wing Press felt no such restraint and welcomed the unexpected gift, to which it gave considerable prominence. It was a distinct own goal as far as the Labour Party was concerned, for it prompted one of the Russians to say that if he lived in Britain he would vote Tory.

I experienced an incident which spotlighted this weakness when a dinner was given in a London hotel from which the Press was again excluded, and I was detailed to hang around the lobby and buttonhole anyone – guests, waiters, waitresses – and try to extract some crumbs of copy. But everyone who left the dining room remained close-lipped, and I retired to the bar with a reporter from the Press Association with the intention of having another crack when the function ended. Suddenly a diminutive but vociferous left-wing MP stormed in, demanding to know if there were any reporters around. His face lit up when we introduced ourselves, and he urged us to produce our notebooks as he had a good story for us.

It was a savage attack on some of the Party leaders, and I phoned over the story which made the later editions.

Next morning I was called in by the Editor and told that the MP had denied ever talking to me and was demanding a retraction and threatening legal action. I had no intention of committing professional suicide, and insisted that the interview had taken place and said I would take private action if an apology was published. Furthermore, I pointed out, the Press Association would verify my story. Unfortunately, when I contacted PA I was told that as the story had not been circulated they did not want to become involved. They had saved my skin in the past, but now I learned the hard way that the ploy could not be relied on. To his credit, the Editor stood by me and there was no retraction, and the threatened writ did not materialise.

What prompted the MP to seek me out, then deny it, I never understood; I suspect he was mainly interested in discrediting people whose views he did not share, and, having done that, wanted to emerge with clean hands.

It was the first, but not the last time, that I was let down. Over the years I discovered that most sections of the community, and politicians in particular, can summon up convenient bouts of amnesia when they read something they regret having said. No phrase has done more harm to the reputation of the Press than 'I was misreported', for it has been stated so often that it has acquired a ring of truth. But from my experience I found that, nine times out of ten, it was merely an excuse to avoid embarrassment. When you analyse it, what good would it serve a reporter? He would only be making a rod for his own back.

It would be misleading to say that the incident was instrumental in my leaving the *Herald*, but it played a part. I felt, rightly or wrongly, that because of its umbilical tie with the Labour Party and the TUC, the paper was becoming dull and over-prone to outside pressure, and was consequently signing its own death warrant.

The paper I admired most – as did a great many reporters – was the *Daily Express*, then being edited by Arthur Christiansen, the stocky bespectacled son of a Danish shipwright. He had revolutionised newspaper techniques with bold, brash headlines, and crisp well-written stories. He had flair and imagination and was famous for his cryptic bulletins and pithy comments. 'Shun clichés like the plague,' was one memorable piece of advice to his reporters. Many said he made the *Express* – but never within earshot of its proprietor, Lord Beaverbrook, who would not tolerate the suggestion that anyone was his equal.

Chris's meteoric rise began when, as Assistant Editor of the *Sunday Express*, he scooped all his rivals with an exclusive front-page splash on the R101 disaster. A news-flash of the airship's crash came in very late when he had retired home to bed, but he was back in the office within minutes, stopped the presses and replated the entire front page while special trains were hired to deliver the scoop to all parts of the country.

Not long afterwards, Beaverbrook decided to appoint him Assistant Editor of the *Daily Express*, then being edited by Beverley Baxter. Baxter, very much a man-about-town who

preferred the theatre to long gruelling stints on the Back
Bench, resented the appointment and tendered his resignation. Beaverbrook expressed his regrets, but would not
alter his decision. Baxter paused and then said, 'In that case, I
withdraw my resignation.'

I dearly wanted to join the paper, but so did a lot of
ambitious young men and it was only through the personal
recommendation of Donald Seaman that I finally made it.

I had first met Seaman on a murder story, where the
detective in charge of the investigation was rather hostile to
the Press. However, he was a superb darts player, one of
those who carried his own darts around with him, and Don
challenged him to a game in a local pub, casually enquiring if
'Three in a bed' won. Don, who was normally lucky to hit the
board after a dozen attempts, walked up and put three darts in
the treble twenty – a not inconsiderable feat, considering how
much we had been drinking. Don declined to play another
game on the grounds that it would be so obviously one-sided.
The detective promptly became a friend and confidant on
whom we could rely for a steady stream of information.

Don had already acquired a high reputation as a reporter
and foreign correspondent, and I was intrigued by the
buttons on his blazer which he assured me were solid gold.
Gold, he explained, was a useful commodity if you were
stuck anywhere without funds. Any paper that provided its
men with such a portable Fort Knox was irresistible. (Don
assures me he was not leg-pulling.)

I still have the letter of employment welcoming me to the
'team' on the then princely salary of £30 a week.

Soon afterwards, Christiansen was to leave the Editor's
chair for a high executive position, and his place was taken by
Ted Pickering. I heard that Beaverbrook had pushed Chris
upstairs because someone had written that he was responsible
for the success of the *Express*, but colleagues close to The
Beaver have assured me that he did it in order to save Chris's
life after a serious heart attack.

Ted Pickering, now Sir Edward – a tall, pencil-slim man
who does not appear to be paying a lot of attention to what
you are saying, but has a mind like a gimlet and is able to
absorb the most complicated explanations as to why a story

should be pursued – would look up, peer over his glasses and give you the go-ahead if he approved; from then on, you could count on his wholehearted support. He may not have had the external charisma some Editors flaunted, but in my opinion he had no peer. He was a many-faceted man; not only was he a very accomplished pianist, he was an acknowledged expert on a variety of subjects. In the office he was 'Sir', in Poppins he met his reporters on equal terms. He later became Chairman of the *Mirror* group of newspapers, and then of *The Times*. He remains one of the most respected figures in the newspaper world.

I served under several Editors subsequently and all were brilliant men – you did not get the job if you weren't – but I always retained a particular regard for 'Pick'. Editors came and went on the *Express* with astonishing rapidity – security of tenure did not go with the position. Some of them deserved to be replaced, others did not; sometimes they went on the whim of the proprietor, but that was a risk they were well aware of when they took the job. Some departed with the staff feeling a genuine sense of loss; the demise of others was celebrated in Poppins. But one quickly learned that Fleet Street was a cruel place at times, and one where you did not wear your heart on your sleeve – it was too obvious and tempting a target. Long after Christiansen had retired and gone into television, I happened to bump into him at Southend Airport where I was covering a very unimportant story about a beauty queen. Chris had clearly not lost his zest for newspapers, and he followed the activities of the reporters with great interest. When he casually remarked to one young reporter that he was the ex-Editor of the *Daily Express*, the young man replied, 'Well, you can't get much more ex than that.' That – to a man who was acknowledged as one of the finest Editors the newspaper industry has ever had.

But no matter how brilliant the Editor of the time happened to be, the controlling voice was Lord Beaverbrook's. Although much has been written and said about him, he still remains an enigma long after his death. There was an unquestionable magic about him, and even today, when people ask me what he was really like I have to say, 'I don't really know.' He seldom appeared in the office, and, apart

from a favoured few, I doubt if he knew his reporters other
than as by-lines. I can only recall seeing him once in the office
but his presence was felt. On a plinth in the front hall was
Epstein's head of the 'Old Man', and such was his authority
that when you passed it you expected it to bark out an order.
I remember the inquest that was held when somebody
committed sacrilege by sticking a cigarette end between those
rather sensual lips.

He was a short man with a pronounced paunch and an
almost round head with a wide slash of a mouth. He had made
a vast fortune in Canada before coming to this country, but it
was unwise for anyone to probe too deeply into how he
acquired his immense wealth. It was buried in shadow, and
Beaverbrook saw to it that the shadow was never lifted.

Few knew him better than Percy Hoskins, one of Fleet
Street's most highly regarded crime reporters, and Beaverbrook's chief trouble-shooter, who said of him, 'He could be
obdurate, formidable, kind, cruel and whimsical.' It is neither
a tribute not a condemnation, and that is about as fair a
description as you are likely to get.

Beaverbrook ruled his empire through fear and was totally
ruthless, as the list of casualties bears witness. He had the
power to hire and fire, and he did both things with great zest.
It was *his* paper and he was entitled to do so, but there were
too many times when he deprived a man of his livelihood for
petty vindictive reasons which had nothing to do with ability.
He sacked one man for having nicotine-stained fingers, and
another for wearing yellow socks. Others were asked for their
frank opinion of his newspapers, and when they gave it were
dismissed. Certainly, Alan Dick's advice – 'make sure you
remain at the bottom' – did not apply; as far as Beaverbrook
was concerned there was no hiding place. He relished telling
his staff that they were married to the paper and there was no
divorce, but there were certainly some abrupt separations.

I make no apology for giving the impression that I did not
share the admiration he commanded. In my opinion the tiny
man was inflated into giant proportions by people who
mistakenly saw warts as stigmata. Undoubtedly he was a
newspaperman of genius with an uncanny knack of making
money, but he contributed little to history except an ability to

back lost and hopeless causes. The nasty aspect of his character was the pursuit of petty vendettas to their illogical conclusion. Many of his victims were men who have altered the course of history, and nothing Beaverbrook said or did can alter that fact.

His choice of personal friends was certainly bewildering; he surrounded himself with the most unlikely company, considering his right-wing politics. But not all fell for Beaverbrook's undoubted ability to charm. Malcolm Muggeridge considered him to be an evil man who had sold his soul to the devil, while Evelyn Waugh expressed his dislike more wittily: 'Of course I believe in the Devil. How otherwise would I account for the existence of Lord Beaverbrook?'

When Beaverbrook was in London he ruled his empire from his eyrie apartment in Arlington House in fashionable St James's, and an invitation there could spell make-or-break in a man's career. I went only once to Arlington House and that was not by invitation, but as a reporter covering some crime or other which I can no longer remember. What sticks in my mind, and my craw, is the strict enjoinder that on no account was I to attempt to interview any of the residents or try to enter the citadel. Beaverbrook did not want his privacy invaded, although he wanted the story to appear in the *Express*. So I had to hang around in a nearby pub until one of my friends from an opposition paper, who had no such restrictions, but was aware of Beaverbrook's perversity, filled me in. Anyone else's house, and I would have been expected to gain entry by fair means or foul.

He was a human Rubik Cube who ran his newspapers by remote control, summoning his editors to Arlington House, the floors of which were littered with newspapers which he had read and tossed aside. There his regular briefings took place, often followed by a stroll in Green Park where a dutiful editor, notebook in hand, jotted down an endless stream of directives barked out in a drawl that was mimicked in every Fleet Street pub. Little escaped his attention and events of momentous import along with items of the utmost triviality were jotted down. Theirs was not to reason why. They knew the alternative. He not only paid the piper and called the tune, he expected everyone to dance.

Apart from his personal briefings, he inundated his editors with memos written on any old scrap of paper, for he was obsessed with economy and it was quite common for his executives or heads of foreign bureaux, when they wrote to him, to soil new envelopes so that they appeared to have already been used. He also made extensive use of the dictaphone, rasping out his commandments at breathtaking speed.

To pin him down is like trying to trap a globule of quicksilver with your thumb. I was told two stories that reveal his mercurial nature. One of the *Express*'s drivers told me that he was driving Beaverbrook and an editor through London one day when he was suddenly told to stop. 'When they got out, Beaverbrook pointed to a steeplejack working on a very tall chimney stack. "Everyone has his price," he said, and got back into the car.'

Arthur Brittenden, one of the *News Chronicle*'s top reporters when Beaverbrook spotted him and invited him to join the *Sunday Express*, told me how one day, when he was in New York, he received an invitation to walk with Beaverbrook in Central Park. This, he thought, was the big break he wanted and a turning point in his career. After a short stroll together, most of which was spent in total silence, Beaverbrook paused to study dozens of pigeons pecking at scraps of food. He remained silent for several minutes, then remarked, 'Pigeons, Mr Brittenden.' Arthur at a complete loss for words, could only respond, 'Pigeons, Lord Beaverbrook.'

'Yes,' said Beaverbrook. 'Greedy birds. Eat a great deal. Do very little work.'

Recalling the incident, Arthur told me, 'The inference was quite clear – that nothing reminded him so much of pigeons as me and my fellow journalists.'

I remember the occasion when I was suspended for falling down on a most insignificant story in which Beaverbrook had been personally interested. Largely because of this I left the *Express* and went to work for the BBC for a time. The story concerned an MP who was said to have used his influence to delay the departure of a train when he was late leaving the House. I was detailed to find out who was the arrogant Member who considered himself so important he could inconvenience hundreds of commuters. The efforts I made to find him are not worth detailing, but I put in hours of work without success. The next morning, the MP was named in the *Daily Herald*, and all hell broke loose in the office. Apparently Beaverbrook was furious at my failure. On reflection I find it amusing that a man who himself so blatantly abused his authority should have been so incensed, but he was. Bob Edwards, the Editor, summoned me into his office and subjected me to a gruelling and most humiliating third degree. That, I thought, was the end of the affair, but no, I was called back again and given another roasting. Eventually I was suspended and sent home. I'm sure that Bob would not have minded too much, he was a good enough journalist to know that everyone falls down now and again, but with Beaverbrook breathing down his neck he had to pursue it.

Ironically, the *Herald* had named the wrong man, and I was able to confirm this with a pal from that paper. But it did not make any difference. Keith Howard, the News Editor, telephoned me at home and said he had a good story for me; it was obvious that he was doing his utmost to forget the whole silly incident, but, foolishly perhaps, I felt I was entitled to an apology, which I did not get. It rankled, and soon afterwards I went to the BBC to work on *This Is Your Life*.

When the programme ended its long run with the BBC – it was revived by Independent Television – I was without a job, but soon I was fortunate enough to be invited to join the *Daily Mail*. Two years after leaving the *Express* I rejoined. I was to have been interviewed by Roger Wood, who had replaced Bob Edwards, but when I turned up Bob was back in the chair. I thought, that's the end of that, but Bob gave me a handsome rise and the subject of the MP and the held-up train was never again mentioned. 'Everybody here is delighted at the news that you are coming back,' Bob wrote to me. By then Lord Beaverbrook was a sick man, and his son, Sir Max, was virtually in control. If the Old Man had still been at the helm I'm sure he would have scuppered any chance I had of returning. He had no time for prodigal sons. As far as he was concerned, if you left him there was no question of coming in from the cold.

On my first day back I went into the library to get some cuttings and the librarian greeted me with the words, 'Glad you're better, Alf.' I had been missed so much he just thought I had been off sick.

Sir Max Aitken had none of his father's genius and when he took over the reins he was not very good. Perhaps too much was expected of him. The sons of famous fathers so often have a cross to bear that proves too great a burden. Although there was no doubt that Lord Beaverbrook loved his son, and admired him for what he did in the war, he was extremely cruel and unkind to him. He seemed to take a perverse delight in ridiculing him in front of guests, many of whom worked on his newspaper.

It seemed to me that Sir Max tried to model himself too closely on his father instead of trying to do things his own way. One of the first things he should have done was move the bust of his father from the front hall and given it a place of honour elsewhere. As it was, Beaverbrook's brooding presence seemed still to be there. Max was a distant and remote employer who seldom appeared in the Big Room. On one occasion he threw a magnificent party for the editorial staff, and the drink and food was lavish and plentiful, but it was completely devoid of atmosphere and everybody I spoke to seemed to have turned up because it amounted to a near Royal command. If we had not been formally announced I don't think he would have known many of our names. Someone had to stand behind him with a pile of cards containing details which he whispered like a prompt.

Without any doubt the circulation of the *Daily Express* began to decline under Sir Max's control, and many placed the blame on his shoulders, but that I think was unfair; circulations were plummeting everywhere. What was true was that he lacked his father's flair for picking men of outstanding talent to fill some important positions.

You can go into any Fleet Street pub today and at some time or another a story will be related about Lord Beaverbrook, but you don't often hear one about Sir Max. At least, not relating to newspapers. His not inconsiderable talents lay elsewhere.

I can only remember being involved in one story in which he was personally interested, and I relate it because it seems to shed some light on the reason for his failure.

Keith Howard called me in one morning and said, 'Go to the Isle of Wight and expose the scandal at Cowes.' When I asked him what it was, he merely said, 'Ring me when you get there.' The mere mention of Cowes was enough to set any reporter trembling, because Sir Max, who had a splendid house overlooking the harbour, was the uncrowned king of Britain's yachting Mecca. I duly phoned when I arrived there and was made no wiser; it was up to me to find out what the scandal was and expose it. Broad hints were dropped that Sir Max was very interested and it would be unwise to fall down on the story, but, to make things doubly difficult, I was not to approach him.

I had been to the island on numerous occasions and over the years had made some very good contacts and friends, but after a few days I still had not got a whiff of any scandal. I telephoned Keith and reported total failure, and he put me out of my misery by recalling me. I had hardly set foot in the office, however, when he said rather apologetically that I had to go back and expose the scandal at Cowes. Again I did the rounds, drawing a blank everywhere. Having no other trail to follow, I began to hang around a pub near the ferry point, which was frequented by yachtsmen and professional cameramen, and kept my ear to the ground; still I remained in the dark. I can't recall the exact details, but I met a member of Sir Max's staff who insisted on giving me a conducted tour of his house. He showed me the magnificent dining room and what I took to be a swimming pool until the man said, 'Sir Max uses that for washing his sails. I've seen it filled with champagne.' Thereupon he became rather confiding. I emphasised that I was not a *friend* but an employee and did not want to hear anything I should not because I could end up being fired. I beat a hasty retreat.

Eventually I did unearth a minor scandal. It concerned a local dignitary who had gone off with 'another woman'. It certainly wasn't worth writing about, and when I told Keith he called me back once more.

On my way up to the Big Room I shared the lift with John

Coote, the General Manager, who observed, 'You have got the wrong story', or words to that effect. I just had time to pick up some money before I was on my way back to the Isle of Wight.

This time I did get the story, which was related to me in great detail by someone in the know. It was so unimportant that I can't remember the details, but it had something to do with a decision by the local council which would affect Sir Max's moorings. The particulars had been given to my informant by Sir Max himself. I was not even required to write a story.

I never found out what the object of the futile exercise was, and frankly I did not care. It just seemed totally pointless and did nothing to enhance Sir Max's image in my eyes. Why on earth he could not have given the News Editor the details in the first place mystifies me.

But such idiosyncrasies were not a rarity.

Sir Max took a deep personal interest in the Rhodesia problem and was most anxious to see that a settlement was reached, and on his own initiative he met Ian Smith in the hope of getting meaningful talks going. His involvement was due more to his friendship with Smith, which went back to their Battle of Britain days, than a desire to go down in history as a diplomat of statesmanlike proportions. But certainly he paved the way for the famous talks aboard HMS *Tiger* in Gibraltar.

Although Sir Max was probably more *au fait* with what would be discussed than anyone apart from the British Prime Minister and Smith, Norman Smart was sent to Gibraltar in the utmost secrecy to keep an eye on things. In order to appear like an ordinary tourist, he was told to take his wife and book a suite at the Rock Hotel, the finest in Gibraltar.

Norman entertained everyone within sight and had a wonderful time at the office's expense, and when the talks concluded he took his wife on a motor-boat trip to Algeçiras to have lunch with an old friend.

In the middle of lunch his host's telephone rang with instructions for Norman to ring the office immediately. It was a matter of great urgency, he was told, and he experienced that deep sinking feeling all reporters get when an urgent call arrives from out of the blue. 'We hurried back to Gib,' said Norman. 'I was worried something had gone wrong, that I had been scooped ... It was Max, who had heard that disposable lights were available in Gibraltar and would I bring him back a dozen.'

6

Spare No Expenses

In its halcyon days, the *Express*, with a circulation of well over four million, was a Colossus which bestrode the world. Its foreign coverage was unmatchable. Money was no object, and if there was a story worth covering in the remotest part of the globe the *Express* sent a man. Its maxim was, 'First in, last out.' In fact, part of that slogan provided many an introduction to a story when a reporter arrived in a trouble spot and had to file before he had had time to size up the situation. 'I was the first man into bullet-riddled ... ' was a great stand-by. Much as the taxi driver who took you from the airport to your hotel became 'a well-informed source'.

The paper had bureaux manned by staff men in Paris, New York, Rome, Beirut, Berlin, Washington, Moscow and many other capitals. And, dotted around the world, were men known as 'stringers'. They were of many nationalities, but their by-lines were always anglicised when they appeared in the paper – Beaverbrook would not permit a foreign name to appear above a story.

Sadly, the foreign side of the *Express* today reflects the great changes that have taken place in the newspaper world. Nearly all the bureaux have been closed, and that famous breed of globe-trotters for which the *Express* was renowned has become an endangered species. Today there are no René MacColls, Sefton Delmers, Donald Seamans and Noel Barbers or James Camerons, to name but a few. They not only looked the part, they played it to the full. Whenever one of them set foot in the office he received the red-carpet treatment, sometimes with embarrassing results. One day a rather shy young man arrived in the Big Room and was escorted to the Foreign Desk where he was introduced as the New South Wales correspondent. Derek Stark, who handled all the travel and financial arrangements, was instructed to take him out for a slap-up lunch. After a splendid meal the bewildered man asked Derek why he merited all the fuss, and Derek explained that anyone from Australia was automatically given VIP treatment. It slowly dawned on the visitor that a terrible mistake had occurred. 'I said I was the new South Wales man.'

The Foreign Desk was sited in a corner of the Big Room opposite the subs' table, but in clear view of the reporters' desks. I used to cast a covetous eye at the really great men as they ambled over to the Foreign Desk – René, the jewel in the *Express* crown, debonair and always sporting a red carnation; or Delmer, with his trilby pulled down low over his forehead like a gangster in an old Hollywood movie – to be briefed about some exotic place which existed for me in name only. I imagined myself in their shoes, only to be brought back to reality with orders to hot-foot it to Paddington where the fire brigade were trying to extricate a child who had managed to jam his head between some railings. In time I was to see young reporters do exactly the same as I had done, when I walked over to pick up my airline tickets and travellers cheques. One thing about the *Express* was that if you bided your time your chance would eventually come, and if you made good there would be more foreign trips.

Norman Smart was one of the Foreign Editors I worked under and one I came to like very much, but it was a slow process. A tall, broad-shouldered man with a slight stoop, he put the fear of Christ into me until I got to know him better and found he was a charming man with a great deal of consideration for the people who worked for him. The hard-boiled approach was a thin veneer. Executives had to appear tough – it was part of the expected image, and certainly part of their survival kit. Foreign Editors changed as frequently as Editors.

Norman, who began his career at a time when reporters were treated abysmally, has told me a great deal of his early struggles to reach Fleet Street and they are an object lesson in tireless endeavour and undiminished optimism, which should serve as an inspiration to any aspiring journalists who fear they will never make it. It is a cliché that journalists are born not made, but in my experience nothing is truer; there has to be a burning desire that is not motivated by the attraction of money. Anyone who put in as much hard work as a *Daily Express* man was expected to do would have succeeded anywhere.

Norman's first job was on the *Portsmouth Evening News* for 10 shillings a week, and his duties included not only reporting but proof reading – which embraced the adverts as well – for as long as twelve hours a day. Later, he covered the Isle of Wight and one of his many duties was to travel up and down the mile-long pier at Ryde several times a day to collect maritime news. Each trip cost one penny, but he discovered he could get a season for five pounds. 'From then on I charged the office for each separate journey. That was my first expense fiddle,' he told me. It was the start of a brilliant career in that direction. His second, more ambitious, fiddle was when he moved to another paper in Norfolk where, weary of doing his enormous round on a pedal cycle, he decided to ask for a motorbike. He saw one for sale for £20, and asked for the Editor's permission to buy it. 'I thought I might make a little on the transaction so I rushed back to the garage and asked the proprietor if he would give me a fiver if my firm bought it for £25. He was only too pleased to oblige.' Eventually he got a job with the *Express* on the iniquitous space system, which meant you were only paid for what appeared in the paper. Sometimes he ate, sometimes he did not.

People have often asked me if reporters had to appear so tough and cynical, and I have always explained that it was a protective pose. Norman told me a story which perfectly illustrates the point. He was sent to Hammersmith mortuary to find out something about a beautiful girl who had gassed herself. When he arrived Sir Bernard Spilsbury, the leading Home Office pathologist, had just completed a post mortem: 'The mortuary assistant was just stitching her up when I arrived smoking a cigarette, which I shouldn't have been. As he sewed away he was singing a popular song, "My sweetie's due on the one-two-two". I watched the jogging body as he worked, and looked around for an ash tray. "Here, give it to me," he said, and stuffed it into the girl's belly – and went on whistling and stitching.'

It doesn't do to brood on such things.

By the time war broke out, Norman was a highly regarded reporter but he immediately volunteered for the RAF, only to be told by Christiansen that he would be far more valuable to the war effort as a journalist, for which he had been trained, than as an airman for which he hadn't. It was a wise observation, and Norman became one of the most celebrated war correspondents in the world.

He served for a considerable time aboard the aircraft carrier *Ark Royal* which Lord Haw-Haw was always sinking. Eventually there was no need for the traitor to fantasise: the Royal Navy's most famous carrier was torpedoed thirty miles off Gibraltar. Norman walked down the sloping deck of the sinking ship with an Ordinary Seaman named Fred Ellis who remarked, 'You've got a — good story here, mister.' (Later Fred became City Editor of the *Express*; his frequent use of 'mister' as a form of address became his trademark.)

Norman had a world scoop, but his problem was to get his story past the censor and back to the office. By means that were not entirely ethical he did so, and when he got back to London he was lionised. Many more scoops were to follow. But among his Fleet Street colleagues nothing could better the story about the expenses he submitted after the sinking. He put in a claim for £150 – a staggering amount in those days, but he explained that they included the cost of a complete set of the *Encyclopaedia Britannica*. Eyebrows were raised, but the expenses were eventually passed. Some time later there were reports that an attempt was to be made to salvage *Ark Royal*, and it was recounted that Beaverbrook had remarked, 'For Smart's sake, there had better be a complete set of *Britannica* aboard.'

The salvage attempt failed, and Norman has always maintained a dignified silence when I have asked him about it.

In late 1942 he was aboard the cruiser *Cairo* when it was sunk in the famous convoy sent to relieve Malta. Norman got another scoop and another £150. 'The *Express* paid up promptly. After the argument about my *Ark Royal* expenses, they recognised the rate for the job.'

Many years later, when Norman was no longer Foreign Editor, he was given the job of vetting expenses. I sensed the hand of Beaverbrook, who knew better than most that poachers make good gamekeepers.

As far as Fleet Street was concerned, the imagination that went into the filling up of the 'swindle sheet' more than justified the appointment of a watchdog, but not even the finest experts were able to curb the imaginative dodges that reporters and photographers got up to.

The most frenetic time in any newspaper office was when the warning cry echoed round the Big Room: 'There's going to be a purge on expenses.' Then reporters, photographers, feature writers and people who never left the office, would sit down in order to catch up on their expenses before the axe descended. Surprisingly, what were known – out of earshot of the accountants – as 'swindle sheets' were not filled in for weeks, sometimes months, and the periodic purges were a sure way of forcing people to get up to date, for there was always the nagging fear that what would have been automatically approved a couple of weeks previously might fall under the pruning secateurs of the departmental heads who had to countersign all claims. The reluctance to fill in expense forms regularly was inexplicable, for it wasn't a difficult task, and, furthermore, it was what kept everyone in beer and cigarettes. Yet if you left them uncollected for a long period it was often the deciding factor on whether or not the family had a holiday.

No one was a greater offender in failing to submit his expenses than Sefton Delmer, known affectionately to his friends as 'Uncle Tom'. He was a prodigious spender of His Master's cash, and believed implicitly that he should fulfil his image for living high on the hog. But he repaid it all in full with the brilliant despatches he cabled from trouble spots around the globe.

I was told he once arrived at London Airport to catch an aircraft for an important foreign assignment when an announcement was made over the public address system that he was to ring the office immediately. When he got through to the Foreign Desk he was told that he was to return to the office at once and would not be allowed to leave the country until he had cleared up his outstanding expenses. The sum was astronomical.

He duly returned to the office, went straight to the accountant who dealt with such matters, and solemnly tipped the contents of a small attaché case onto his desk. Out tumbled receipts, bills for hotels and car hire, and countless others for items he had been required to purchase. 'Make that up to what I owe,' he said, and smartly left for the airport.

Tom globe-trotted as other people commuted, and he invariably stayed at the best hotels where, understandably, he was greeted with open arms. In Karachi it was always the Palace Hotel, a stately pile reminiscent of the great days of the Raj. There he had a punkah wallah in his room; the hotel's restaurant was renowned for its cuisine, and Tom, a dedicated gourmet, used it frequently to enhance his ample waistline. On one occasion when he was due to depart he instructed the local stringer to present himself in his room with fifty pounds' worth of silver rupees – a considerable amount then – and, as he was leaving, Tom had the manager line up the entire staff, which literally numbered hundreds, and walked down the long file like Royalty, individually tipping each one.

In the mid-fifties, Don Seaman was working with Delmer in Beirut and, although they were working in harness, Don was at a cheap hotel while Delmer was residing at the St George's, the most expensive in town. Don called round one morning for his regular briefing and was greeted by Tom sitting in his bath, sipping orange juice while the local stringer was scrubbing his back and translating the local Arab newspaper to him.

On another occasion, he was locked in a room and told to stay there until he had accounted for thousands of pounds of outstanding expenses. For hours the sound of furious typing was heard. Soon after Tom had handed the sheets in, Morley Richards, the News Editor, declared, 'Not only has he finished on time, but he's made a profit!'

Tom's star, which everyone thought would shine for ever, began to wane as a result of the Hungarian uprising which was ruthlessly crushed by the use of Russian tanks and troops. It was a tragic and totally unfair demise of a brilliant career. Quite unreasonably, Beaverbrook considered he had let the paper down. I was told the truth behind the story by Noel Barber, the *Mail's* top roving correspondent, now a best-selling novelist. Barber and Delmer were both covering the uprising when suddenly there was a clamp-down on information, and all outgoing telephone calls and cables were banned. Barber was the only one with a motor car and he had wisely built up a cache of petrol, which he used to drive up to the Austrian border where he passed over his cable to Jeff Blythe, another *Mail* man. During one trip he was shot in the head and badly wounded, and the British Legation gave Delmer special permission to send a story about the incident to the *Mail*. As a result, a by-lined story appeared in the *Mail*, as it was the first time the *Express's* star correspondent's copy had appeared in a rival paper. Legend has it that Delmer received a cable from Beaverbrook asking: 'Why you unshot?' True or false, the fact remains that Delmer went into eclipse after that.

The mere mention of Noel's name was enough to set the *Express* Foreign Desk shivering in their shoes. Whatever he did made news – often bad news for Beaverbrook's pride, and whenever Barber set off on his travels, there was near panic in the *Express*. Once, they rushed a senior writer to London Airport to dog the footsteps of Barber, who had just flown out. The *Express* man arrived in Cape Town and tracked Barber down. Unfortunately, his quarry turned out to be Stephen Barber of the *News Chronicle*. Noel had gone on to the South Seas, where he landed another world exclusive.

Such incidents bore out the claim that in those days the slogan 'spare no expense' meant what it said. Most of us bastardised it into 'spare no expenses'. The often outrageous, hilarious claims that were submitted provided endless gossip in the Fleet Street hostelries, and developed into an 'anything you can do I can do better' challenge.

One astute photographer who had enjoyed the comfort of a German prostitute asked her to give him a signed receipt 'For services rendered'. He submitted it with his expenses and was duly paid. An item 'Money for old rope' was explained away by a photographer who said he had purchased it in order to haul himself up onto a vantage point to obtain a picture.

Another cameraman, who had just painted the exterior of his house, did not see why the office should not pay for his new ladder, and he attached the bill to his expenses explaining that he had bought it in order to get his camera above the heads of a dense crowd lining the route of some procession.

Some did not trouble to explain at all. When I was with the *Herald*, Maurice Fagence had his expenses returned with a note demanding the production of a bill for some hefty entertaining he had claimed for. The fact that he could not do so worried him not at all. He simply put a paper-clip on his original form and wrote on the form: 'Bill attached'. When told that nothing had been attached, he calmly insisted that the accounts department must have lost it.

Sometimes the office refused to pay when they should have done, and on occasions forked out when they should not. Mike Brown (who later became Bureau Chief in Paris and opted for voluntary redundancy when the *Express* decided that, in the face of the mass exodus to Dockland, survival depended on a ruthless pruning of staff) was a victim of the former. During the troubles in Angola he submitted an item: 'To entertaining tribal chiefs – £3'. 'There's no way you're getting away with that,' he was told, and it was erased from his expenses sheet. When Mike related the story to me he was obviously still bitter that his integrity had been questioned. 'You know, Alf, it happened to be true.'

Mike had been in Leopoldville, kicking his heels while pulling every conceivable string to get to Angola. 'Everybody wanted to get there but no one had been allowed in since the massacre of the whites there.' One night, he landed himself in trouble, having slugged his way out of a club where he had refused to pay for the grossly overpriced drinks. Troops cordoned off the hotel where he was staying and he was told 'Pay up or go to jail.'

It was only through the intervention of the hotel manager that Mike was saved. By sheer good fortune it turned out that the manager's brother was the Portuguese Consul and the only person who could arrange a visa for Angola.

'He told me, "You must be sure to take some gifts for the chiefs", and I did. I bought thousands of old V-for-Victory cigarettes which had been issued to British troops during the war and which someone had been hoarding for years. At one place I visited I found myself surrounded by local chiefs and men carrying spears. I was told they were expecting me to make a speech, and a box was produced for me to stand on. I just jabbered on, and a television chap standing nearby remarked, "You look like a big white queen." I burst out laughing and the entire audience joined in, not because they found it was funny, they thought they had to. Afterwards I dished out my thousands of cigarettes. But they wouldn't believe me in the office.'

Evelyn Waugh couldn't have improved on that in *Scoop*.

I myself took a merciless ribbing over an expense claim which no one would believe, and for several weeks whenever I walked through the Big Room I was greeted with the refrain 'Alfie, where's your trousers?', a parody of the old Scottish music-hall song.

I had flown out to Skagen in Denmark with photographer Terry Disney to cover the story of the Frenchman, Jan de Kat, who had been forced to abandon his trimaran *Yaksha* in a transatlantic solo yacht race and was rescued from his dinghy by the 10,000-ton *Jagona*. By a stroke of luck, Terry and I bumped into a French journalist who had flown in with de Kat's fiancée Catherine Debergie. The idea was to stage a tender reunion, but a high-seas mix-up foiled the plan. The girl was naturally upset, but not as much as the French reporter who saw his exclusive story sinking as surely as the trimaran. So, together we hired a trawler and with Catherine aboard we set off to try and salvage the story. She waved and shouted to him as he stood on the upper deck but de Kat did not seem to recognise her. Then a pilot boat from Skagen went alongside the *Jagona* and took him aboard. Ashore, however, he shouldered his way past the television crews, waiting newsmen and the welcoming reception party of local people. Terry and I were lucky. He had some superb pictures and I had a good story of the heartbroken sweetheart, together with an interview with de Kat passed on to me by Catherine when she had spoken to him from Paris on a ship-to-shore line.

As Terry needed to get to a wire machine, we went straight to Copenhagen. When we had finished sending the pictures

and story, we set off to find an hotel, but the only
accommodation we could get was aboard the *St Lawrence*, a
liner which had been converted into an hotel and was
permanently moored alongside the harbour wall. It was pitch
dark by the time we booked in; I undressed, flopped onto the
bunk and fell asleep. When I woke up in the morning there
was no sign of my trousers, which I had draped over the back
of a chair near the porthole. Inside the back pocket were my
spectacles without which life became a continuous game of
blindman's-buff. To start with, I wasn't unduly worried,
thinking that Terry was playing a prank, but when I woke
him from a deep sleep he retorted angrily, 'Why should I
want your bloody trousers?'

I had left the office in such a rush I had only the clothes I
was wearing. Terry, fortunately, had a spare pair of trousers
which he loaned me so that I could nip into town and buy
some. Terry was like a bean-pole whereas I had a distinct pot,
most of which was attributable to Poppins and The Bell, and I
couldn't fasten his trousers round my waist, while the fly
would only zip up half-way. But we made it to a menswear
shop.

'I would like to buy a pair of trousers,' I said to the owner,
who could only speak broken English.

He looked at this strange Englishman desperately trying to
keep up the pair he was wearing: 'Not like those?'

'Of course not. They aren't mine. They belong to my
friend.'

'Why do you wear them when they do not fit? You look
very silly.'

I tried to explain, but he was too convulsed with laughter to
hear. Eventually I was fitted out, and I made sure I collected a
bill. When we returned to the ship I discovered there was a
steel ladder running from the quay up the side of the ship and
past the porthole of my cabin. The thief had simply reached
through and lifted my pants. I saw the manager who offered
to let me have the cabin free of charge, but I pointed out that
the offer did not solve the problem. For one thing I was still
without my glasses. The police were called and the ship was
searched from bow to stern without any luck.

When I got back to the office, I put in my expenses and

claimed for the trousers, my glasses, and £12 in cash. Norman refused to approve the claim, firmly convinced that it was a made-up story. The truth, more likely, was that I had had them pinched by a member of the oldest profession, and it served me right for falling for such an old stunt.

The story got round and the singing started. I felt so aggrieved that I consulted the Legal Manager, who advised me to write and find out whether the ship was covered by the Inn Keepers' Liability Act. I got no reply.

Weeks later, I went on holiday with my family to Devon, and the matter of my trousers had still not been sorted out. Norman, however, relented and wrote to me asking to re-submit the claim and attach a memo explaining what had happened. 'In case you are short of expense sheets, I enclose a couple, and you can sit on the beach and fill them in, you lucky chap – it's raining here.'

I did as he suggested, but, determined to exact my pound of flesh and silence the choir in the Big Room, I pointed out that the trousers were part of a suit and the jacket *sans* pants was like *Hamlet* without the Prince of Denmark.

I was given permission to buy a suit. I had one made which cost far more than I had ever paid. As the replaced suit had been tweed, the jacket made an admirable sports jacket. I still have it. Whenever I put it on I whistle the refrain which haunted me for so long.

There were, however, occasions when the office forked out when they should not have. Another reporter fared better after returning from a lengthy stint in Africa. He put in his expenses and looked forward to collecting a little surplus, but to his horror and consternation he was told he was £400 short. Not only a brilliant reporter, he was an old hand at expenses and could not believe that he had been guilty of such an unpardonable error. But the department responsible for cabling money had discovered that £400 had been sent to a bank in some town, which he hadn't accounted for. He couldn't remember receiving it, let alone spending it, but knuckled down, rewrote his expenses to everyone's satisfaction and collected the surplus. Some weeks later a cable arrived from the bank manager asking the *Express* what he should do with Mr So-and-so's uncollected £400. When asked for an explanation, he said he had been forced to use his own money to fund *Express* activities at the time because he had moved on before the cash arrived.

Every newspaper claimed to have an expenses story to cap them all; one of the best I have heard concerned Freddie Salusbury, an Australian and a bit of a Beau Brummel who spoke with an impeccable English accent. After working on the *Express* he joined the *Daily Herald* as a War Correspondent, and established a well-earned reputation with his coverage in the Western Desert. One item he claimed for was a camel; it was a very expensive camel, but when the amount was queried, Freddie replied, 'It's not a normal one. It's a racing camel. I need it to keep up with the ebb and flow of the battles with Rommel's Panzers.' Salusbury's expenses became a near obsession with the accountants. Month in and month out, vast sums were claimed for fodder and the upkeep of the beast. They only ceased when Montgomery routed Rommel at El Alamein and the Germans were subsequently defeated. As the person responsible for vetting expenses perused Salusbury's last expense sheet, he noticed that there was not a word about the camel, and he sent off an urgent cable demanding an explanation as to why the animal had not been sold and the office reimbursed. 'Thank you for pointing out the omission,' came Salusbury's answer. 'Unfortuntely the camel died. I forgot to charge for the burial. It was bloody expensive. I'll put it on my next sheet.'

During one purge, Hannen Swaffer was taken to task for a luncheon bill at the Savoy. His own lunch was scrubbed through. 'You would have had to eat even if you had not been entertaining. Why expect the office to pay?' it was pointed out to him. Hannen accepted this with equanimity. 'Just as well he didn't turn up page three and see, "Taxi up front hall stairs",' he told colleagues.

Barry Devney, now the distinguished Industrial Correspondent of the *Express*, managed to claim aphrodisiacs on his expenses when he was a young reporter. He was covering the trial of an elderly woman accused of murdering three husbands for their money. It came to be known as the Widow of Windy Nook case. Her defence counsel, the redoubtable Rose Heilbron, QC, claimed that the accused was not trying to kill them but to stimulate them sexually and the drug she'd used was a minor aphrodisiac which could be purchased at any chemist's. Barry was despatched by the News Editor to purchase some of the drug and write a story on how easily obtainable it was. But he could not find any chemist who stocked it, and ended up doing the rounds of the rather sleazy sex shops which have now been replaced by blatant sex parlours. At one he found an elderly lady behind the counter who said she stocked the drug and Barry bought a bottle for 1s 6d. As he left, the woman wistfully remarked to another customer, 'And such a big lad, too.'

'They didn't work,' Barry told me. 'I tried them on one of the young secretaries.'

The ultimate accolade must, however, surely go to the Moscow Correspondent who claimed for 'purchase of fur coat for Russian winter', and on his return put in for 'loss on resale of fur coat'.

7

IN PURSUIT OF ROYALTY

When Sir Donald Bradman was introduced to King George VI it is said that he congratulated the Monarch on being England's finest change bowler in the history of Test cricket. The King, somewhat puzzled, asked him to explain, and the great batsman, who was captaining his country, said that whenever His Majesty visited Lord's it was always after lunch, and usually when Australia had made a splendid start; the two teams would be lined up outside the pavilion to meet him, and when play resumed Australia would invariably lose a quick wicket. Such lese-majesty would not be permitted in Fleet Street.

Today, if the Editors of the national dailies were lined up in similar fashion to meet the Queen, I am sure they would give three rousing cheers, for without doubt she and her family are the greatest-ever circulation-builders, bingo and page three included. Despite the strictures of the Willy Hamiltons of this world, 'The Royals', as they are known in The Street, continue to exercise a magic that nothing can diminish. And it is a fascination that extends to many other parts of the world, including those which have got rid of their own monarchs by way of the ballot box or the executioner. The public just cannot get enough of them, and newspapers make sure they are sated. Whenever there is a fresh romance, a birthday, or a new baby, a kind of euphoria grips the country, and with it an unquenchable thirst that is cynically exploited by the Press. It was so in my day, and will remain so. In private, newspapers' Editors might question the worth of Royalty, or they might speak derisorily of it, but they would not have the folly to express their views in print. They are like bald barbers selling hair-restorer. There has recently been a considerable mellowing in the image presented by the Royal Family, who make a tremendous effort to appear more human and less god-like – but Editors don't want this to go too far: they would abhor the thought, say, of the Queen cycling down The Hall. The pedestal may be shortened but must not be toppled.

Editors encourage some reverence; should a gust of wind lift the hem of the Queen's dress, it makes headlines, and 'No comment' from a Palace official is drummed up into something of immense significance. Ironically if, as the Duke of Edinburgh and Prince Charles are apt to do, members of the Royal Family make serious, often sensible, observations about industry, unemployment, or social conditions in deprived areas, the Press is quick to rap them over the knuckles for stepping out of line: like the figureheads of ships, they must remain ornamental but useless. No wonder that, in my time, Philip got a reputation for being abrasive to the Press. He is an intelligent man who wants to be recognised as one, not just an authority on coach and horses, or a conservationist who loves shooting.

The Royal Family's news value is so immense that every paper has its own Court Reporter, who specialises in their activities. Although they never get to know their subjects personally, some of them affect a familiarity that is often quite nauseating. Many of my pals, though, men and women, would have been content to do nothing but report the doings of Royalty. It was an enviable job in many respects as it took them to some of the most colourful corners of the world, and they loved nothing more than to prop up the bar on their return, and regale anyone who would listen with the inside stories they could not write.

Although I did more than my fair share of covering Royal events, I never shared that enthusiasm; not through antagonism to the Royal Family, or fervent republicanism – I think they do a good job – but because I was dogged by misfortune which at times incurred Royal displeasure. I started off badly, and my away results were every bit as bad as the home fixtures.

One of the first tours I covered was the visit of the Queen

and Prince Philip to the Channel Islands in 1957, the first time she had been there since her accession to the throne. The *Daily Herald* may have been the voice of socialism, but when it came to the Royal Family the symbolic flat cap was doffed in homage and all stops pulled out, the Red Flag hauled down and the Royal Standard hoisted.

It was a pleasant enough trip to start with, although there were long periods of unutterable boredom not appreciated by newspaper readers. One had to hang around for hours at night, such as when a dinner was held on the Royal Yacht and you had to be on the quayside in case some VIP fell into the water when returning ashore. They never did, of course, and there were times when you were sorely tempted to nip off and buy a pound of bananas. But I did my best to inject some life into stories as flat as a chapati – the Queen chatting to a group of women knitting Guernsey sweaters, or Philip talking to members of a netball team who suddenly erupted into great bursts of laughter. At that, I darted into their midst, notebook in hand, pencil at the ready, to record for posterity the gem of wit which had convulsed them. It turned out to be an innocuous remark, eminently non-quotable, and the laughter indicated nothing more than relief from tension. Yet my photographer had taken a splendid picture of the hilarious incident and I had to provide words to match it. It was hard work, and I envied the talent of my friend Vincent Mulchrone of the *Mail*, who could write a brilliant piece around the remark 'How interesting'.

The first real story came when the Queen, wearing a beautiful gown adorned with various orders, addressed Guernsey's Court of Chief Pleas, where an extraordinary session had been convened in St Peter Port in order that the islanders could pledge their homage. Some five hundred VIPs and dignitaries had assembled for the eight-hundred-year-old feudal ceremony. Standing outside were the island's eight convicts who had been released for the day, given twenty cigarettes, civilian clothes, and escorted by warders in plain clothes. It was that important.

The Queen read aloud from a parchment scroll; I found the phrases, in the 'My husband and I' vein, stilted and lifeless, and in the stuffy, overwarm chamber I felt myself dozing off.

I was roused by the elbow of Herbie Machon, the Editor of the local paper and the *Herald*'s 'stringer', digging into my ribs. 'Did you hear what she said, Alf?' he asked with genuine amazement. I had to admit that I had only been half listening. So had Vincent. The Queen, said Herbie, had just dropped a monumental clanger. She had said, 'We have the happiest memories of our visit here in 1948.' But she had got the date wrong, and that, to the islanders, was unpardonable, for at that time the island had not yet fully recovered from the effects of the German occupation.

Why hadn't the Queen realised her error? Could she not remember? It may seem a trivial matter, but one has to have experienced the immense loyalty of the Channel Islanders to appreciate the impact it had. It was up to the reporters to find out how the error had arisen. So for the rest of the day we dogged the footsteps of Mr R.A.B. Butler, then Home Secretary, who did his utmost to evade us, and had us dodging through hoopla stalls and displays of local works of arts and crafts trying to corner him. Eventually we did, and he knew damn well what we wanted. A compromise solution was reached. The blame was placed fairly and squarely on the shoulders of an anonymous typist whose fingers had slipped. The Queen had ordered her speech to be officially corrected. Although it was a most implausible answer, honour all round was satisfied and the headline on my story was 'Typist puts the Queen all wrong'. Needless to say, we made no effort to track down the young lady. In any other walk of life such a slip of the tongue would not have merited attention, but of such trivia are Royal stories made.

The news soon reached us on the grapevine that the Queen was most displeased with us. It was not an auspicious start.

The Royal party was due then to visit the tiny island of Sark, ruled by the Dame who had yet to discover that the twentieth century had been around for some time. Among her many feudal idiosyncrasies was a decree that she was the only person permitted to use a motor car, everybody else had to walk or cycle. Tractors were the only other means of mechanised transport allowed. I decided to go over in advance to see if I could find anything newsworthy, and found the islanders engaged in a frantic search for any old iron: nuts, bolts, screws, discarded saucepans. They were needed for the six and a half muzzle-loaded cannons, first fired in the reign of George III, which had been unearthed from the undergrowth as they were the only weapons available for firing the Royal Salute. The half-gun was all that remained of one of the cannons which had been blown over a cliff top the previous time it had been fired.

I sensed an amusing story, and discovered that the gun crews would be provided by the local branch of the British Legion. One of them, a farmer, told me, 'We'll also stuff a copy of the 1951 Stark Constitution down the barrel of one because we disagree with it.' The careful choice of words reflected what they thought of the archaic manner in which the island was governed. The story was by-lined in the *Herald* the next morning, and was read, I was informed, by the Queen who diligently saw everything that was written about her. Like her distinguished predecessor, she was not amused.

When the Royal party arrived on Sark, the Queen travelled in the Dame's car, with Prince Philip, accompanied by his detective, following in a horse-drawn trap. The Press corps had to follow on Shank's pony. As we tramped up the steep hill from the harbour to where the official welcoming reception was to take place, I noticed that a slight breeze was lifting the Prince's trilby, which he had placed on the floor at his feet. A lost hat can assume the headline proportions of a lifted hem, and I said to photographer Gerry Warner, 'Keep your eyes on his trilby. It could blow away.' It did, and we watched it bowling down the hill. We then set off in pursuit, but two out-of-condition newsmen were no match for a rolling trilby, and when we got to the bottom there was no sign of it. A man and a woman were trudging up the hill, and we asked them if they had seen it. The man, a Mr Smith, on holiday there with his wife, said he had tossed it into the graveyard of a nearby church. His wife had apparently pointed out the Royal Warrant inside and suggested it could be Prince Philip's, but 'I told her he would never wear a brown hat with a blue suit. Anyway, I never wear a hat,' said Mr Smith.

Gerry and I went into the churchyard to find it; a few minutes later a panting detective arrived on the scene and

began to search for it on his hands and knees. When he had
recovered it he tucked it inside his jacket and warned us of the
dire consequences if we wrote about it. We followed him
back up the hill and saw him surreptitiously slip the hat to the
Prince. Mr Smith's views on what a gentleman should wear
appeared in the paper next morning.

My stories had not helped what was intended as a solemn
occasion.

But more was to come. The next halt was Alderney, where
I learnt that the taxi drivers were proposing to boycott the
Royal visit; not because they objected to it but because their
loyalty had received a snub. They had been informed that a
Rolls was being brought over from Guernsey to convey the
Queen, and would be driven by the Governor's chauffeur.
The spokesman for the taxi drivers protested, 'One of us
should have been allowed to drive it. It is a slur on us.'

It would have been a storm in an egg-cup but for the fact
that many officials who wanted to follow the Royal
procession had no means of transport. As one said plaintively,
'We can't follow on bikes.' It seems incredible that such
piffling incidents could make headlines, and even worse that
we were happy to see our by-lines above the story.

The visit ended with a garden party, in the grounds of the
official residence of the island's Governor, attended by the
local dignitaries and representatives of the various charitable
and voluntary organisations. The Press were invited to have a
drink in the kitchen, and while I was half-way through mine
an official appeared and ordered me outside for the Royal
presentation. I tried to explain that I was a reporter, but he
would not listen and I found myself in a long line of people.
The Prince came out and began shaking hands. My heart was
in my boots as he got closer to me. He did not say anything
when he reached me, but his look was enough to convince me
that I had not made a friend for life.

I covered a number of Royal visits in the ensuing years,
during which I encountered the Prince, and if he harboured
any resentment he certainly did not show it. I admired him
because he showed that he was not content to be bogged
down in the Royal rut. What's more, he developed a sense of
humour.

In May 1968 he visited the London Zoo to address the Fellows, and during a tour of the animal hospital he halted to admire a recent acquisition, a young orang-utan named Napoleon. The theme of his speech was to be that modern methods and a more enlightened approach was helping the animals to live a more natural existence. Napoleon, perched up a pole and surrounded by his harem, obviously agreed for he let fly from a great height an accurate stream of urine.

I waited for the order committing Napoleon to the Tower. An embarrassed expert tried to pour verbal balm on the water. 'Orang-utans are our closest relations. At home in Sumatra and Borneo, they live in trees where they relieve themselves without seeing the consequences.'

Prince Philip mopped his suit and went in to make his speech. 'I apologise for any faint whiff of animal that might emanate from my end of the room. Napoleon has just widdled all over me.'

He had once described the *Express* as 'that bloody awful newspaper', so I felt I was heading for the doghouse once more. But there were no repercussions when the paper appeared next morning with a picture of Napoleon alongside one of the Prince laughing off the incident.

Beneath the picture of Napoleon was the caption: 'A star is born'.

Certainly the orang-utan was applauded in Fleet Street for having evened the score for the ill-tempered occasion when Philip had doused reporters with a garden hose. On the other hand, Napoleon may have been motivated by more personal reasons: he might have heard on the simian grapevine of the occasion when the Prince was feeding the apes on the Rock of Gibraltar and tossed a handful of peanuts to the onlooking Press. The comparison could have been considered offensive to his species.

There was an unforgettable occasion when I was given a lesson in the art of reporting by Noel Monks of the *Mail*, an Australian who was a brilliant War Correspondent. I was sent to cover the Royal Fleet Review in the Firth of Cromarty on the east coast of Scotland, and given a berth along with Noel aboard HMS *Ark Royal*, the Navy's biggest and newest aircraft carrier. Her communications system was reputed to be the finest in the world and would play a vital role in the event of war. Its efficiency would be demonstrated when the time came for us to file our copy.

Unfortunately, when that time arose there was a mix-up and our copy couldn't be got away in time to catch the edition. Full of initiative and enterprise, I got the officer of the watch to lay on a motor boat to take me ashore to the nearest telephone. There, I dictated a story about the impressive fly-past, the splendour of Britain's sea power on display, what the Queen wore, and how Prince Philip had joined in calypsoes in a hangar concert.

Noel wrote a powerful piece about a serious flaw in our early warning and defence systems, and the inadequacies of *Ark Royal*'s communications system.

Why, I was asked, had I missed such an obvious story?

One of the most enjoyable Royal stories was that of the romance between Princess Margaret and the handsome Group Captain Peter Townsend. It was a fairy-tale story of the Battle of Britain hero-commoner and the beautiful daughter of the King. They had first met when he was equerry to King George VI. But there was one insurmountable barrier, at least as far as the Establishment was concerned – Townsend had been divorced. The Princess could, of course, have told the Establishment where to go, but she was only twenty-three and could not marry without the Queen's consent for two years. Tactfully, the love affair was temporarily nipped in the bud when Townsend was sent to the British Embassy in Brussels as Air Attaché, and Margaret went off to darkest Africa.

With his return, the romance blossomed again and Margaret was warned that she would lose all Royal privileges and income if she married him.

Naturally, the world's Press descended on London and the story was front-page news for several weeks. There were crazy car chases through the streets and country lanes with the Group Captain dropping hints as to where he was heading. Sometimes he was not so accommodating, and I saw an enterprising reporter trap him inside a telephone booth and then refuse to move his considerable bulk from the door until Townsend disclosed his destination. There was a hair-raising occasion when Fleet Street's mobile cavalry was pursuing Townsend down The Mall and police motor cyclists formed a human barrier across the road. Undeterred, we just drove round them, mounting the pavement and ploughing through the flower beds.

Eventually, Princess Margaret decided to put duty before love, and stated that as a devout Christian she could not marry a divorcee.

I also covered the romance between Margaret and Anthony Armstrong Jones, who did a lot of photographic work for the *Express*. How times and values change! Hardly an eyebrow was raised when they divorced. I often wonder what the outcome would be if the Abdication Crisis had taken place now.

I only met the Duke of Windsor once, but was more impressed by the Duchess for whom he had renounced the throne. I had been sent to Gibraltar with a photographer, Leslie Lee, to cover the seemingly never-ending dispute between Britain and Spain as to who was the rightful owner of that impressive chunk of sheer-faced rock. While there, we received instructions to go to the Marbella Club across the border to interview the Duke who was staying there with the Duchess. It seemed that the Duke did nothing but attend parties and play golf, except on Sundays which he always strictly observed. The Duchess greeted us at the Club and gave us a brief lesson on etiquette. I had heard a lot about her, much of it unflattering: she was scheming, ambitious and very much acted the Queen she would never be. Understandably, I was apprehensive. I had no need to be. She struck me as extremely charming and astonishingly frank, especially when I talked to her about the house they were rumoured to be building there. They had owned a plot for some time and were now thinking of building a small villa; after a short time, though, I began to doubt if they ever would – the Duchess had a low opinion of Spanish sanitation and not a very high one of the social climbers who aspired to be their neighbours. 'Everyone tries to find out what you're doing and when you're going to build.' To my knowledge, the villa was never built.

When the Duke appeared he was wearing dark glasses, and

as I was interviewing him Leslie let off his flash. The Duke recoiled and the Duchess gave us a piece of her mind. We were unaware that the Duke was still suffering the after-effects of a serious eye operation, and Leslie had not contributed to a speedy recovery. The story and picture appeared in the William Hickey column for which I was devoutly grateful: at least I had retained my anonymity. I did not want to go down in history as the man who had aided and abetted the sabotage of the surgeon's skills.

I never saw the Duke again, but I did cover the return to England of his body when he died in Paris. It was the end of his long exile which had begun with his abdication in December 1936, and the finish of the love story that had divided the nation. Some never forgot the young monarch. Others never forgave.

His death brought about the much sought-after reconciliation between the Duchess and the Royal family, for the Queen invited her to stay at Buckingham Palace until after the funeral.

I wrote a piece about the scenes outside Buckingham Palace when the Duchess arrived, and interviewed several people, most of whom sympathised with her. Among them was Bob Shepherd, an ex-Navy man who was in Portsmouth when the Duke arrived after his abdication, to be spirited away into his long exile aboard a Royal Navy destroyer. 'The Duchess should have been allowed to marry him. Who would take any notice today of the fact that a woman is divorced?'

Another ex-naval petty officer, Gunner Mr Tommy Warner, who had become a tourist guide at the Palace, said, 'What a great misfortune it is for her to be welcomed in only when her husband is dead. They should have gone in together.'

There was a deep resentment among many onlookers that she was made to enter through the door used by tourists who wished to sign the vistors' book. It would have been their thirty-fifth wedding anniversary, and the Duke had died without his dearest wish being fulfilled: that the woman he loved for so long should be given the title Her Royal Highness.

'Yesterday the woman known to history as Mrs Simpson conducted herself like a Queen,' I wrote.

I had no personal feelings about the rights and wrongs of the

Abdication Crisis; I was solely concerned with doing a professional job. Keith Howard dropped me a note, congratulating me on the story: 'You might like to know that I heard a back-bencher describe your effort as "a story that needed no subbing". Praise indeed when it comes from our usually taciturn brethren!'

I felt I had made amends for the best-forgotten incident in Spain so many years earlier.

When the Duchess died, the whole controversy was revived in the Press and on television, with the phrase 'the love story of the century' repeated *ad nauseam*.

Belatedly, the Royal Family decided that the time had come to forgive, if not forget, and the Duchess was allowed to be buried alongside her husband at Frogmore, but it was a very low-key affair.

Although Earl Mountbatten was not strictly a member of the Royal Family, he was considered by many to be a powerful influence behind the throne. For years, Beaverbrook had conducted a quite unworthy vendetta against him, the origins of which have never been satisfactorily explained. Those close to the Old Man said it began when Noël Coward made the film *In Which We Serve*, based on Mountbatten's experiences when he captained the destroyer *Kelly*. In one of the scenes, the *Daily Express* is seen floating past the stern bearing the headline which became the Beaver's personal albatross: that there would be no war this year or the next. He also linked Mountbatten with the surrender of the Empire because he was the last Viceroy and did so much to speed Indian independence. I think the former explanation is more likely, for Beaverbrook was only interested in the white empire.

When the vendetta was brought to an end, or why, the staff never found out – there were other vendettas which were continued with an almost Cretan intensity and only ended when Beaverbrook died. Stanley Meagher, one of the *Express* photographers, was among the first to know that this particular hatchet had been buried. He was covering a ceremonial occasion at Sandhurst when Mountbatten, dressed in his Admiral's uniform, strolled out onto the lawn for a formal photograph of himself and several Commonwealth dignitaries. As he passed Stan he stuck his tongue out. Stan was so taken aback he could not bring his camera into action in time, and he was sure that he had missed a picture that would have made the front page. To his surprise, however, Mountbatten repeated his gesture, and this time Stan did not miss.

When Stan got back to the office, the Editor and Chapman Pincher were waiting for him in the front hall. Stan was told to develop and print his film without delay and hand the prints over to the Editor. Stan, concerned at the unexpected interest, was relieved to find they were pin-sharp. He had one print blown up to twenty inches by sixteen, which he proudly showed to the Editor. 'I never saw the picture or the negatives again,' he told me.

That the hatchet had been buried was confirmed for me when I went with a photographer to cover the opening of a club for Royal Marines by Lord Mountbatten. Neither of us had much heart for the assignment, for we knew, or thought we did, that any story about him would be spiked. But we went through the motions. No one could have been more co-operative; when the photographer said that a picture of Mountbatten in uniform was too run-of-the-mill even to stand a chance, he obligingly removed his jacket and played a game of darts in his shirt-sleeves and braces. The picture and story were given the treatment.

I first met Serge Lemoine when he was Chief of Bureau for *Paris-Match*, which had a London office in the *Express* building. Later he became a free-lance and established a world-wide reputation as a Royal photographer, and the last time I saw him was when we were working on a book together, when he had covered more than fifty tours. Serge, who speaks with a pronounced Charles Boyer accent and knows more about the Royals than any Pressman I know, once remarked, 'It's more fun photographing Prince Charles than Princess Anne.'

They are sentiments that are echoed by everyone I've encountered who has had to cover stories involving Princess Anne. When she first began public engagements she clearly believed that she was entitled to every Royal privilege, but expected to offer nothing in return, certainly not as far as the Press was concerned. She was acid-tongued and downright rude. A habit she shared with Princess Margaret who could be very informal one minute and very regal the next, which could be disconcerting to people who were treated like equals for a short time then expected to act as serfs soon afterwards. As Serge remarked to me, 'You can never be sure when you're with Anne whether it's going to be smiles or scowls.'

There were occasions when the Press, both home and foreign, criticised her for being bad-tempered, sulky and unco-operative, and the Queen was known to have ticked her off for publicity which reflected badly on the whole family. Familiarity with her brought, if not contempt, a well-delivered snub. In Canada, where the people are less formal and stuffy than here, an official once asked her, 'How is your mother?' to which she replied, 'Still Queen, thank you.'

In fairness, the passage of time has mellowed her; and she works very hard, especially for the Save the Children Fund.

Fleet Street is a notable haven of gossip, and I only know of two members of the Royal Family who have been exempted – the Queen and her mother. With the help of her husband, the Queen has done much to modernise the Royal image. Invitations to the informal luncheons at Buckingham Palace are now much sought after, which is a great improvement to what in the past were considered Royal commands.

I first reported on Prince Charles when he attended an infants' school in Kensington, and later went to a prep school somewhere in the country. I hated dogging the little boy whose every move was photographed. It seemed crazy to write lines that suggested he was 'just like any other schoolboy', when you were going out of your way to show he wasn't. At his prep school one photographer even carved young Charles's initials on a church pew and took a shot at them, passing the work off as that of the Prince. There was something Orwellian in the way Fleet Street treated him – equal, but a little more equal than the rest of us. It's a miracle he managed to survive intact. Indeed, Serge Lemoine says he is one of the finest men he has ever encountered – and that coming from him says something, for he has been Charles's shadow for so long the Prince addresses him by his Christian name. And no one appreciates more than him that the Press has a job to do: to accommodate Serge, he once dived sixty feet under the Arctic ice in a frogman's suit so that Serge could get a picture. It was not only an uncomfortable descent, it really was dangerous.

Harry MacNally – a genial Irishman built like an amiable grizzly bear, with white hair which resembled snow on a mountain peak, and almost as tall as some of the stories he told – had an unrivalled capacity for drinking vast quantities of bitter. He had spent so many years on the *Express* that he was allowed to spend most of his time in Poppins, only leaving his favourite seat when he was needed to do some work. He loved to tell the story of when he was doorstepping Sandringham at the time when George V's life was drawing to a close. He thought it was the most pointless and time-consuming vigil he had ever mounted as he was certain no one would come out and give him a personal bulletin; the news when it came would emanate from Buckingham Palace. Nevertheless, he had to ring the office every hour on the hour and report progress, or rather lack of it, from the only public telephone available, an antiquated machine that had to be handcranked in order to get through to the operator. His calls became so frequent that he and the Post Office operator became quite chummy. 'Usual number?' the operator would ask whenever Harry came on. The ritual went on for several days with Harry merely repeating the same message when he got through to the office, 'Nothing from this end.'

Then one day the operator said, 'Is that you, sir? Just hold the line'; and Harry found himself listening in to a call to Downing Street announcing the death of the King. As soon as it was finished he telephoned the office and dictated the story, wisely keeping mum as to how he obtained it. The golden rule was to make out that nothing came easily – 'Congratulations!' is so much more rewarding than 'You jammy bastard.'

8

WATERING HOLES

There were two watering holes in Fleet Street where anyone could go without arousing the suspicion that they were looking for a job, or had been sent on a skirmishing expedition to sniff out what the opposition was up to. They were El Vino, about half-way between the Law Courts and the Old Bailey, and the Press Club, then in a narrow alley at the rear of St Bride's Church. Both were male bastions. El Vino, the haunt of lawyers and the higher echelons of The Street, was – and still is, to some extent – one of the few places to have retained an olde worlde appearance; it sold only wines and spirits (the latter dispensed from pewter measures: newfangled gadgets like optics were taboo), and was avoided by general reporters who did not want to be accused of hobnobbing with the bosses, and who in any case preferred a pint. It was overseen, with an almost naval discipline, by Frank Bower, a Dickensian character who favoured a cravat fixed with a pearl pin, and flowered waistcoats, and managed to give the impression that he was doing everyone a favour in dispensing drinks. And they had to be the 'right' drinks – a casual visitor once had the temerity to ask him for a beer: 'The only beer I know,' said Frank, 'has four wheels and carries a coffin.'

Like Beaverbrook, Bower had a blacklist which was not too difficult to get on: your appearance, if it did not meet with his approval, was good enough grounds, while foul language was met quite simply with a disapproving finger pointing towards the door. Levity did not go down too well, either – out of doors Bower always wore a bowler, and Vicky, the *Standard*'s famous cartoonist, was banned for life from El

Vino for attempting to wear it. Those who were unwelcome were told to go over the road to Peel's if they wanted a drink; embracing a near-empty bar with a wide sweep of his hands, Frank would say pointedly, 'As you can see, sir, we are full.'

George Melly, the jazz singer, once grabbed Bower by the lapels and accused him of being racialist when he overheard him pronounce, 'They're all right in their own country, perfectly acceptable, even likeable. But bring them across here and they're no good at all.'

Having broken himself free from Melly's grasp, Bower said, with crushing aplomb, 'I was speaking of some German wines.'

Men had to wear jackets and ties (except on Saturdays), and women were not allowed to stand at the bar, served instead in a small room at the rear, shut off from the main bar by a screen. But many women objected to it being a male bastion, and it was stormed by a hostile crowd of female journalists demanding an end to sexual discrimination. Regulars fought them off with soda syphons. Now women serve behind the bar. I was there one lunchtime when a male chauvinist pig was expressing his personal indignation at women being treated as equals. It was all for the benefit of a woman standing nearby, and she rose to the bait and began berating him. 'Do you always listen in to other people's conversations?' he asked primly.

Today El Vino still refuses to be dragged into the twentieth century and a number of the old regulations still stand – and just as men must wear ties, women must not wear trousers – but not many people really mind; it is like a pair of old and comfortable shoes, too loved to be thrown away.

The Press Club, on the other hand, was a haven for everyone. Rank did not count – as long as they paid their subs all were equal. It was a wonderful place, smoke-filled and human, the walls adorned with cartoons of many of its more famous members. It had a snooker room where you lit your cigarettes from naked gas jets, and a library which was a bolt hole where you could sleep off a hangover. It moved some years ago to a tower block in Shoe Lane where it lost most of its magic. Unlike El Vino it marched with the times, women came not only to be entitled to membership, but also to sit on the committee. No one seriously objected to that, but not everyone took kindly to the modernisation which made it resemble the lounge of an airport hotel. The old cartoons still hung on the walls, but they somehow looked out of place among the chrome and modern furnishings.

While writing this book, I visited the Club to check on some fact or other, and it was the first time I can recall not having a drink. The bar was closed. The bailiffs were in, and desperate efforts were being made to raise the money to guarantee its survival. They failed, and the library and the priceless collection of Press memorabilia went under the auctioneer's hammer.

The old Press Club was at its best late at night when the pubs had closed and men who had been working late dropped in for 'one for the road'. For some of the stalwarts it was a long, long road: they had been there since lunchtime. It was said of some of its regulars that the cleaners swept round them, thinking they were part of the furniture.

For newcomers it provided an opportunity to get to know some of the giants who would otherwise have remained just names. The bar was invariably propped up by some of the finest raconteurs The Street has produced: 'Cassandra', Ian Mackay, Tim Healey, Noel Whitcomb, Percy Hoskins, and scores more. Editors were thick on the ground, sometimes literally. If only someone had had the good sense to bug the place.

Bill Connor – Cassandra – who was knighted for his distinguished services to journalism, had the most devastating wit which was not always confined to his column. A celebrated wine connoisseur, who could be extremely verbose when discussing his favourite subject, one day interrupted Cassandra during a conversation at the club to remark, 'I'm off to Bordeaux in the morning.' Bill blinked behind his thick glasses and murmured, 'Who's Deaux?'

Early in the war, Bill became a thorn in the flesh of the Establishment with his frequent criticisms of the way the war was being conducted, and it was suggested that it would be better for everyone if he went into the army. Bill was delighted as that was what he had been trying to do since the outbreak of hostilities, but had repeatedly been told his pen was worth a full brigade of troops. That opinion, however, soon altered with his scathing comments in the *Mirror*, by then dubbed The Forces Newspaper, and he was allowed to enlist. When he returned to the paper after the war he began his column: 'As I was saying when I was interrupted, it is a powerful hard thing to please all the people all the time.'

A few years before his retirement from the *Express*, Bernard Hall was admitted to the Fleet Street Ward at St Bart's Hospital for a hernia operation and there several nurses told him of two men who had kept the other patients in fits of laughter shortly before his own admittance.

One, they said, was a burly Cockney docker named Alf, the other, occupying the adjoining bed, was Bill, a Fleet Street journalist. The docker, intrigued by the massive pile of newspapers which were delivered each morning to his neighbour, addressed him: 'Tell me, mate, why do you read all those every day?' It was his duty, the journalist told him, to keep abreast of events, and was something that a spell in hospital could not be allowed to interrupt. The docker, confessing that his own reading was strictly limited, commented plaintively, 'I just don't understand some of the lingo you people use. What the hell, for example, are invisible exports? I've been a docker for thirty-five years, and all the exports I've handled have been very visible.' (He then conceded that certain imports did become invisible – but that was due to pilfering.)

Patiently, Bill explained how the enormous revenue that Britain earned from overseas through shipping, insurance, banking, investments and so on, were classified as invisible exports. Thus was begun a firm friendship. Alf asked the journalist to provide him with an easy-to-understand breakdown of the news each morning, which Bill did, with a brisk summary of all the outstanding news, delivered in such an entertaining manner that doctors and nurses used to pause by his bedside to listen.

One morning Bill did not give his bulletin: he had died in the night. The journalist was Sir William 'Cassandra' Connor. A few days later the docker died.

When I joined the *Express*, Joe Meaney was still working, although he could have retired long before. His memory was phenomenal and if you caught him in the right mood he would recount stories that have long since become a part of history. He even covered the Crippen case and the transatlantic chase which ended with the arrest of the doctor and his mistress, Ethel le Neve. When the remains of Crippen's wife were unearthed in the cellar of his home in Hilldrop Crescent, North London, one of the greatest-ever manhunts was launched in London. Joe's pay-off line to his account of that had everyone in stitches. A policeman shining his torch into a cellar saw the figure of a crouching man. 'Are you Crippen?' he asked. 'No, I'm crapping.'

While writing this chapter I saw Bill Tovey at a lunch to celebrate his ninety-second birthday. A man who joined the army in the First War as a drummer boy, and served again in the Second as a rear gunner, he is one of the *Express*'s most remarkable products. Among his greatest achievements is the only photograph of Frederick Bywaters, who was arrested with his mistress Edith Thompson and charged with the murder of her husband. During the committal hearing at Ilford Magistrates Court, Bill took the two prison warders out for a drink thinking they would be a great help in getting him a picture. They anticipated that the hearing would last a considerable time, but their calculations were sadly awry: it lasted just two minutes, and the warders returned to the court to find they had no prisoner, while Bywaters had found he was without an escort. Even worse, Bill had no picture. They found the accused waiting very patiently in the police canteen. There Bill bought him half a pint of beer and, with the warders' permission, took a close-up portrait of him. 'They're still using it today,' he told me.

Every effort was made to stop anyone getting a picture of Edith Thompson, but Bill found a flat-roofed building overlooking the Court's yard, got hold of a ladder and concealed himself there until she came out. When the police spotted him they clambered onto the roof and tried to snatch his camera, but he shinned down the ladder, pulled it away and left them stranded on the roof.

Bill had a marvellous record, but to hear him talk nothing came easy. He was sent to Maidstone with reporter Jack Frost where a young soldier had run amok with a loaded rifle and shot two women. When Bill tried to take a photograph of the scene of the murders his camera was knocked from his hand by an over-zealous policeman; Bill promptly knocked him flat, and the two *Express* men were arrested and taken to the police station where a crowd of reporters had gathered outside, champing at the bit because they could get no information. As the *Express* men waited in the charge room, they overheard a detective in an adjoining room on the telephone giving the details of the murder in minute detail to the Chief Constable. Jack took it all down in his notebook. When they were seen by an inspector he said he would not charge them with assaulting a police officer if the *Express* did not claim for the ruined camera. A deal was struck. But the police were amazed when the full details of the double murder appeared in the *Express* next morning.

One of the Club's most talented habitués was Ian Mackay, the *News Chronicle*'s columnist, who spurned all offers to lure him away from the paper he loved. He was a big man in every respect, and made a mockery of the tailors' art. He too was renowned for his ripostes, and when Ramsay MacDonald died aboard a ship during a cruise, Ian, who considered him a traitor to the socialist cause, wrote his obituary which included the phrase: 'He died where he had spent most of his political life – at sea.'

Ian had asked for his ashes to be scattered in Lincoln's Inn Fields. So, after his funeral a party of his closest friends duly assembled, and, with Ian's ashes in a shoe box, headed for the small park at the rear of the Law Courts. But when they arrived a park keeper strongly objected to the ceremony, and so they adjourned to the King and Keys to talk it over. They then moved to the Punch, the Falstaff, and finally the Press Club, still in possession of the shoe box. Over drinks they decided that Ian would approve if they scattered his ashes on the Thames near Cleopatra's Needle. But when they got to the Embankment the box was empty – it had a hole in it. They returned to the Club and consoled themselves with the thought that they had left a little of him in all the places he loved best.

Fleet Street funerals had an unfortunate reputation for producing the unexpected. On the morning of Hugh Saker's, a group of his friends met in the *Mirror* pub before setting off for the crematorium. They stayed much longer than they should have done, and set off in convoy at great speed, fearing they would be late. When they entered the chapel a clergyman was delivering the funeral oration, which was full of glowing tributes. They stood discreetly at the back listening intently and endorsing the sentiments being expressed – although they had not heard Hugh's name mentioned. It was only when the coffin was disappearing that the dead man's name was given, and it was not Hugh's. They had gone to the wrong service. But everyone was sure that Hugh would have chuckled at their embarrassment.

One of the Club's proudest possessions was a wall plaque presented by the Winnipeg Press Club, bestowing 'The Order of the Walrus' on members. It bore what appeared to be a thick leather thong above an embossed caption which described it as 'the genuine article'. When the Queen Mother paid a visit to the Club, she expressed great interest in the object, much to the consternation of the Chairman who was showing her around. He was at a total loss for words for the simple reason that he could not explain to Her Majesty that it was the penis of a giant walrus. When the Club moved, the plaque went too, but it was put on a wall a few feet away from the cloak room. Discretion was considered better than embarrassment, especially as the Club now had lady members.

That incident resurrected memories of the costly visit Lady Kemsley made to the *Daily Sketch* when she saw the photograph of a prize-winning bull on the Picture Editor's desk. The best was well endowed, and the proprietor's wife considered it unseemly for such a picture to appear on a paper read by countless women. 'Remove that at once,' she commanded; an artist obliged, and the bull appeared in the next day's paper devoid of his masculinity and his money-earning potential. The owner sued and was awarded substantial damages.

Such stories were invariably told in subdued voices. They could boomerang if they reached the ears of the person who was being laughed at. One Editor threatened instant dismissal to anyone on his staff who was overheard relating a particular story that held him up to ridicule. He insisted that there was not a word of truth in it, and that may well have been true, but it was too good a yarn not to go the rounds. Apparently his proprietor had telephoned and asked how the young coloured journalist who had come to London from Nigeria to study modern newspaper techniques was getting on; something the Editor had known nothing about. Later, when he paid a visit to the gents he found himself standing alongside a coloured man who was using the next stall, and automatically assumed that this was his new charge and invited him to the morning conference. The pre-lunch conference at a morning newspaper is the non-event of the day when executives with clipboards file in and report on what they have for the next morning's paper. As very little news has come in, much of it is make-believe and no one has the vaguest idea of what will fill the paper until the evening conference. The young man listened attentively and made the appropriate noises when the Editor explained that the really important conference would be later in the day and he should attend that. The young man apologised and said that that was not possible as he had to get on with the pipes. It turned out he was a plumber.

9

PHOTOGRAPHERS AND SNATCHERS

Oscar Hammerstein's wife is said to have described Jerome Kern as the man who did the tum-ti-tum-tum part for her husband's lyrics. Clearly to her mind the words were far more important than the music. I have encountered many reporters and photographers who held a similar view of the other's job. I have worked with photographers who would selfishly bitch up a story in order to get a picture, and reporters who would do likewise in reverse. They had little or no respect for the other's role. The shrewd ones, however worked together as a team, which was the only sensible and rewarding way: a good story complements a good picture, and vice-versa.

I was fortunate in that I worked most of the time with photographers who had the good sense and professionalism to work in harness. Men like Terry Fincher, George Stroud, Wally Bellamy, Stanley Meagher, Gerry Gerelli and Bill Lovelace. They could all snatch pictures without the subject even being aware that an entire roll of film had been exposed, often against their express wishes.

Wally Bellamy was outside Old Street Magistrates Court where a Maltese was accused of distilling illegal alcohol. When the case was adjourned, Wally snatched a picture of the evil-looking crook – the Maltese were the underworld's king-pins then – and the next minute he was surrounded by a gang of thugs, one of whom held a vicious-looking stiletto against his stomach. 'Take a picture and you'll get this,' he warned. 'So take it easy.' Wally promised he would.

'I looked around, hoping that someone would see my problem. It was a nice sunny day, the pavement was full of pedestrians, the traffic was thundering by and I could see a shirt-sleeved constable sunning himself on the top step of the court. But no one could see I had a damn great knife pressed against my belly. I was able to promise the gangsters I wouldn't take a picture because I knew I had a good one. Next morning it was on the front page.'

Some photographers can go back to the days when their cameras held clumsy reversible glass plates, which meant they literally had seconds in which to get *the* picture. If they missed it the opportunity had gone for ever. Life was made very much easier with the introduction of small cameras capable of firing off thirty-six exposures in as many seconds, but I suspect that the old hands still hankered for the old Speed Graphics; they separated the men from the boys.

Wally recalled the time when photographers would take a picture of the start of the Derby, then jump on to a waiting motor cycle and take another of the finish. A crowd of motor cyclists, their engines revving, would be standing by to take the plates, which were placed in special developing tanks attached to their machines, to Fleet Street. A mini TT race would take place, for the first pictures back were always the most valuable, especially for the agency men. I think the record time was something like twenty minutes. Even more remarkable, the evening papers carrying pictures of the finish were on sale at the course before the last race was over.

An assignment with George Stroud was always a delight. A chirpy sparrow of a Cockney with a weakness for eye-dazzling bow ties and an incredible fund of stories, in his company hours passed like minutes. Once we were instructed to link up at London Airport and fly to Reykjavik in Iceland, and do a picture story about a Grimsby trawler skipper who had been arrested for illegal fishing. Although he would not have agreed with us, the story had a Keystone Kops flavour about it. After his ship had been arrested, the skipper made a dash for freedom, with two Icelandic policemen locked in his cabin.

But he did not get far. Spotter aircraft were sent up, and two gunboats set off in pursuit; and, after a twelve-hour chase, one of the gunboats caught up with him, put an armed party aboard and escorted the trawler back to port.

The office wanted an immediate story – which was a pretty tall order as we arrived on a Sunday, and the skipper was being held in a cell until his court appearance, which would not be until the following Tuesday as the Monday was May Day.

George and I took a taxi to the home of the judge who would be presiding, and requested permission to interview the skipper in the local jail. It was an outrageous suggestion and one we would never have dreamed of making back home – a British judge would have locked us up for contempt. Understandably, the judge was rather indignant; although the escapade was extremely funny to us, to the Icelanders it was a national affront. With my fingers crossed I told the judge that at home we frequently interviewed prisoners awaiting trial, and George, with his customary saucy eloquence, backed me to the hilt. Reluctantly the judge gave us permission to visit the skipper in his cell.

George got a wonderful picture of him sitting gazing out of the small window, still wearing his sea-going waders, and I got an exclusive interview.

When the skipper appeared in court, George even managed to convince the authorities that it was quite common to photograph the proceedings. The truth is that at home no one is allowed to take a picture within the court precincts, and these can stretch as far as the judge deems. When other photographers tried to follow George's example, they were unceremoniously bundled out of the court-room.

The skipper really played to the gallery, and in a short time even the judge and the Icelandic audience were rocking with laughter. He was jailed for three months, heavily fined, and his fishing gear and catch confiscated. He immediately lodged an appeal and was told he would be released when the trawler's owners lodged £10,000 with the authorities.

We got to know the crew who were still living aboard, and the night before their skipper was due to appear in court we had a phone call at the hotel from a member of the crew, telling us that if we went to the docks we would get a good story. When we arrived, smoke was belching from the trawler, its plates almost pulsating with the heat, and firemen

in breathing apparatus were busy rescuing members from the
ship. Some of the crew had been celebrating a little too
enthusiastically and had fallen asleep when a fire broke out in
the paint locker.

We were on the quay when the trawler sailed for home.
The crew lined the side waving and cheering, and I wrote,
'Their cheers of joy were equalled by those from the
Icelanders on the quay.'

George had a talent for surviving near-disasters with
colours flying. On one such occasion, we had been covering a
story in Southend, then a very popular seaside resort for
Londoners; the story, long since forgotten, had petered out
and we were anxious to get back to town. But whenever we
put in a check call and asked to return we were told, 'Hang on.'
We were staying in a rather large and rambling hotel opposite
the famous pier, not far from the Kursaal, kicking our heels
and playing the pin tables, and running up a vast drinks bill. I
remember meeting a thoroughly miserable-looking young
detective who explained that he was on vice duty at the
Kursaal which entailed him concealing himself in a ventilation
shaft in the gents in order to keep observation on the activities
of homosexuals, which in those days were an offence. 'When
someone comes in for a crap, it's like a breath of fresh air,' he
confided. He was as brassed off as George and I were, but at
least we were doing our utmost to impoverish Beaverbrook.
Finally, we decided to make our way slowly back to London;
every so often we halted and put in a check call, only to hear
the inevitable 'Hang on.' Even so, we continued our home-
ward journey and ended up at George's home where we put in
another call. By this time it was late evening. When George
spoke to the Picture Desk he was asked, 'Where are you?' and
answered, 'Still in bloody Southend.' 'Good,' said the Picture
Editor, 'a big story's just broken.'

'What is it?'

'Look out of the ruddy window and you'll see. The pier is
on fire.'

We broke all records getting back to Southend, and George
had a big picture in the paper next morning and I had a good
story, thanks mainly to the co-operation of the local
correspondent.

If a reporter or photographer fell foul of his colleagues he could be given a very rough ride, and I recall an occasion when one young man was brought to the verge of a nervous breakdown. Out of town or abroad, newsmen tend to book into the same hotel in order to keep an eye on each other, and on this particular occasion we were ensconced in a very fine hotel in Amsterdam not far from the red light area. There, in narrow streets on the side of muddy-looking canals, near-naked women sat framed in windows, illuminated with fluorescent strip lighting, beckoning to passers-by to pop in and enjoy their clearly visible charms. Some succumbed, others just went window shopping. One day a group of us were sitting in a bar when a young man, not renowned for his sense of humour, came in and began to bore everyone with a long, turgid story about his worried friend who had purchased the services of one of the more amply bosomed ladies of the night, and was now worried whether she was clean. It was abundantly clear to us all who that 'friend' was. But in a short time his concern for his friend, and what he should tell his wife should he have contracted an anti-social disease, grew a trifle boring and Eric Kennedy, the *Mail* man, who had travelled down from Brussels, decided to play a rather cruel hoax: 'Tell your pal that there is black pox in Amsterdam which is a real killer unless treated immediately.'

On hearing this the young man dropped his pretence and admitted that he was the one who had been exposed to infection. Eric emitted a low ominous whistle that sounded like a death knell. 'This kind of pox is so deadly they have special detectors in the hotel in the slim hope that they can catch it in time.'

The hotel was the first I had encountered to have pocket bleepers, which were issued to residents who were expecting urgent calls and did not want to hang around the switchboard. At the time, only Eric knew this and he dashed off and returned with one. We sat in a circle and Eric ran it round our private parts. When he reached the worried young man it began to bleep furiously – Eric had arranged with the girl at the switchboard, who could see us quite clearly, to set off the gadget as soon as he reached his victim. The young man broke out into a cold sweat until Eric told him there was nothing to worry about, there was one man in Amsterdam who could effect an immediate cure. Eric gave him a telephone number, and much-relieved, he rushed to the phone and blurted out his tale of woe. 'Why are you telling me this?' asked a voice 'I am the mayor of Amsterdam.'

Stanley Sherman was another photographer it was always a delight to work and relax with. The first foreign job I did with him involved Jacqueline Kennedy and her husband's brother Robert, who was later, like John F. the President, to be assassinated. While staying in London, Mrs Kennedy had been robbed of some very valuable jewellery, but before the story broke they had left for Zurich, and Stanley and I were rushed off to intercept them there and get the story. By a stroke of good fortune and some excellent planning by the Foreign Desk, we were able to catch up with the Kennedy party at Zurich. But Jacqueline refused to say a word. The party clambered into a huge limousine, wrapped rugs around their knees and sped off. In classic style, we hailed a taxi and uttered the immortal words, 'Follow the car in front.'

We drove through a blinding snowstorm for what seemed hours before the car in front stopped. Robert Kennedy got out, came up to our taxi, and asked us how far we intended following them. 'As far as you're going,' I answered.

He shrugged and replied, 'You're in for a long cab ride. We're going to Klosters.'

Neither of us knew Switzerland very well, but we did know that this meant taking a taxi ride right over the Alps. We conferred with the driver. Would he be agreeable to us paying him when we had arranged for more money to be sent from London? No, he was not, was his answer. So we made our way back to Zurich and caught a train early the next morning.

We looked a most incongruous couple when we arrived at the famous ski resort, where every face had at one time or another adorned the Hickey column. Stan was wearing a long black overcoat which almost reached the ground, while I was wearing a rather grubby raincoat similar to the ones worn by all screen reporters. We were both wearing shoes with slippery soles, and as we made our way up the main street we continually had to help each other to our feet. Everyone else was wearing thick boots, windproof ski-jackets and pants, and dark goggles, and had suntans the colour of well-seasoned mahogany. We began a Cooks tour of the hotels, asking at each reception desk if the Kennedy party had booked in. Everywhere we met with the same negative response, and finally, Stan said, 'Sod it. Let's have a drink.'

We went into the best hotel, ordered two large scotches, which cost as much as a bucket of radium, then got our heads together to work out what we would tell the office. Clearly our quarry had gone somewhere else.

When Stan went to the bar for 'the same again', the English barman looked at him quizzically, and said, 'Don't I know you?' It turned out that Stan had met him somewhere in England.

'What brings you to this neck of the woods?' he asked.

'We're looking for the Kennedys,' said Stan.

'You mean the Smiths.'

'No. The Kennedys.'

'Same thing. They're upstairs. They booked in incognito. Sit tight, they'll be going out to dinner soon.'

As soon as they appeared in the foyer, I buttonholed them and Mrs Kennedy conceded defeat. She agreed to give me an interview and to pose for pictures on the condition that we would promise to leave them alone to enjoy their holiday. I had no hesitation in giving my word. All I wanted was a story, and all Stan wanted was a good picture.

After I had phoned over my copy and Stan had wired his picture on the nearest wire machine, we decided to make an evening of it. Stan asked the barman where the best restaurant was, and we went there intending to blow a big hole in the office's money. It was a tastefully decorated place with lots of music and boisterous skiers who seemed to think that throwing bread rolls was part of the meal.

Then to our alarm we saw the Kennedy party being escorted to the table next to ours. Chilling glances were thrown in our direction and we were reminded of our promise. We could only say, quite unconvincingly, that we were there by pure chance. Nevertheless, as the evening wore on, the Kennedy party gradually relaxed and began to enjoy themselves and take part in the festivities.

Stan's camera was as much a part of him as the Sheriff of Dodge City's six-shooter was of him, and he could use it with such speed that his victims were unaware that they had been 'shot'. And I would not have needed to take out a pencil and notebook – I could remember everything. But Stan shook his head and I did the same. As soon as we had finished our meal we returned to the hotel, where we propped up the bar.

We never mentioned the encounter to the office. They would have wondered what had happened to our news sense.

Apart from the time when President Kennedy visited the Prime Minister, Harold Macmillan, at his country home, I was never again to write about the family. But I shall never forget the day he was assassinated although I was thousands of miles from Dallas at the time.

I had been given the job of tracking down a beautiful young girl, described as a 'pocket Venus', who had run away from the home of her well-to-do parents to go to sea as a 'deck-hand' aboard a yacht skippered by a swashbuckling but somewhat dubious character with whom she had fallen in love. Eventually I traced her to Holland, where the skipper was under arrest for theft. I managed to persuade her to return home on the Harwich ferry, and at the docks I wrote my story and made a reverse charge call for Foreign copy. I got no further than dictating my name and the date line when the copy-taker said, ' —— off', and hung up. I booked another call and said plantively, 'I've spent two weeks getting this exclusive – ' Again the unfriendly advice and a dead line. The next time I rang I asked to be put on to the Foreign Editor, to whom I repeated the copy-taker's remark, only to hear him utter the same sentiments. Then he mellowed: 'Sorry, Alf, but President Kennedy has just been shot dead.' This time I hung up. I wandered out of the phone booth feeling physically ill. My photographer asked what was the matter, and I told him. My remark was overheard by several people in the lounge, and as the news was passed on a deathly silence descended as if everyone was paying homage.

One photographer I always enjoyed working with was Stanley Meagher, a wiry redhead who had the courage of a lion, and had risked his life in many parts of the world, covering wars, military coups and uprisings. He was always given the privileged task of photographing Lord Beaverbrook on his birthday, and I assumed this was in recognition of his considerable talent until Stan told me how it came about. It endorsed how enigmatic the Beaver was.

Stanley had been sent to door-step the Wiltshire home of Sir Anthony Eden around the time of the Suez Crisis. Several reporters and photographers had assembled there, all with the same brief: to watch the comings and goings of visitors, but on no account to approach the Prime Minister. As the days passed, everyone became extremely bored, and to pass the time they held races with boats made of twigs on the stream that flowed near the main gate. A Putney-to-Mortlake course was mapped out, with various spots on the bank named after the Thames bridges. For hours the cries of 'Come on, Oxford!' or 'Come on, the Light Blues!' disturbed the pastoral silence.

As the size of the bets increased, the game became more competitive, to the extent that everyone bought a toy boat from a local shop. One day, as they were cheering their craft on, a Rolls-Royce appeared with Lord Beaverbrook walking slowly behind it. Naturally, Stanley asked him to pose for a picture, but His Lordship declined, saying it was a private visit. Instead he pointed to a nearby cottage and said, 'Find out who owns it and how old it is. Also what breed of cattle they are in the field.'

Beaverbrook then disappeared into the house. Stanley made the necessary enquiries, then telephoned the office and told the Picture Editor that Lord Beaverbrook was visiting Eden. He was told not to be daft, the Old Man was in Canada; and was torn off a strip for causing an unnecessary panic.

When the Rolls reappeared, Stanley went towards it but it drove right past him, with Beaverbrook in the back staring straight ahead. Then it stopped up the lane and Beaverbrook got out. 'He seemed to be peering over the hedge studying the landscape, and I rushed up and blurted out the name of the man who lived in the cottage, how old it was, and told him the cows were Friesians. Lord Beaverbrook said, "Do you mind, young man", and I realised he was having a pee. He then asked me my name and drove off.'

When Stan made a check call to the office he was told, 'You were right. He did visit Eden. He's just been on the phone asking for details about you.'

Stan's heart skipped a beat – he was convinced he was in for a ticking-off for interrupting His Lordship's piddle; but he was told that Beaverbrook had requested that he should always take his birthday picture.

Lord Beaverbrook was indeed a most unpredictable man. A penchant for taking a personal interest in things – which bewildered his executives, though none of them ever questioned his idiosyncrasies – led to one of the strangest assignments undertaken by Wally Bellamy. Wally, who always carried his camera in a paper bag tucked under his arm, told me how he was given the task of obtaining a photograph of Sir John Ellerman, who had just succeeded to the title following the death of his shipping magnate father.

The nineteen-year-old youth was said to have inherited a fortune of over thirty million pounds, which made him the richest boy in England. It was further claimed that he had never been photographed, owing to his father's obsessive fear that he might be kidnapped and held to ransom; so stringent was the security that he had not even been allowed to appear in a classroom group photo. The two claims were an irresistible challenge to Beaverbrook, and Wally was instructed to take it up.

'I waited until the day of the funeral and posted myself outside the family home in South Audley Street; but, to shield the boy's departure, a canvas tunnel was erected, that stretched from the front door to the pavement, and I just managed to get a glimpse of him but no picture.'

A year passed before Wally was given another opportunity. A stop-press item in one of the London evenings announced that the lad had eloped with his girlfriend, Miss De Silva, and, after a register office wedding at Weybridge, had disappeared.

Wally and reporter Jack Frost were summoned into the office of J.B. Wilson, the News Editor, who announced, 'I have a hunch the couple are within a fifty-mile radius of Eastbourne; go and find them.'

Wally worked out that the area would include a part of France and a fair proportion of outer London, and felt so angry at the stupidity of the suggestion that he was on the point of resigning until Jack, ever practical, said, 'Why get annoyed? We'll have a few days at the seaside in peace.'

They took the next train to Eastbourne and began a tour of the local estate agents to find out if anyone had let a plush residence that was suitable for a couple of extremely wealthy newly-weds. By nightfall they had drawn a complete blank and retired to a pub for a sandwich and a beer.

'There we started a conversation with a local man, who invited us to play billiards at his club.' said Wally. 'We got into his car and had only been driving for about five minutes when a man ran across our headlights and without thinking I shouted out, "Ellerman!" I jumped out and followed him to a phone box where I got a better look, and although he looked like Ellerman I had my doubts because of his shabby appearance. But I followed him until he went inside a humble-looking terraced house.'

Wally and Jack decided to try and find out who lived there. While they were making discreet enquiries without any success they came across a nearby garage in which were parked about a hundred cars. Wally had done his homework very thoroughly and had the numbers of four cars owned by the Ellerman family. They included two Rolls-Royces and a Standard; one of the cars in the garage was a Standard, and the numbers matched.

'We both went to the house and knocked on the door. It opened in complete darkness and Jack said, "Could we see Sir John Ellerman?" and from the darkness a voice, heavily laced with a large plum and obviously that of a butler, said, "I'm afraid you have made a mistake. Sir John Ellerman does not live here." Another voice, farther up the passage, called out, "All right ... Show them in." We were shown into a small parlour with a minimum amount of furniture and crammed with bric-à-brac, and there was the bride playing bagatelle on a small pin table. On the sideboard was a half-crown bottle of British sherry. Sir John said, "I'm sorry, I cannot give you an interview", to which Jack replied, "I do not require one. I have my story, but my colleague would like a picture." I then said, "Surely, Sir John, a pleasant informal picture of you both will do no harm?" but he said, "Sorry, that is out of the question". '

Jack then tried one of Fleet Street's favourite ploys; he pointed out that his story would bring the rest of Fleet Street to the doorstep in the morning, but he was prepared to leave the address out if Sir John agreed to a picture. It worked.

'Sir John agreed, and I took one picture and caught the next train to London. The photograph remained the only one of Sir John for many years. I have to admit it was a hundred-million-to-one chance that we found him.'

It was only later that Wally discovered the reason for the rather humble hideaway; it had been arranged by the butler whose plumber brother was on holiday.

Wally's triumph was not allowed to remain unchallenged; the paper got tired of printing the same picture, and George Stroud was given the job of getting a more-up-to-date photograph. It was a task that, on and off, lasted two years. 'It was very difficult, as you dared not make any enquiries because if it reached Sir John's ears he would go to ground. It was also a waste of time trying to pay anyone money because he would double your offer.'

George and reporter Bill Allison, who later became Deputy News Editor, kept watch on his chauffeur and followed him to Eastbourne where he would pick up his boss, drive him to the beach and then collect him when he had completed his regular walk. But Sir John always managed to elude George's lens, although Bill once was very near to getting a picture; he came across Sir John by accident and grabbed a camera from a holidaymaker, but the picture did not come out.

Eventually George bought himself a peaked cap and joined the rank of chauffeurs who were always standing outside the Dorchester waiting for their masters to emerge. 'No one saw me taking my picture of Sir John,' he told me.

That was not the end of it; every now and then, Beaverbrook would announce it was time a picture of Sir John appeared in the paper, and the carnival would start all over again.

As well as photographers, there was a strange breed of men without whom no Picture Desk could function. They were known as 'picture snatchers', and led such a ghoulish existence that they were suspected of being descendants of

Burke and Hare. They never carried a camera, and it is doubtful if they even knew how to operate one. Their job was to obtain pictures of people who were no longer in a position to be photographed, such as murder victims, or people who had died in some disaster or other. Although I admired their skill, I was not too enamoured of their ethics. They were usually well-spoken, far better dressed than the average reporter, and they were as silk-tongued as any conman – which of course they were, their role in life being to obtain photographs from people who were usually reluctant to part with them.

I remember one of them accompanying me into the home of a distraught mother who had lost a child and did not want a photograph to appear in the paper. The picture snatcher, all solicitude, comforted her, shared her feelings, and suggested that she popped into the kitchen to make a cup of tea, which would take her mind off the rather sordid business we had been discussing. While she was putting the kettle on he stripped the walls, sideboard and mantelpiece of every picture of the child he could lay his hands on. He was off and away before she reappeared. When they had been copied, he just pushed them through her letter box.

These men used to make a lot of money because they claimed expenses on every picture they obtained – none ever came without a price tag. And, if they were first on the scene and collected more pictures than they needed, they were not averse to selling the remainder to the opposition, who would then double the price when they charged their own office. I am told they are now a dead breed. I'm sure no one laments their passing.

10

BEAVERBROOK – THE RUBIK CUBE

Much has been written about Beaverbrook, and, as I have already remarked, 'mercurial' was the adjective most often applied to him. But it is the most apt. He could be magnanimous one minute and insensitively cruel the next; he could command total respect and allegiance in some, and intense loathing in others. Ironically, although he believed that no one was exempt from the spotlight of publicity, he could go to great lengths to protect someone if the spirit moved him. He went out of his way to save Tom Driberg, who wrote the Hickey column, from public disgrace when he was arrested for importuning in a public lavatory. Obviously, the Beaver did not want the reputation of his paper tarnished, but he could have sacked Driberg, as he would have done in most cases. Instead, he instructed Percy Hoskins to see that not a word appeared anywhere in print, and this Percy did, with the exception of the *Morning Advertiser*, which he had overlooked. Beaverbrook also gave Driberg £8,000 towards the cost of his defence.

Driberg – who became an MP and Chairman of the Labour Party – later repaid Beaverbrook by writing a biography of him which was less than laudatory. Yet, although the Old Man was in a position to suppress it, he made no attempt to do so; and he was not alone in protecting Driberg, who clearly believed that he was immune to exposure as his exploits were already common knowledge in Fleet Street and the House of Commons. Indeed, he made no secret of his homosexuality, and his autobiography, *Ruling Passion*, fairly

gloats over his escapades, many of which were pretty
loathsome, going into explicit details of his casual encounters
in public lavatories and air-raid shelters. When Beaverbrook
read it, Percy Hoskins told me, he hurled it across the room
exclaiming, 'To think I saved that bastard!'

Some years ago, when I was working for Percy on the
crime beat, and long before the publication of Driberg's
book, I received a telephone call from a police contact who
asked me to meet him as he had a good story to give me. We
met in a small drinking club not far from Scotland Yard where
he explained that although I could not write the story at
present, he would give me the details, and when the time was
ripe I would have the exclusive. He was, he said, nearing the
end of an investigation concerning Driberg and young
Guardsmen. He had all the evidence necessary and would
tip me off when he was about to make an arrest. He told
me enough to convince me that the story was not a stumer;
two Guardsmen were willing to talk, and the description of
the bedroom had been checked out, and was found to be
reliable.

Several evenings later, just as I was about to leave the office,
my contact telephoned me and asked me to meet him for a
drink. I could tell from his speech that the last thing he
needed was another drink – he had obviously been at it for
some time – but he was persistent and said it was about the
Driberg story. When I arrived he was quite tipsy. But he was
not celebrating – the investigation, he told me, had been called
off. He had no idea if there had been any strings pulled, and I
never discovered why the investigation had been dropped,
but dropped it had been.

That anybody should have wanted to protect Driberg
bewildered me: not only did he personally court disaster, he
was the personification of political hypocrisy. Percy assured
me that Beaverbrook had certainly played no part in a
cover-up, if there had been one. But there was a suggestion
that Driberg worked for MI5, and there seemed some
justification for the claim. He definitely went to Moscow to
see Burgess, and even there he managed to pick up boys in a
large toilet in the centre of the city which was a known haunt
of people with similar tastes.

I was involved in one story which was suppressed where, although I missed a scoop, I was grateful that Beaverbrook and the Editor killed it. One day in the office I noticed a well-known public figure deep in conversation with the Editor, and soon afterwards a bottle of champagne was produced. The gentleman had once worked for the paper. I was introduced to him and told that the next morning the paper would be exclusively announcing his forthcoming marriage. I went clammy with apprehension when told the name of the young lady. A disaster was in the offing.

Some time previously I had met a young part-time actor who was totally without scruples, and not averse to a little blackmail. He had been living with the young lady. Once the announcement appeared, I was fearful, he might try to capitalise on it. I confided my fears to the Editor, who instructed me to get in touch with this young man and keep an eye on him.

As the wedding day approached, he told me that he intended to attend the wedding and, when the vicar asked if there was anyone present who had just cause for the wedding not to proceed, he was going to stand up and shout 'She is the mother of my child.' I had no idea whether this was the truth or not, but he did produce a pile of love letters.

The day before the wedding I was instructed to make sure that he got nowhere near the church, although I was to pretend to drive him there. Peter Kinsley, another reporter, was detailed to assist me as an extra bodyguard.

When we got into the car the young man asked me to provide him with a bottle of Scotch, which I happily did. Then we drove into the country, miles away from the wedding venue and booked into a hotel. Peter and I continued to ply him with drinks, and when he flaked out on his bed we locked the door, went down into the bar, burned the letters on the open fire, and had a drink we could enjoy.

Then the girl at the switchboard called out, 'The *Mirror* is on the line.' The actor had made a reverse-charge call to the paper. Peter and I rushed upstairs just in time to stop our ward from giving the story to the *Mirror*.

He let me know what he thought of me, but I did not care. By the time we got back to town the ceremony was over.

I met him several times later, and if he bore me any ill will there was no sign of it. It was just water under the bridge as far as he was concerned.

I have also seen the gentleman whose marriage I saved; we have never spoken but I can't help wondering if he is aware of the role I played.

Percy Hoskins was undoubtedly the Beaver's Number One Fixer. He was even called in to extricate one of Beaverbrook's sons – he later died in tragic circumstances – from a particularly unpleasant scandal. If he had not become a crime reporter, Percy would have made a first-class detective. His own favourite piece of sleuthing related to the late Brendan Bracken, proprietor of the *Financial Times*, who boasted that he was the illegitimate son of Winston Churchill. He was so plausible that Randolph Churchill used to refer to him as 'my bastard brother', and even Lady Churchill had her doubts; so much so that she often tackled Winston about it, but he remained enigmatically vague. 'How old is he?' he would ask, and on being told would shake his head in a manner that neither confirmed nor denied it. As his name never appeared in any reference books it was difficult to check on Bracken's story.

Bracken incurred Beaverbrook's wrath when he attacked him in the *Financial Times*, and Percy was summoned: 'Find out who he is. One minute he says his parents died in a fire in Australia, the next that he's Churchill's illegitimate son.'

Percy had no idea where to start, until Lord Castlerosse gave him a clue, 'Go to Dublin.' There, he met Oliver St John Gogarty, who was a member of the London Press Club, and the original 'stately plump Buck Mulligan' of Joyce's *Ulysses*. Gogarty introduced to him W.B. Yeats, the poet, who advised Percy to go to Templemore, near Tipperary. 'But watch out for the natives, they could be hostile,' he warned.

Percy arrived there disguised as a hiker, an unlikely cover as Percy never walked anywhere if a taxi was within hailing distance. After running up and down the road until he was exhausted, he called on the local doctor and said he felt unwell after climbing the nearby Devil's Mountain. The doctor examined him, pronouncing him fit, but advised him that, with his surplus weight, he should not be indulging in such strenuous activities as mountaineering. Percy then casually mentioned that Brendan Bracken was his local Member of Parliament, for North Paddington, and did the doctor happen to know him? 'Know him! I brought him into the world,' he exclaimed. Within a short time Percy knew everything there was to know about the childhood of the red-haired politician, including the fact that he was the son of the local stonemason.

When Percy returned and passed on the information, Beaverbrook made no attempt to expose Bracken but simply kept the information on ice.

'Fifteen years later,' Percy told me, 'Beaverbrook invited me and my wife Jeannie to dinner at Cherkley. I had no idea why, but there were a number of distinguished people there, including Bracken, who I thought was an arch-enemy. After dinner Beaverbrook took me aside, put his arm around my shoulder and said, "Aneurin Bevan has resigned and there may be a General Election. If the Tories get in Bracken will be Home Secretary. I want you to bring him up to date on the workings of the Metropolitan Police Force." Then he took Jeannie in to watch his favourite film, *Destry Rides Again*, while I spent two hours explaining the functions of the police to the man I had been sent to expose.'

Many years ago, when the Irish Republican Army launched a bombing campaign in London, blowing up telephone booths and left-luggage offices, Beaverbrook wanted to know where they were operating from.

J.B. Wilson, the News Editor, a tall elegant man, always impeccably dressed, concealed a heart of steel beneath his suave man-about-town exterior, but when Beaverbrook called he jumped. He summoned his entire reporting staff and commanded, 'Find the IRA's headquarters.' He was a man who demanded the near-impossible, and invariably got it.

Even Bernard Hall, who was assistant to Bill Barkley, the Parliamentary sketch writer, was detached from his duties and seconded to the team. The reporters toured every Irish area in London, but apart from getting sore heads from too much Guinness, they had nothing to show for their endeavours after days and nights of hard grafting.

Percy, as Chief Crime Reporter, even with his vast array of contacts, also seemed to be getting nowhere. One morning he rang J.B., who went into an angry tirade about his lack of success. Percy let him finish before saying, 'I'm phoning to tell you I have some bad news. I've found the arsenal. The bombs are being made in your cellar. The Special Branch are there now, removing explosives – and your butler.'

J.B. grabbed a camera and leapt into a taxi for his house in Brunswick Square, Bloomsbury, where he arrived just in time to take a photograph. As his butler was being led away under arrest, he turned and said, 'I'm awfully sorry, sir, there'll be no supper tonight.' J.B. not only wrote the story of the raid on his own home, but was responsible for the arrest of another member of the gang, whom he saw slipping away from the house with an attaché case. J.B. promptly alerted the police, who were able to catch the man. The case was filled with explosives, fuses, and french letters, which played a vital part in the bomb-making; the last appeared in J.B.'s story as balloons – the correct description was not considered fit for the *Express*'s delicate readers.

J.B. was ragged unmercifully for having dined for months above a basement packed with explosives. but the last straw was a request from his jailed butler: 'Please send me a reference, sir.'

Beaverbrook was a prolific writer, and one of his earlier books was called *Don't Trust to Luck* – he did not believe the elusive lady existed. It was not a view I shared. The difficulty was not in finding the lady, but in recognising her when she appeared, and grasping her firmly by the hand. I certainly did that when Sophia Loren was burgled.

When she was filming *The Millionairess* with Peter Sellers at Elstree Studios, she rented the Swiss Chalet, in the grounds of nearby Edgwarebury Country Club, so as to be near the studio. It was aptly named, for the house resembled something from the Hollywood set of *Heidi*. As I was not living far away when she was robbed of all her jewellery, the office naturally assigned me to the job, and I was on the scene before anyone else had even left The Street. When I arrived, a burly constable was standing sentinel at the front door, but luckily, the person who had tipped off the office had also given the name of the detective-inspector in charge of the investigation, who happened to be someone I had met on a previous story. When the constable asked me what I wanted I simply gave him the name of the officer, and to my astonishment he opened the door and allowed me to enter. The detective-inspector, who was busy interviewing Miss Loren, merely looked up, said, 'You made it quickly,' and waved me to a chair. There was a team of detectives combing the chalet, while others were busy dusting for fingerprints, and Carlo Ponti, the filmstar's husband, was offering words of comfort to his clearly upset wife. I listened to Miss Loren's every word, where she kept her jewels, how she discovered their loss, and how much they were worth. I had never had a story dropped so neatly into my lap. God, I was grateful to the police officer; not many carried friendship that far. I continued to sit there taking notes, as the famous star was fingerprinted for the purpose of elimination. Already, the story was writing itself in my mind. Then the proceedings were interrupted by the appearance of the constable keeping watch, who announced that my photographer had arrived and was asking for me.

The detective, perplexed, at last turned his attention towards me, and asked me who the hell I was. 'Alf Draper, *Daily Express*,' I replied as nonchalantly as possible.

He ushered me outside and said, with some vehemence, that although he recognised the face he had mistakenly thought I was the extra detective he had telephoned for. I felt sorry for him, but I had done nothing wrong except take advantage of his mistaken identification. And when he said I could not use a word of what I had overheard I politely said I could not agree to that.

Obviously, I could not remain in the chalet, and we arranged to have a drink in The Artichoke in Elstree village. When he turned up he had a suggestion to make, which when I heard it I readily agreed to: Miss Loren had no detailed description of her jewellery which, if I remember correctly, was not insured. But if I contacted my picture library and got them to dig out all the photographs in stock of Miss Loren wearing jewellery, and had them sent to him by despatch rider, I was free to use the information I had obtained. This was done, and the actress was able to identify a great many pieces, which was of great assistance to the police when it came to circulating their description. The photographer was rewarded with a first-rate picture of the actress and I got a scoop for which I was congratulated.

Naturally I did not let on as to how I had enjoyed such a stroke of luck – that would have diminished my enterprise. My expenses showed that it had been achieved by hard work, lavish entertaining, and payments to informants.

Needless to say, I've never read Beaverbrook's book. It would be as rewarding as telling a turkey Christmas doesn't exist.

11

THE DOYEN

Fleet Street has always loved attaching labels to people: a label makes a person's status immediately identifiable with a minimum of mental effort. But the most overworked word of them all is 'doyen'. If a person showed the slightest inclination to stoop, or his paunch was cutting off his view of his own feet, or his hair was starting to grey, he became the doyen of his particular field. There is only one man I know, however, who has been granted that accolade without a single murmur of dissent. He is Percy Hoskins, for more than sixty years Chief Crime Reporter and Consultant for the *Daily Express*. His reputation is world-wide, and such has been his influence over the years that he is known as Scotland Yard's Doctor Watson. But his relationship with the most famous police force in the world is not purely professional; he comands the deepest respect and affection. No one man has done more than Percy to promote the image of the dedicated professional detective. He detests the crime novelist's depiction of the detective as a bumbling thick-head who has to rely on brilliant amateurs to solve his murders. Likewise he hates the public image of the crime reporter. Addressing a conference of British and American lawyers, he once said:

> There are those who, under the influence of Hollywood, are quite sure that all reporters are tough cynical rowdies, always with a bottle of gin in one pocket. Another school had derived its mental picture from the popular novel in which the crime reporter tracks down gangsters, rescues the millionaire's daughter and dashes into the office shouting, 'Clear the front page!'
> Believe me, if I rushed into the office shouting, 'Hold the

presses!', the Editor would either send me to a psychiatrist
or transfer me to the *Junior Express* (now defunct).

Nevertheless, there was something of the chameleon about
Percy, for he could adapt to any conditions when working. (I
write in the past tense, although he is still very much alive and
vigorously kicking – he has simply retired.) He lived a life of
champagne and shadows, mingling easily with the famous and
infamous. He could dine at Claridge's with a judge after
having spent hours drinking with a crook in a low dive. Few
men knew as much about crime from both sides of the fence.
And no man has covered so many murders, some of them so
gruesome that I have never ceased to be amazed that Percy
has managed to remain so warm and trusting towards his
fellow humans.

People asked to name his profession on meeting him for the
first time would probably hazard a guess that he was a Harley
Street consultant or a successful gentleman farmer – anything
but a crime reporter. He could also pass as the double of his
friend Alfred Hitchcock, having similar features and the same
ample waistline. One of his proudest possessions is a stunted
picture of his own head peering from behind one side of a tree
trunk with Hitchcock's peeping from the other side: the
master of real crime alongside the maestro of make-believe
suspense.

Percy has always maintained that he had no desire to
become a crime reporter, that it happened by sheer chance;
but anyone who knows his background will disagree. He was
destined for the job. Fate had already decided the morning he
was born – on Holy Innocents Day, 28 December – in the
small town of Bridport, where they used to make the
hangman's rope, known in Elizabethan times as the 'Bridport
dagger'. Now in his eighties, he still has that warm, leisurely
West Country burr, which gives a shock quality to his
remarkably astute observations.

Before his retirement, reluctantly taken in order to be at the
side of his sick wife, he lived in a seventh-floor flat
overlooking Hyde Park, which was as famous as the fictional
one in Baker Street. If you were invited there for a drink you
could never be sure who would be there. Most likely you

would find yourself drinking with someone who was a household word as far as crime was concerned; or it might be a Cabinet Minister, an Ambassador, a judge, or one of the several eminent pathologists he worked alongside in so many cases. On a less professional footing there could be stars of the stage and cinema. One evening his friend Bing Crosby gave an impromptu concert there for a group of visiting detectives. Whenever Percy held court the hospitality was lavish, but people like myself would have been content to die of thirst just for the pleasure of listening to the conversation, especially when it turned to crime, as it invariably did. It was spell-binding to hear old crimes relived, and the true story behind unsolved murders recounted.

Practically every inch of his wall space was occupied by photographs and cartoons reflecting his astonishing career; he is pictured with the Queen, the Queen Mother, Prince Philip, Prince Charles, the Archbishop of Canterbury, and J. Edgar Hoover, founder of the FBI. One that could never be shown in public is of a dinner party Percy gave to the heads of all the Intelligence Services when the war ended. Another photograph reveals his impish sense of humour. He is with a friend, both wearing the coronet and scarlet and ermine robes of a peer of the realm, with Westminster Abbey in the background. It was taken at the time of the Coronation, and sent to friends who would have given their eye teeth to have been there. They thought it was a genuine photograph. But Percy had borrowed the robes from Bud Flanagan and another member of the Crazy Gang, who used them on stage. After they had been photographed in Percy's flat, an *Express* artist superimposed the Abbey.

There is a document granting him the Freedom of London, and another awarding him the CBE, personally signed by the Queen and Duke of Edinburgh. The shelves are lined with one of the finest collections on criminology, in which his own contribution figures largely. Today they all adorn his flat overlooking the sea at Hove, and although he has retired the company is still as lively.

A measure of Percy's status can be judged by a conversation he once overheard. He was seated behind two eminent judges, Mr Justice Davies, and the Recorder of

London, Sir Anthony Hawke, when one remarked to the other, 'You know, if Percy ever got into trouble it would be difficult to try him. We know him too well personally.'

'You are right,' came the reply. 'We should have to set up a special neutral tribunal.'

Yet Percy might well have remained at Bridport working for a local newspaper if a ship had not gone down one Christmas Day with the loss of thirty-seven lives. He happened to be the only reporter on duty, and covered the disaster for all the national papers. He had the front-page lead in all of them, and on the strength of that was invited to join the staff of Beaverbrook's *Evening Standard*, not as a chronicler of major disasters but as the writer of a showbiz column.

He was busy writing his column, in long hand, when he was told to get to Crowborough in Sussex where Scotland Yard had been called in to investigate the mysterious disappearance of a young woman. 'I was the only reporter available,' Percy told me. 'So, with many doubts and misgivings, I quit showbusiness and started my career as a crime reporter.'

Percy was later to cover many much more celebrated murders: Haigh, the acid-bath killer; Christie, the necrophiliac mass murderer; Neville Heath; the Yorkshire Ripper, and countless others. But none of them took precedence over that first murder, which was in many ways rather mundane compared to what was to come. But it was his first experience of the dedicated work of the Murder Squad and of what makes a brilliant detective, and from it he developed a deep respect for the police force at its best, which never deserted him. It also revealed that Percy had found his vocation, because he interviewed the main suspect before the Scotland Yard men, and guessed – quite rightly – where he had buried his victim.

As the Yard team hastened to Sussex, they must have thought that the circumstances which had involved them in the case were similar to scores of missions they had undertaken. The parents of a young woman had reported her missing, not having seen her since she had set out from her Willesden home to visit her fiancé, Norman Thorne, who ran a chicken farm. A week after her departure they sent him a telegram enquiring about her whereabouts, and he replied that she had never turned up, and he was as worried as they were.

Unable to trace her, the local police eventually called in the Yard. The facts were pretty straightforward. Norman Thorne was a young man of impeccable background, who had served in the latter part of the Great War and, although he worked hard, still found time to be a Sunday School teacher and assist at a boys' club. During a trip to London he met Elsie Cameron, a rather dowdy young woman whose appearance was not improved by the severe steel-rimmed spectacles she wore to correct her myopia. She fell hopelessly in love with him and soon became his mistress, often spending the night with him in a converted chicken house on the farm. In November 1924 she wrote him a letter pleading with him to marry her as she was pregnant. Thorne, however, was not too anxious to comply with her appeal for the simple reason that he had met someone else and fallen in love.

None of this, of course, was at the time known to the Scotland Yard detectives. When I knew and worked under Percy, his personal contacts were legendary and the envy of every other Fleet Street crime man, but when he went to Crowborough he did not know a single detective at Scotland Yard. But luck, or fate, stepped in, otherwise Percy could well have gone back to his showbiz column. By coincidence he travelled on the same train as Chief Detective-Inspector John Gillan, the Yard man in charge of the investigation. He was a complete stranger to Percy, but his sergeant, who turned out to be the son of a superintendent from Bridport and knew Percy by sight, introduced him to the 'guv'nor'.

Gillan suggested that Percy should call on Thorne and see what he had to say and report back to him, which Percy did. They talked surrounded by squawking chickens, and Thorne repeated his story that Elsie had never arrived.

As they spoke, the postman delivered two poison pen letters which accused him of being a murderer, and he handed them to Percy saying, 'How can I stop them and their gossip?'

'That's easy,' replied Percy. 'You've got to invite the police to come and dig up every inch of your farm.'

Thorne agreed to the suggestion, but with one proviso: they should not disturb his chickens.

That night Percy met Gillan and told him the missing girl was buried in the chicken run. She was – just where he had been standing.

For the first time, Percy saw a judge don the black cap. 'A moment never to be forgotten by anyone,' he told me. Since then he has witnessed the grisly ritual many times, but that first occasion still preys on his mind. Not because he is opposed to capital punishment, but because he has doubts about Thorne's guilt.

Although Thorne admitted dismembering her and burying the body, he claimed that she had hanged herself while he was out, and that, in panic, he had decided to hide the body, thinking that the police would not believe him. Several doctors and the eminent pathologist, Dr Robert Bronte, supported his story; but Sir Bernard Spilsbury, who had established a reputation for infallibility, ruled out the possibility of suicide.

The jury accepted Spilsbury's evidence, but it sparked off a controversy that was to last until Spilsbury's own death. Was his reputation alone enough to secure a conviction, irrespective of what others said?

Many years later Percy covered the murder of Vera Chesney, which went a long way to prove that Spilsbury was capable of the most serious errors of judgement. It was one I was personally interested in.

Percy had no illusions about his own fallibility, and I know he suffered considerable torment when he took his solitary stance in the Bodkin Adams case. Dr John Bodkin Adams, an Eastbourne doctor, was charged with murdering elderly patients after getting them to leave him money in their wills. Before his arrest he had been subjected to a scurrilous Press campaign, which virtually condemned him as a mass murderer. It was a disgraceful episode in Fleet Street's not always untarnished history. Percy, although he had no personal knowledge that the doctor was innocent, was appalled at the idea of trial by the Press and refused to join in, determined to see the bulwark of British justice – that a man is innocent until proved guilty – upheld. In the event he was justified – Adams was found Not Guilty at the Old Bailey trial – and, thanks to Percy, the *Express* obtained Dr Adams's exclusive story.

Percy received a brusque telephone call from Beaverbrook, who said, 'Two men have been acquitted today. Adams and Hoskins.' It was hardly a paean of praise, but the best that might be expected.

Understandably, the other dailies, although privately admiring Percy's lone stand, would not publicly admit that he was right: the blame was pinned on the Attorney-General, Sir Reginald Manningham-Buller (widely known as Bullying-Manner), who prosecuted, and 'Adams owes his life to M&B' became a frequently heard remark. Michael Foot, on the other hand, later wrote of Percy: 'His campaign, conducted almost single-handed, to ensure that Dr Adams should receive the proper protection of British justice, stands out as one of the finest examples of honest and courageous journalism in living memory.'

Percy delayed writing his own account until after both the doctor and the police officer in charge of the case were dead; not because he feared any libel action, but because he knew it would revive painful memories for them. Dr Adams left Percy £1,000 in his will, which he donated to the Liver Cancer Research Unit.

Percy was always something of a loner, preferring to rely on his own judgement rather than fall into line with the generally held view. It did not always make for popularity, especially if it spoiled a good story.

One occasion was the celebrated case, in 1949, of Timothy Evans, who shared a house with John Reginald Christie, the mass murderer. Evans was hanged for the murder of his baby daughter, and had at one time confessed to the murder of his wife. That was before the discovery of Christie's horrible deeds, and when they were revealed there was an outcry that Evans had been wrongly executed – that the real murderer was Christie. A great deal was written about a gross miscarriage of justice, notably by Ludovic Kennedy, whose brilliant anatomy of the case convinced most people that the necrophiliac had killed Mrs Evans and the child. I was certainly convinced. Percy was not. He told me that, at the time of his arrest, Evans said to a detective, 'After I killed my wife, I took the wedding ring off her finger and sold it for six shillings in Merthyr.' When detectives called at the jewellers they recovered the ring. That had been enough to convince Percy.

There was an interesting sequel to the story, which Percy recounted to me. In October 1949, a wildfowler found a large bundle floating in the Dengie Marshes off the Essex coast. Inside was the headless torso of a man. The late Professor Francis Camp, a longstanding friend of Percy's, deduced that the massive damage done to the bones was consistent with the body having been dropped from a great height. But that was not the cause of death: the man had been stabbed to death. Fingerprints established he was a kerbside car dealer named Stanley Setty.

A most exhaustive inquiry produced evidence that a man named Donald Hume had hired an aircraft at Elstree airfield and had been seen at Southend airport where he was forced to land. He was also seen loading two big parcels aboard the aircraft. And later he had made a return trip.

It was a long and frustrating investigation, and an example of perfect team work on the part of the police. Hume was charged with Setty's murder, but managed to convince the jury that he had not killed him but had merely been paid for disposing of the body. The money he received was found to be part of a thousand pounds that Setty had been paid for a car sale.

Hume was acquitted of murder, but sentenced to twelve years as an accessory after the fact. Percy never believed his story.

With remission for good behaviour, Hume was released in February 1958, and among the first things he did was to call on Percy, to whom he boastfully admitted to having killed Setty. He then offered to sell his story to the *Express*, but Percy turned down the offer, telling him it was not the kind of deal the paper would ever consider. (He sold it elsewhere for £10,000.)

Percy did not disclose his personal disgust; instead he used Hume to put his mind at ease over the Evans case. He knew Hume had met Evans in prison when he was awaiting trial, and he asked Hume how he had persuaded Evans to withdraw his confession. 'I told him it was stupid to have made all those confessions to the police,' Hume replied. 'I told him to admit nothing in court, just to think of the best story and stick to it.'

Hume went even further and confided to Percy that Evans had told him of the arrangements he had with Christie for disposing of Mrs Evans's body, and that Christie had also killed the child because it would not stop crying, while Evans stood by and watched him do it. That doubly confirmed Percy's belief that he had not been wrongly hanged.

To Percy, Hume is the most evil and coldly calculating killer he has ever encountered. It was not long before Hume was again in trouble on a murder charge. He had flown to Switzerland after carrying out a series of bank raids in London, and continued his criminal activities in Zurich. While making his escape from a bank he shot dead a taxi driver and was sentenced to life imprisonment in Switzerland.

I was only minimally involved in the Setty murder, but I did get an exclusive on Hume for the *Express* – though I never dared tell Percy how I got it. I happened to be at Zurich airport when I saw Hume's picture staring at me from the front page of a Swiss newspaper. I bought a copy and asked a Swiss air hostess to translate it for me. It was a story of how Hume had gone berserk in prison and attacked another prisoner with knives he had fashioned from parts of his cell bunk. I found a telephone and put the story over. (He was then transferred to Broadmoor, where he remained for twelve years, until his removal in April 1988 to a hospital for low-risk patients.)

One of Percy's earliest contacts was the Chief Constable of the Metropolitan Police Force – now known as the Commissioner – who came from Somerset. He did not himself talk to the Press, but would telephone his son-in-law, an inspector at City Row, with any news, which the Inspector would then pass on to Percy. Through this ruse no rules were broken while Percy was able to obtain scoop after scoop.

He once telephoned a story that a man had been arrested for attempting to blackmail a well-known peer. Later the same day, Percy attended the court hearing, where the magistrate announced, 'We will not divulge the name of the prosecutor, who will be referred to as Mr X.' Through the open window, Percy could hear the voices of the newsboys selling copies of the *Evening Standard* which carried the peer's name. He was lucky not to have been prosecuted for contempt of court.

There were times, too, when Percy deliberately risked his career and faced possible imprisonment for a point of principle.

Neville Heath was a sadistic killer who was hanged for the murder of two women he had sexually mutilated before death. The second need not have happened because Scotland Yard knew his identity, and a picture of the wanted man had been circulated to all police stations. But the Press had been requested not to use it. Percy, who has always considered the crime reporter to be the police's greatest ally in the fight against crime, believed, and still does, that if the newspaper had been allowed to publish the picture, a life would have been saved. 'When the trial was over,' he said, 'I wrote a story that I illustrated with the picture of Heath which had appeared in the official *Police Gazette*, saying it was the one which every policeman in the country had memorised but which no member of the public had been allowed to see. I was later told that the Home Secretary had seriously considered prosecuting my paper for reproducing an official document.'

This incident, however, did little damage to his relationship with the police. When he was awarded the CBE in the Birthday Honours List, a special tribute was printed in *The Job*, the Metropolitan Police's own newspaper, with a message, signed by Sir Robert Mark, the Commissioner, reading: 'This award will give real and personal pleasure to many serving officers. He is the doyen of crime reporters and has long enjoyed the confidence, respect and indeed affection of many members of the Metropolitan Force. Scotland Yard as a whole is delighted by the news.'

Such a tribute would have been unheard of when Percy started. 'In the old days it was often a case of suspension if an officer was seen talking to a newsman,' he told me.

The present close liaison between the media and the police is largely due to Percy's efforts. Today's Press Bureau is comfortable and well equipped, and a steady stream of information is handed out to the crime men. When the first

Press Bureau was opened, however, in a disused storeroom on the Embankment, it was so dank and squalid that it was dubbed 'the Black Hole of Calcutta'. It was economically run, too: the civil servant in charge there was forced to supplement his wages with a music hall act, and would often disappear without warning to appear on the stage at the Victoria Palace, while, 'No outgoing calls were allowed,' Percy told me. 'When we had a story we had to run to Westminster Underground station where the nearest phone was.'

While he was covering an Old Bailey trial at that time, a police witness mentioned the Press Bureau. The judge exploded: 'I have never heard of the Press Bureau and I never want to hear it mentioned again.'

Another delightful story Percy tells about the Old Bailey was the trial for murder in 1932 of wealthy socialite, Mrs Elvira Barney, who shot dead her lover.

'In those days crime reporters were not entrusted with the task of covering the trial. Famous writers were hired to do that. At the trial there were Edgar Wallace, Sidney Horler, Gilbert Frankau and other best-selling novelists. I was sitting alongside George Arliss, the distinguished actor. Sir Patrick Hastings, who was appearing for Mrs Barney, turned to the jury and said something like "You and I have not come here as specially hired writers to paint a picture in words of this woman's agony ... " There was a pause and all eyes turned towards the novelists. Then Hastings resumed, "Neither have we come here as distinguished actors to study this woman's emotions, to use them for profit in the make-believe world of the stage." All eyes turned towards Arliss, who whispered to me, "The dirty bastard, he invited me." '

With the commencement of the war, Percy joined the Army and spent two fruitless years on the South Coast waiting to repel the invasion which never came. He reminded his friends of his continued existence with a stream of telegrams, 'Remember Poole Harbour.' Thankfully, someone had the good sense to realise his immense talent was being wasted, and he was attached to a radio unit, on Eisenhower's staff, which had the job of boosting morale among the troops. Guy Burgess produced some of the programmes Percy wrote, and, many years later, Percy was to scoop the world with the story of his defection to Russia with the diplomat Donald Maclean.

While on Eisenhower's staff, Percy often had to look after visiting VIPs, among them Bing Crosby, Fred Astaire and Glen Miller, who invariably ended up in his flat. When he went to America, Bing made him a member of a private dining club, and from that visit sprang the famous Saints and Sinners. Percy decided to start a club, with the impresario, Jack Hylton, in order to repay the hospitality enjoyed in America. It started with fifteen people and was limited to a hundred members. It still is, but the guests number hundreds, and it has raised large sums of money for charity. Prince Philip is a regular guest. One unbreakable rule is that no people of similar professions should sit next to each other, so that 'shop' will be avoided – thus, Sir Malcolm Sargent would be seated next to Bud Flanagan. Saints wear white carnations, Sinners red. Percy always sports the latter.

Towards the end of the war he wrote a series of radio programmes called *It's Your Money They're After*, which exposed crime and explained the workings of the police. For the first time he took a microphone into the secret Information Room at Scotland Yard to explain how the 999 system worked. The number of calls from the public rose by sixty per cent in one day.

Yet Percy can recall an earlier Commissioner who, when he saw a telephone on his desk, thundered: 'Take it away! The next thing we know is that the public will be ringing us up.'

Percy has had many honours bestowed upon him for his services to journalism and charity, but he remains an essentially modest man. The honour he values most is the suite at King's College School of Medicine named in honour of his late wife Jeannie. It is a measure of the man that he is more interested in the achievements of others than in his own.

Many years after I had left Fleet Street I was standing in Scotland Yard's Black Museum, gazing at two forearms preserved in a glass-sided tank, and I was transported back in time to a pavement outside a house in Montpelier Road in Ealing, and another case covered by Percy. Inside, detectives were investigating the murders of Lady Menzies, and her daughter Vera Chesney, who ran an old people's home there.

In a short time their killer was named as Ronald Chesney, Vera's husband, who, in February 1954, shot himself in a wood near Cologne, realising that he was about to be arrested for their murders. The severed arms belonged to him, but their great interest to the criminologist was that they had finally provided the answer to a controversial crime which had been a matter of debate since 1926. And for many it confirmed that the unquestioning faith in Spilsbury's judgement had been misplaced, reviving the question: how many innocent men had been condemned through his arrogance?

Chesney was John Donald Merrett, who, in 1926 when a seventeen-year-old student at Edinburgh University, walked into the kitchen one March day and calmly informed the maid: 'My mother has shot herself. I have been wasting her money.'

Bertha Merrett was found slumped over her desk with a near-fatal bullet wound in her head. Nearby was a .22 pistol. She died in hospital not long afterwards, and it was assumed to be suicide – until it was discovered that Donald had been forging her signature on cheques; suspicions then arose as to the manner of her death, and he was charged with murder and forgery.

His chances of escaping the noose seemed slim indeed; there was a complete absence of 'tattooing' or 'blackening' round the wound, consistent with suicide. How could she have held the pistol so far away as to avoid this and yet kill herself? Even more puzzling, the wound was *behind* the right ear.

But Merrett had an unexpected champion – Sir Bernard Spilsbury, who for the first time in his career appeared for the defence. He won the day. Any blackening could have been removed by bleeding or cleansing. Neither the position nor direction of the wound were incompatible with suicide. He argued with his customary eloquence and obstinacy which implied that any other opinion was ridiculous. The jury returned a verdict of Not Proven – unique to Scottish law.

Merrett was sentenced to twelve months' imprisonment for

forgery. After his release, he eloped with Vera, the seventeen-year-old daughter of Lady Menzies. Not long after that he inherited a large sum of money from his grandmother – some of which he settled on his wife, and the rest of which he soon went through. He then resumed a life of crime, 'Merrett' disappearing when he adopted the alias of 'Chesney'. When the war came, he joined the Royal Navy, and when it ended, he deserted Vera and went to live in Germany, where he survived on black-market activities.

Lady Menzies and Vera in the meantime set up their old people's home.

However successful his criminal activities, though, Chesney never seemed to have enough money, and it occurred to him that his problems could be solved if he got hold of the money he had settled on his wife. He made plans for the perfect murder, and began to put them in action. First, he flew to London on his own passport, visited his wife and presented her with a bottle of gin, to which she had become addicted. Then, having made sure he had been seen by a neighbour, he flew back to Germany, where he shaved off his beard and put on horn-rimmed spectacles before taking the next flight back to Britain, this time on a false passport. That night he plied Vera with gin until she was incapable, and then carried her to the bathroom, where he drowned her. But as he crept down the darkened stairs, the meticulously planned crime misfired. Standing at the bottom was his mother-in-law. Despite his disguise she recognised him, and he bludgeoned and strangled her to death. He flew back to Germany, knowing he had left too many clues, among them his fingerprints.

It was not long before he learnt that Scotland Yard had alerted Interpol to look for one Ronald Chesney, also known as John Merrett. He made a desperate attempt to contact the German girl he was in love with, and to whom he had confided that he had killed his mother. Unable to find her, he shot himself.

At the Ealing inquest on Vera and her mother, a jury ruled that he had killed them. His arms bore bruises and scratches, and under his mother-in-law's finger-nails were fragments of flesh torn from them during her struggle for life.

Today those pickled arms are used to help young detectives in the never-ending battle of crime detection, and to remind them that no murder can be considered unsolved.

12

CHARACTERS FOR A NOVELIST

It was during my time on the *Daily Express* that I wrote my first novel, *Swansong for a Rare Bird*, which was runner-up in the Panther-Macmillan First Crime Novel Competition. Much of it was written during the idle hours of night shifts – a difficult task as I had to whip it out of sight whenever one of my numerous bosses approached – or at home, competing with the demands of my young family and television. I was reasonably well qualified to write about crime as I had been involved in reporting it for a considerable time, but it is one thing to know a subject and another to write a novel. When reporting you deal with the facts, whereas a novel makes great demands on your imagination – the one quality that is discouraged in a reporter. The first thing you need is a peg on which to hang the story. My peg came when I became involved in a sordid yet very tragic murder case, although I doubt whether it would rate any interest today now that we no longer have the death penalty. I have deliberately blurred the facts here, because some of the people involved, especially the young woman, may still be alive and I have no wish to revive painful memories. I hope it is all forgotten in their minds and the young lady in particular has found the happiness she so richly deserved.

The seeds of the idea were sown when I was sent to cover the brutal killing of a young man who had become engaged the day previously. He was returning home after having spent the evening with his fiancée, and, as he was walking down a narrow alley, was waylaid and mugged by a group of youths who kicked and beat him so savagely that he died the next day. They had been looking for someone to roll in order to get some cash to continue their drinking. Although the dead man's wallet was empty, they were charged with murder 'in the furtherance of theft', a capital offence. None showed any remorse for their senseless and vicious crime, seeming more concerned with the sentences they would receive. Some thought they would only get a few years' imprisonment; one thought they might 'dangle'. At their Old Bailey trial all pleaded Not Guilty, but they were convicted by their own statements, in which they said that they had had a 'few shants' (drinks) and decided to 'jump' somebody.

All were found guilty and two were sentenced to death; one, being a minor, was ordered to be detained During Her Majesty's Pleasure, and another was sentenced to life imprisonment.

But long before the trial I had been gathering what is known as 'background material', only to be used if they were found guilty. My particular interest lay in an eighteen-year-old labourer who admitted to having put the boot in. His decent, hard-working family could not believe that the son they idolised, who had shown such promise at school, could be guilty of this monstrous crime; but, in the presence of a detective, he said to his mother, 'I'm sorry, Mum, but I did it, and that is all there is to it.'

He had a very pretty teenage girlfriend who was pregnant by him, and I got to know her and his family extremely well, and made arrangements for the *Daily Express* to have their exclusive story. It is hard even for the most cynical and hardbitten reporter not to be moved by the agonies of a family suddenly caught up in a crime that made headlines nearly every day. What made a bunch of youngsters attack and kill a man they had never set eyes on before simply because they wanted some more to drink? I wondered, and remembered the dying man's last words: 'What do you want me for?'

I was also deeply sorry for the young girl, a pathetic little creature, totally bewildered by the events, who still professed her love for the youth. I spent many sleepless nights thinking about it all. But the seeds of my idea were beginning to germinate.

One day I met her father, a well-read man who told me that he too had spent hours wondering why his little girl had been caught up in it. He quoted some of the authors he had read, Freud, Jung, and so on, in an attempt to find a satisfactory answer. Suddenly he turned to me and said, 'Then it hit me, she is sex mad.' Somehow the words summed up all his bitterness and frustration. He didn't know the answer any more than I did.

The youth was one of those sentenced to death; although I had only seen him in the dock, I felt I had got to know him through his mother and girlfriend, who were able to present sides of him unknown to the jury; and I sympathised with the public outcry against the hanging of someone so young and callow, hoping that he would get a reprieve, for he was young enough to survive a long prison sentence and emerge wiser and penitent and able to pursue a worthwhile life.

I took his mother regularly to the prison, and spent many nights with her, watching her endure an agony of suspense, hoping and praying that the Home Secretary would intervene. The girl also wanted to see him, but her father, who did not approve of or understand her affection for a killer, refused his consent, so that although she went to the prison she was turned away until he gave his written consent.

While he was in the condemned cell, the boy wrote surprisingly moving and eloquent love letters to her, which she gave to me to be printed in the paper. One letter was little more than a series of strung-together pop-song titles. It seemed tragically trivial considering what awaited him:

When you ask about love I always remember those magic moments we spent together. I know that my living doll aint no schoolboy crush and that she'll always be my high class baby. Dont leave me now as I've already got a mess of blues and if you dont whisper sweet nothings to me there'll be 16 reasons for me to say I'm sorry. There's nobody sweeter than you. You're my top ten baby who leaves me shaking all over. Just ask your heart about togetherness. That's all you've got to do and dont give me no summertime blues as that's when my heart aches begin and I get restless. I keep on saying hallelujah I just love her so and asking when I will be loved by my dream lover from that wondrous place.

A note of grim reality crept in like the blade of a stiletto as he ended: 'Don't think it's because I want to. It's just I have to give the pen back.'

No reprieve came, and I took the two women for their last visit to the youth in the condemned cell. When they emerged through the massive gates of the prison I hustled them into a waiting office car to prevent any of the opposition from interviewing them; on the way to the mother's home I asked her what her last words to him had been. She said, 'Keep your chin up in the morning.' The words struck a chill of horror through me, and it was only later when we were having a cup of tea in her neat little house that I realised that she was quite unaware of the import of the words. In her grief she had simply repeated his words of comfort to her on a previous visit.

The atmosphere in the house was doom-laden and there was very little conversation. I spent some considerable time dealing with persistent Pressmen trying to get interviews. The family, however, still held out hope of a last-minute reprieve as a result of a telegram that had been sent to the Queen asking her to exercise the Royal Prerogative of Mercy. I had sent the telegram, not as a stunt but in the sincere hope that it might bear fruit, but I was not very optimistic. I had made the fatal error of becoming personally involved in a story.

Before he was hanged he sent two final telegrams – to his girlfriend and unborn child: 'Always remember my star will watch over you both and give you the love and strength you so richly deserve my angel.' And to his mother and father: 'Keep smiling I shall be watching over you both.'

The tragic story preyed on my mind, but it was nearly ten years before I wrote the book, by which time crimes of violence by gangs of youths had become depressingly common. Although my canvas had broadened, I still centred it around a young tearaway reflecting on his past while waiting to be hanged. But as I wrote, it became more than an anatomy of one particular murder. I found myself introducing underworld characters I had encountered during my work, hatchet men, safe-breakers and big-time gangsters. The girl's words – 'He had to be big. Big all the time' – summed up what had led to the downfall of so many youngsters who saw glamour in crime and violence.

One of the characters I introduced, who I named Gorgeous George, was based on an old-time hoodlum I had encountered several times. I forget what stories I was working on, but do remember that he kept me well informed, for which regular payments to him appeared on my expenses sheet. He always wore a black snap-brim trilby and dark blue suits, the pockets of which were always sewn up, 'To prevent the Old Bill planting a shooter on me,' he explained. It also prevented him from buying a drink as he had no place, he said, to keep his money. He lived in a very seedy lodging house and had a wardrobe full of identical suits, with the top covered with identical black trilby hats. He loved to sit on the edge of his bed and play sentimental songs such as 'Home Sweet Home' on a battered accordion with more emotion than skill. I asked him how he had come to play the instrument, and he explained that it had been sent to him when he was doing a long prison stretch. 'It was filled with snout, and when I finished smoking it I was left with the squeeze box and four years still to do. I didn't have no option but to learn to play it.' His face had more lines than a road map, the never-fading reminders of how he had been cut to ribbons by members of a rival gang armed with cut-throat razors. He would recall the incident in all its gory details. 'They chased me up the street and into one house and out of another until I ran out of doors. Then it was chop, chop, chop, chop. There was claret on the ceiling and claret on the walls.' He enjoyed regaling me with how many stitches had been needed to patch up his face, and how many pints of blood to keep him alive. There was a kettle permanently on the boil on the gas stove, and when I asked him why he never made tea he explained that it was there in case any pals arrived, 'tooled-up and mob-handed', to carve him up again; he would throw the boiling water over them and leg it through the window. Surprisingly, to me, he never expressed any hatred for the men who had shivved him – it was all part of the job, an occupational hazard.

He himself could be incredibly brutal, and quite immune to any criticism of such behaviour – again, it was just a job to him. I never saw him drink anything but rum and blackcurrant, and after a few he would suddenly turn on me and say, 'Who the —— are you? You've been following me round all day. Now scarper.' I think the beatings he had received over the years, and the injuries that had been inflicted on him, had made him a little unbalanced, for, seconds later, when I had moved up the bar he would search me out, demanding, 'What's the matter with you? Don't you like my company?'

One evening he sought me out in the King and Keys, adjoining the *Daily Telegraph* office, and asked me for money. As he had ceased to be of any further use to me I declined, but he became very insistent, so insistent that I decided to go into the office and ask the News Editor to approve a special payment – but, unsurprisingly, as the man was no longer providing us with information, he refused. When I relayed this to my erstwhile informant, he announced, 'I'll go and see him', and set off for the office. He returned a short while later, flourishing some notes: 'He's a great fellow. Didn't need much persuading.' I was gratified that my boss had experienced at first hand the kind of people I had to fraternise with in order to get stories.

I met many so-called gangsters, all of whom seemed to have no moral values whatsoever – although they could be morbidly sentimental. I once attended the funeral of a get-away driver who had piled his car up after a robbery, and almost decapitated himself.

It reminded me of the news-reel films I had seen of Chicago mobsters' funerals. A long cavalcade of cars, and the most incredibly vulgar floral tributes. Friend and foe filed through the parlour to pay their last respects to the dead man, stiff and cold in his coffin. The tributes included a ladder made of white chrysanthemums – presumably to give him a leg-up to heaven – a vacant chair, and a miniature snooker table, complete with appropriately coloured flowers to represent the balls. There were also dice, and the Gates of Heaven.

I was told that after the funeral some of the mourners

stopped at the dead man's favourite pub to toast his memory, and a rumpus broke out because they thought one of the customers who was smoking was showing a marked lack of respect. While it was going on, someone vaulted over the bar and emptied the till. Yet they thought they had style.

During the fifties, Billy Hill, the self-crowned King of the Underworld, fell out with Jack 'Spot' Comer, a brash and flash gangster who thought the time had come to stage a comeback. It culminated in a vicious knife fight in a Soho Street between Albert Dimes, one of Hill's lieutenants, and Jack Comer. It was described by Fleet Street as 'the fight that never was', although in fact both men were badly wounded. Witnesses said that Spot had attacked Dimes, and he was arrested and sent for trial. But gangland had no time for the courts, they liked to settle their own differences, and a succession of witnesses came forward to say that Dimes had attacked Spot. Spot was acquitted, and when Dimes later appeared in court the case was dropped.

It would never have been anything but a sordid gangland vendetta and consigned to the gutter where it had originated, but for the dramatic appearance in court of the Revd Basil Andrews, an ancient silver-haired cleric with an angelic expression. He was presented as a zealous Christian with a mission for reforming ladies of the night, which accounted for his habitual presence in Soho. But he was no more than a seedy old reprobate who blatantly committed perjury and then turned Queen's Evidence, which resulted in three key witnesses being jailed. He later sold his story to a newspaper for a hefty sum.

Naughty vicars, however, have always commanded a soft spot in the hearts of news editors. Ever since the infamous Rector of Stiffkey, who got his just deserts in a side-show lions' den, newspapers have pin-pointed the folly of men of the cloth who have not learned the wisdom of wearing their trousers back to front like their collars. Headlines such as 'Vicar runs off with mistress of the hunt', 'Parson elopes with Sunday school teacher' are meat and drink to circulation managers. In my time the accolade went to the Revd Philip St John Ross, whose photograph for many years occupied a place of honour in the news room of the *Daily Express*.

The story of 'The Vanishing Vicar of Woodford' occupied the attention of Fleet Street for eighteen months before it was brought to a successful conclusion by the brilliant work of Bill Allison, one of the *Express*'s most talented and tenacious reporters. Although the vicar might not have agreed with the description successful.

Bill, a burly Scot with the build of a lock forward, employed tactics that were to say the least unorthodox. They may have met with disapproval from the 'quality' papers, but they made him the envy of the 'populars'.

It began in 1955 when the fifty-two-year-old vicar was 'presumed dead' after faking his own drowning whilst on holiday with his wife and family at Hell's Mouth, Caernarvonshire.

It was soon discovered, however, that he had gone away with Mrs Kathleen Ryall, a wealthy widow, and teams of reporters took up the hunt, which led them to the South of France, the Italian Riviera, Switzerland, and other holiday resorts of the well-to-do.

Bill got the equivalent of the non-eating end of the pantomime horse. While other reporters were swanning it abroad and amassing vast expenses, he became part of the furniture in the Red Lion in Bledlow, a village in Oxfordshire. The Red Lion had been the local of the runaway couple who had a love-nest cottage in a secluded wood nearby. Bill was certain that this was where the story would end. During the time they had spent in the area before disappearing, the couple had established close relations with the locals, who were reluctant to talk about them. Bill assiduously cultivated their friendship. And it paid dividends. He got a phone call from a ploughman, asking him to call at his home – after dark so as not to be seen. And there, at a midnight meeting Bill was told that the vicar had twice been seen driving his car along nearby lanes; his whereabouts, however, remained a mystery as the cottage was empty.

Bill continued his vigil at his favourite table in the pub, where the original hostility he had encountered was replaced by a genuine sympathy for his tenacity. But, apart from the ploughman, no one was talking.

It was several days later, when Ted and Florence Bewshea, among the several people who had helped the vicar in his deception, came in, and seeing Bill said, 'Oh, no! Not you again. When we last met we told you the vicar was in Germany. As far as we know he's still there.'

Bill was dubious. It was through tips from Mr Bewshea that the Press had scoured the Continent, and it seemed inconceivable that they should be unaware that the vicar and his mistress had returned. It occurred to him that they might be hiding them in their own home. So, while they were drinking, Bill paid a visit to their large house, standing in its own grounds, well back from the road and surrounded by high walls and hedges. It seemed an ideal spot for a hideaway.

Bill decided to make a late-night call.

Nearly thirty years later he told me exactly what he did. His previous reluctance to discuss it in detail was understandable. 'I decided on getting through the hedge and over the wall at a time when they could reasonably be expected to be enjoying an after-dinner drink in a relaxed atmosphere. My prayer was that there would not be any large dogs prowling around. I was thirty then, so getting over the high-perimeter hurdles was relatively easy. According to my subsequent expenses, I only severely damaged a very expensive suit. But once over I nearly fell into a cunningly concealed trap. I tip-toed towards the lights which were shining behind drawn curtains in a ground-floor room. Below the window was a pile of very dry twigs which I nearly stepped on. Each window had a similar pile below it, which would if trodden on reveal the presence of an intruder.'

He carefully removed one heap and pressed his ear to the glass and heard four voices, two male, two female. 'One voice was predominant, that of the vicar. He obviously knew I was in the area, and was planning a Houdini-style escape. He would conceal himself in the boot of a car in the garage, which could be reached without leaving the house.'

Bill stayed long enough to hear him make some disparaging remarks about the staying power of reporters who were incapable of maintaining a round-the-clock vigil. They were too fond of pubs, for one thing. One, therefore, could always select a suitable time. And he went on to boast that when he had returned from abroad there was actually a reporter aboard the aircraft, searching for him. His only disguise had been a beard, he bragged.

'He was actually enjoying the chase. He was a fox with a lot of useless hounds on his trail, and he was loving every minute of it,' commented Bill, who, recalling the months spent in the Red Lion, was naturally resentful of any criticism of *his* staying power.

Bill was in a dilemma. He could file a story, or he could wait until Monday, the day of the escape, and get a much better one. He decided to file in case the plan was changed. But when he checked in to see if there were any queries he was told the story had been spiked – it smacked too much of keyhole reporting. Furthermore, he could only claim to have *heard* the vicar, not seen him, and that was not enough.

Even worse, news was that someone on the desk had passed the information to the *Sunday Express*, which often employed Saturday stand-in reporters from other newspapers. In no time the information had reached the other Sundays, and when Bill passed the house the next morning it was surrounded by Pressmen. Fortunately, the *Sunday Express* had not been told that Bill had actually heard the vicar, and when their quarry failed to appear, the Press contingent withdrew.

Bill returned the next morning – Sunday – to find the house was again under siege, this time by the dailies. Patrolling policemen made sure there was no intrusion or trespass. The most incongruous sight was that of *Express* photographer Stanley Meagher, keeping observation from the back of an enormous carthorse he had 'borrowed' from a nearby field. As darkness came, once again the reporters gradually withdrew, as news desks became convinced it was a stumer. Something Bill did his utmost to encourage.

But one persistent man from the *Mail*, Stanley Bonnet, refused to budge until Bill announced that he was calling it a day. Even then, Stanley insisted that Bill drove ahead of him all the way to London. When Bill had got far enough in front, however, he did a U-turn down a side road and headed back to the house, where he was joined by some extra help from the *Express*.

'At seven o'clock next morning, bang on the time of the plan I had overheard, Mr Bewshea drove his car slowly down the road. He was driving with such care that Mr Ross simply had to be hidden in the boot.'

One *Express* car got ahead of it and the other fell behind. When the car reached the Buckinghamshire Hills, the two newspaper cars blocked it in. All three cars stopped, and Bill got from Bewshea the key to the boot. But it would not open, and in frustration he kicked it, knocking off the handle and leaving a hole. A reporter promptly started blowing cigarette smoke through it in the vain hope of smoking the vicar out.

Guessing that he had been handed the wrong key, Bill demanded the right one, and this time the boot opened, to reveal the vicar lying down with his head resting on a briefcase. The cameras clicked before he could clamber out.

'I've had a good run. The game is up. It is finished,' Mr Ross said resignedly. And he then swung a few wild punches shouting, 'I also gave you a good run for your money. Now you can go to hell. I'm off to the police station.'

Bill had one regret, which was the way he had pulled a fast one on Stanley Bonnet, an old friend. 'But later, whenever we met in a Fleet Street pub, Stanley would good-humouredly tell the story of how I had hoodwinked him. I like to think if it had happened to me I would have done likewise,' said Bill.

And I know that he would have.

13

THE LAST WOMAN TO HANG

There are people who, in my opinion, should never be released from prison, and the Krays, Myra Hindley and Ian Brady are among them, yet they have their champions. But even the devil will find some misguided fool ready and willing to give a character reference.

As well as the boy who went to the gallows, however, there were others I thought, and still think, should have been reprieved.

One was Ruth Ellis, a night-club hostess who shot dead her racing-driver lover, David Moffat Blakely. It was among the first murders I covered, but a far more important milestone was that she was the last woman to be hanged in this country. She would have been one of the few people to have disagreed with me; when she was sentenced to death by an Old Bailey judge, she murmured, 'Thanks'. The famous Number One Court has heard many statements from the accused standing in the glass-sided dock, but none have brought about such a chilling silence as that single word spoken in a hushed whisper. So soft it was almost inaudible.

In some respects, Ruth Ellis reminded me of Edith Thompson, who was hanged with her lover Frederick Bywaters, for incitement to murder her husband in what became a famous *crime passionel*. It was before my time, but I had read about it and been told about it by newsmen who covered the trial, and was certain that it was for her immorality that she was executed. The most telling evidence against her were the lurid and juvenile letters she wrote to her young lover. But for them, it was a murder that would have attracted little attention, for it was a straightforward killing with no mystery to unravel. She was walking home with her husband after a visit to the theatre when Bywaters sprang out and stabbed him to death. Throughout the trial he insisted that she knew nothing of his intentions.

Judges are renowned for telling juries that they do not preside over courts of morals, but it was her loose morals which led to Thompson being dragged to the scaffold, kicking and screaming, by five hefty warders. And the same applied to Ruth Ellis. Furthermore, I am not alone in thinking that, if Edith Thompson was guilty of incitement to murder, then there is a man still walking free who should have stood in the dock alongside Ruth Ellis, accused of the same grave charge.

Ruth Ellis, an attractive twenty-eight-year-old divorcee with brittle blonde hair, was having a turbulent on-off affair with David Blakely, a pampered ex-public schoolboy making a reputation as an up-and-coming racing driver. It had begun while she was still married to George Ellis, an alcoholic dentist. She was the mother of a boy of ten and a girl of three; and she had had an abortion – which in those days indicated wantonness.

Although he treated her shabbily, even to the extent of beating her up, she was hopelessly in love with Blakely, whom she kept in clothes, drinks and cigarettes. She also, however, had an 'alternative lover' in Desmond Cussen, a wealthy businessman, with whom she lived. Blakely was not constant either – he had other mistresses. Nevertheless, Ellis moved out of Cussen's home and took a flat in Egerton Gardens in Kensington, in order to share her bed with Blakely. There she became pregnant, and had a miscarriage when he struck her in the stomach during one of their frequent and violent rows.

The tragic finale came over the Easter weekend in 1955, when they had parted yet again, and she was deeply depressed after the miscarriage. On Good Friday, learning that Blakely was spending the weekend with some friends in Tanza Road in Hampstead, she turned up there, and pounded on the door, demanding to be let in; twice the police were called to lead her away. She returned on the evening of Easter Sunday while a party was in progress, and waited outside until Blakely appeared with a friend and went to the Magdola, a nearby public house, to get some more drink and cigarettes. As Blakely was leaving it, she shot him at point-blank range with a pistol. She fired six shots, two of which missed, one striking a passerby in the hand. The other four entered his body, two in the back, one in the leg and the other in his left arm. He was killed instantly. She made no attempt to escape, and asked someone to call the police; there happened to be an off-duty policeman in the Magdola, to whom she handed the revolver.

She then went quietly to the police station where she said, 'I am guilty. I am rather confused.' She also made a written statement. She seemed drugged or drunk, or a combination of the two.

Although there was a newspaper strike on at the time, the editorial staff were working as normal, and every newspaper soon had a team of reporters building up background material. I was a member of the *Herald*'s team, and worked with the paper's 'picture snatcher' whose job, by legal or illicit means, was to obtain photographs of the dead man and his mistress. In a short time a hefty dossier had been compiled. Neither emerged as particularly worthwhile characters, both utterly devoid of morals, living in a sleazy twilight world of drinking clubs and promiscuity. Ruth supplemented her income by prostitution and was not averse to modelling for pornographic pictures. Provided that the more sordid aspects were omitted, it was a tailor-made story for the Press.

In those days there were no restrictions on the reporting of committal proceedings at the Magistrates Court, and when details of the torrid love affair were made public, newspapermen from all over the world flocked into London. When her trial opened at the Old Bailey, extra seats had to be provided to accommodate the Press.

Ellis remained completely impassive throughout the short trial, her hands clasped demurely in her lap as she sat in the dock flanked by two women prison officers. She was stunningly dressed and, foolishly, she had obtained permission to re-dye her hair, which had lost its colour during the time she was on remand in Holloway. The tarty appearance this gave her did nothing to enhance her chances.

She looked what the prosecution would make her out to be. And the hopes her defence counsel had held of evoking the sympathy of the jury were firmly scotched. One person in the public gallery said aloud what was in many minds.

Desmond Cussen, to her surprise, appeared as a prosecution witness, although he had been visiting her and sending her gifts and flowers.

She seemed resigned to her fate, almost inviting it, for when Mr Christmas Humphreys, the senior Treasury Counsel, who prosecuted, asked her, 'When you fired at close range at David Blakely what did you intend to do?', she replied, 'It is obvious. When I shot him I intended to kill him.'

It was the only question he asked her during one of the shortest ever cross-examinations. She had sealed her fate.

The jury were out a mere twenty-three minutes before they returned with a verdict of Guilty. She was sentenced to death, and smiled as she was taken to the cells below.

I, along with several colleagues, felt that far more effort should have been made to unearth the truth. Surely her explanation that the gun had been given to her by a man whose name she could not remember deserved deeper probing. I was told by a crime reporter that she had been given the gun by the man who had driven her to Tanza Road on the day of the shooting. Furthermore, he had taught her how to use it during a visit to Epping Forest. Unfortunately, Ellis refused to incriminate anyone else.

Her defence may have doubted the gun story she told, but saw no point in pursuing it; it would only prove a conspiracy to murder, and that could not help her. In those days there was no such thing as diminished responsibility, so little purpose would have been served by stressing that a client who had pleaded Not Guilty had been aided and abetted by someone. As for the police, they had a watertight case, a rare event, and when such a thing is presented to them on a plate there is little point in trying to improve on it. Although the Press had misgivings, there was nothing they could do – the laws of libel inhibited them from writing anything.

There was a public outcry and thousands signed a petition calling for a reprieve, and no paper was more vociferous in its support for this than the *Daily Herald*. Neither were the

Fleet Street's 'doyen' of crime, Percy Hoskins *(right)* with Donald Hume. To Percy – who covered some of the most notorious and horrific murder cases, from Haigh and Christie to the Yorkshire Ripper – Hume remains the most evil and coldly calculating killer he has ever encountered. *(Daily Express)*

Dr John Bodkin Adams, the Eastbourne doctor accused of murdering elderly patients who had left him money in their wills. Percy Hoskins *(standing at his right shoulder)* refused to join in the Press campaign against Adams, and, on the doctor's acquittal, obtained for the *Express* Adams's exclusive story. *(Daily Express)*

Outside the gates of Wandsworth Prison – Alfred Draper with the mother and the girlfriend of a young mugger sentenced to hang for murder. There was no reprieve for the youth, the sad little tale made all the more pathetic by his mother's unthinking last words to him: 'Keep your chin up in the morning'. *(Daily Express)*

Ruth Ellis, the last woman to hang in Britain, in spite of all the efforts to secure a reprieve. Ironically, her execution was instrumental in bringing about the end of capital punishment in this country. *(Daily Express)*

'I've had a good run . . . I also gave you a good run for your money. Now you can go to hell. I'm off to the police station.' The Revd Philip St John Ross, who faked his own drowning in order to run away with a widow, gives in more or less gracefully when tracked down by *Express* reporter Bill Allison, trying to escape the Press in the boot of a car. *(Daily Express)*

A secret trip to Saddleworth Moor in 1968 which did not remain secret long enough. Myra Hindley *(foreground)*, with a woman prison officer, being hurried back to Holloway by the police. This picture, taken by *Express* photographer Harry Dempster as he hung out of a window of a car being driven at 96 mph, nearly earned the driver, Dan McGeachie, a penalty for speeding. *(Daily Express)*

Harold Macmillan is elected Prime Minister, January 1957 – an occasion remembered by the author (seen here standing just behind Macmillan's right shoulder) for the unscrupulous behaviour of an influential rival journalist.

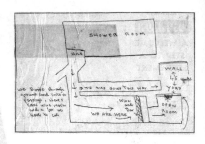

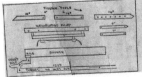

EXPRESS

Weather: Thundery rain, sunny spells

Price 3d

THE GREAT HAMSTER JAILBREAK

By ALFRED DRAPER and PHILIP FINN

A MAJOR break, complete with getaway cars, was planned at Durham Jail's E-Wing for tomorrow, it was revealed last night. But months of work on a tunnel was ruined by the premature escape bid by three men on Tuesday.

Letters smuggled from the "escape proof" prison within-a-prison say that

A HAMSTER, a prisoner's pet was used to measure the tunnel by being posted in with a string on its leg.

A WARDER inadvertently revealed a chink in the prison's armour by knocking a hole in a wall.

A WORKMAN provided a movement tip for tunnel debris by digging a drain in a yard.

THE PRISON itself supplied all the tools of escape, from iron bars to paint as well as a steaming tarkax bath to cover the operation.

In the end, according to the letters, "We were all talking like Mione Splines. It's most death or glory. But in the end, in reality, there was only letter prospector.

The full astonishing story starts on Page 9

The Great Hamster Jailbreak – one of the strangest and most hilarious stories covered by the author, complete with the jailbreakers' letters and plans. *(Daily Express)*

The inseparable twins, Ronnie and Reggie Kray, undisputed bosses of the East End. Jailed 22 years ago, their names still inspire fear in their old haunts. *(Daily Express)*

The Army in Ulster: hated and vilified, shot at and spat at, they were still expected to answer every call for help . . . And 'yet we hear parents telling toddlers, "Don't talk to those murdering bastards."' (*The Times*)

The author *(left)* with Norman Kirkham of the *Telegraph*, Ellis Plaice of the *Mirror*, and Michael Leapman of the *Herald*, flying from Lagos to Port Harcourt in an elderly aircraft. Under the pile of blankets they were seated on they found a lethal cargo of bombs, mortars and shells.

Their reception committee at Port Harcourt – seen descending from the aircraft here is Ellis Plaice. 'Run like ———,' was the pilot's advice.

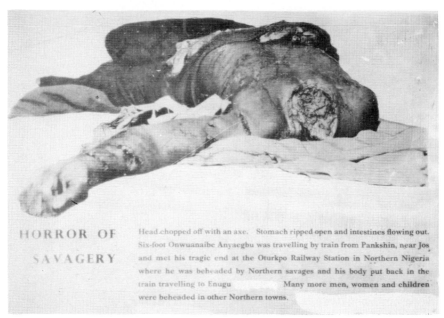

A Biafran publicity shot. The horrors were real, but such photographs were self-defeating, for the world could not face them – and they 'put the average Britisher off his breakfast . . .'

Colonel Ojukwu, the Biafran leader. Once a Sandhurst classmate of General Gowan and Colonel Adekunle, he now saw them as his bitter enemies: 'My people are the victims of systematic extermination . . .'

Helen and Peter Kroger leaving for Poland, released in exchange for an Englishman jailed in Russia. 'We love youse all,' they said. *(Daily Express)*

Christine Keeler who, at the centre of the so-called Profumo Affair, played a part in the ending of 13 years of Tory government, and caused worldwide Press speculation and excitement. *(Daily Express)*

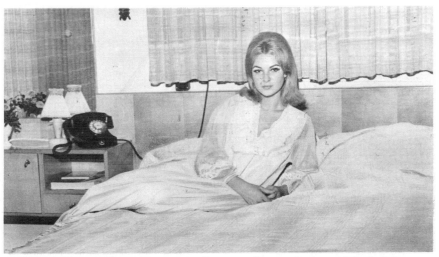

Mandy Rice-Davies, who shared a flat, as well as profession, with Christine Keeler. She stripped naked in front of the author – but as a suspicious reporter he resisted her. *(Daily Express)*

George Blake, a Soviet spy in the British Secret Service and responsible for betraying to Russia at least 40 Western agents, many of whom were executed. Five years after he was sentenced to 42 years, he escaped – suspiciously easily - from Wormwood Scrubs, to reappear in Moscow, where he still lives. *(Daily Express)*

The costume of the 'Jersey Monster', the sex pervert who for 11 years abducted and terrorised women and children, and dabbled in black magic. *(Daily Express)*

The author with Alphonse le Gastelois, who – suspected of being the 'Jersey Monster' – had gone to live, a self-exiled hermit, on the barren reef called the Ecrehous. Now 'King of the Ecrehous', he wanted just to be left in peace: 'I am the law, the police, I am everything.'

appeals limited to this country – Raymond Chandler, the writer of hard-boiled private-eye novels, protested, 'I am deeply shocked that this woman will be hanged until death. And in Britain.'

Threats were even made to blow up Holloway Prison.

No one was more determined to help save Ruth than her friend Jacqueline Dyer, who visited her regularly in the condemned cell, and did her utmost to get her to tell the truth about the gun, without success. Undeterred she saw her MP, Mr George Rogers, and told him that Cussen had given Ruth the gun, made her drunk and driven her to the scene of the crime and encouraged her to shoot Blakely. She gained Mr Rogers's full support; but the Home Secretary refused to budge. Jacqueline then repeated her story to the police and a search began for Cussen; but he had gone to ground – Ruth's brother, Granville Neilson, was also looking for him.

With thirty-six hours to go before her execution was due, Charity Taylor, the Governor, interrupted a visit to tell Ruth Ellis there would be no reprieve. Behind the scenes, however, inquiries continued unabated, for by now most of Fleet Street had learned of the allegations that had been made.

Although resigned to her fate, Ruth was now bitter that Cussen had not stood in the dock alongside her, and, blaming her solicitor, Mr John Bickford, for this, she sacked him. Mr Victor Mishcon, a solicitor who had previously handled her legal affairs, was asked to take over, and Mr Bickford passed on what Ruth Ellis had implied to him, urging him to pursue the question of the gun with her. Mishcon, when he visited her in the condemned cell, persuaded her at last to make a signed statement telling the truth.

Although the newspapers were aware of what was being alleged, they were unable to report it as no one would officially confirm it. It was a hectic time for the reporters on the case, for by now almost the whole of Fleet Street was convinced that, in the light of what they were learning, a reprieve was almost certain. Time, however, was running short – it was 12 July, and her execution had been set for the 13th.

I met Jacqueline Dyer in the Mayfair club where she worked, and wrote a story of her desperate search for a vital witness who could still save Ruth Ellis.

We dogged the footsteps of Mr Mishcon who, having obtained the vital statement, had requested an urgent meeting with the Permanent Under-Secretary to the Home Office, Sir Frank Newsam. In the event, Mishcon saw Mr Philip Allen, Assistant Under-Secretary of State, as Newsam was at Ascot.

Although we all knew what evidence he had submitted, Mr Mishcon, when he emerged from his meeting, refused to confirm it. All he would say was: 'I've had an interview. What I said is being seriously considered.'

Mr Allen got a message to Sir Frank Newsam requesting him to return immediately; he also summoned one of the detectives who had worked on the case. As a result of what was said, a fresh search was made for Cussen. This was again unsuccessful.

Mr Mishcon made a further call at the Home Office, but again he disappointed reporters: 'It is too difficult to discuss. A life is at stake. I can say no more.'

The Home Secretary, Lloyd George, asked to intervene, declined, because an innocent passer-by had been wounded and he was determined that Londoners should be able to walk the streets without being in fear of their lives. A full confession from Cussen was the only thing that might make him change his mind, but that was not obtainable.

Fleet Street would dearly have loved to write the story, but that was impossible.

I was outside Holloway Prison on the morning she was hanged. A crowd of several hundred had assembled in the street opposite the main gates. Many, led by Mrs Violet Van Der Elst, the fervent abolitionist, were there to voice their displeasure and offer up silent prayers. Others were there out of ghoulish curiosity; one man even lifted his small child shoulder-high in order to see the notice of her execution posted outside the prison. Teachers from a nearby school wrote to the *Herald* protesting that the grisly spectacle had been observed by the children who had been deeply and emotionally disturbed.

Ruth Ellis plunged to her death at nine o'clock in the morning of 13 July. Albert Pierrepoint, the hangman, said she was the bravest woman he had ever hanged, and he had had a lot of experience.

Twenty-four hours later her likeness was on display in a waxworks exhibition.

The case convinced me that our legal system is not all that we claim. It should be less of a gladiatorial contest between eminent counsel, and greater importance should be attached to eliciting the whole truth and nothing but the truth, and to letting the jury hear it. There was too much left unsaid and unasked at Ruth Ellis's trial.

Many of us thought that Fleet Street should have been much bolder in their efforts to get her reprieved – but that was merely an effort to purge a sense of guilt. The truth was that the laws of libel made it impossible to pillory a man who steadfastly denied the allegations. He still does to this day – from Australia where he went to live and forget – but not very convincingly, as those who saw the television documentary on Ruth Ellis will know.

To my knowledge, two films have been made, and countless articles and a number of books have been written about the case, and Cussen has been publicly branded as her accomplice. He has, however, never sued anyone for libel.

Ruth Ellis was quite content to pay the supreme penalty for her crime; ironically her death was largely instrumental in bringing about the end of capital punishment.

The trial of Ian Brady and Myra Hindley, for what became known as the Moors Murders, revealed such a chronicle of sexual perversion and depravity that some of the toughest detectives and crime reporters, who thought nothing could shock or sicken them, were forced to leave the court. They felt physically ill.

Brady and Hindley, who killed for kicks, and subjected their child victims to torture and sexual indignities of the foulest kind – and even tape-recorded the screams of one of their victims – aroused worldwide horror and revulsion. Yet they might have remained undetected if it had not been for the murder of Edward Evans, which was committed as 'a demonstration murder'. Tipped off by a young man who had been forced to witness the horrific axe-killing, the police raided the couple's house before they could dispose of the corpse, which was trussed up like a chicken and wrapped in a polythene sheet.

In May 1966, Hindley and Brady were found guilty of the murders of Edward Evans and Lesley Ann Downey; and Brady was found guilty of the murder of John Kilbride, Hindley of being an accessory. Both were jailed for life.

But the strong conviction remained that there were other bodies buried on the lonely moor – a conviction corroborated by recent events. It was known that detectives who had investigated the murders had interviewed the couple in prison not long after they were sentenced. It was not difficult for crime reporters to figure out why.

Nearly two years later, photographer Harry Dempster, with whom I had worked on many stories, told me that he had been tipped off by a contact that Myra Hindley, who was serving her sentence in Holloway Prison, was to be driven to the moor. She had apparently indicated her willingness to point out the graves of people still buried there. Harry and I knew we were on to a big story; just as important was the knowledge that it would also herald the end of an agonising period of suspense and speculation being endured by the parents of missing children. At last they would know the truth, and be able to give their children a decent and proper burial. And that was certainly foremost in the minds of the police officers. After all, Hindley and Brady could not be given greater sentences than those they were serving.

It was very much a top-secret operation and Harry had been told that we must adopt a softly-softly approach. Harry and I teamed up, and the office was informed that we planned to go to Manchester where we would book into an hotel and just wait there until we received the information that the search had been successful.

The News Editor, however, concerned about trespassing on Manchester papers' territory, decided he should inform them of the story and what we intended to do. From that moment it began to collapse around our ears. There was a sad lack of discretion.

Harry and I, in a car driven by a colleague, Dan McGeachie, had discreetly followed the police convoy escorting Hindley from Holloway Prison to Risley Remand Centre, twenty-five miles from Saddleworth Moor. But when we got there, reporters from Manchester were already on the scene. Others had gone to the moor itself.

Coded messages were sent to London on the lines of 'Auntie has arrived for tea' and 'She has not yet started pouring'.

The news soon filtered through to other newspapers that the *Express* was showing an unexpected interest in the moors, and swarms of opposition reporters and photographers descended on the area.

Hindley got no further than Risley. Harry was telephoned at the hotel and told the operation was off. The caller, needless to say, was far from happy at the way things had turned out.

The *Daily Express* had a big front-page story headlined 'Moors killer Myra in jail switch mystery'. It was not the story Harry and I had hoped for.

The police took Hindley back to Holloway soon afterwards, and, as they sped down the motorway, Harry managed to snatch a picture of her sitting beside a woman prison officer. He literally risked his life to get it – he was leaning out of the car window, with me hanging on to his legs.

The photograph appeared in the paper the next day above Harry's by-line, with details of the exposure he had used – and the speed at which our car was travelling. Dan narrowly escaped prosecution for a driving offence.

Now, over twenty years later, the deeds of Hindley and Brady have not been forgotten, and, indeed, they have been revived by recent further visits to Saddleworth Moor, by both of them, supposedly in a bid to help police find other graves; by the discovery of more bodies; by further confessions and claims made by the evil pair; and by a letter Myra Hindley wrote to the mother of Lesley Ann Downey in October 1987, expressing contrition and attempting to prove that she had changed. Other than those who support her, few people are convinced – least of all Lesley's mother.

Hindley and Brady together committed some of the most horrible crimes the world has ever witnessed. Yet she has no shortage of supporters, who claim that she has paid the price and that the time has come for her to be paroled. She is said to have reformed, and to have become a Christian – if that is true, she should show it by expressing a willingness to stay where she is. And read a prayer book: it might remind her that it was in a prayer book that she concealed two left-luggage tickets, which, when found, led to the recovery of suitcases containing incriminating tapes and photographs. At least, Brady has, so far, indicated that he does not wish to be released.

14

CONS AND SWINDLES

Confidence tricksters have always fascinated me; I have a soft spot for many of these plausible, sometimes likeable, rogues who live on their wits rather than work, and I've sometimes thought that if only some of those I had met had concentrated their activities in legal ventures they would have become millionaires. But they were incapable of earning an honest crust or of resisting the temptation of a fast buck. They never resorted to violence, however, and when they were exposed, as often happened, they accepted their punishment with resignation, and never, as far as I can recall, shrieked that they were the victim of a police frame-up or a gross miscarriage of justice. Alas, they never learned, and no sooner did they come out of prison than they were back to their old tricks, confident that this time they would get away with it.

I never ceased to be amazed at the audacity of conmen and their ingenuity, which could not have succeeded without a suspension of belief on the part of their victims. One trickster, a self-styled official guide who touted for business outside Buckingham Palace, earned himself a lot of money by charging his wards an extra pound per head for the privilege of signing the visitors' book. It never occurred to any of his victims to enquire why there was an extra fee – if they had they would have found that anyone was entitled to sign the book free of charge.

Among the cheekiest cons I ever heard of is one that concerns The Cheshire Cheese. One of Fleet Street's oldest hostelries, and one which attracts tourists from all parts of the globe, it is sited down a narrow alley off The Street, not far from Samuel Johnson's house in Gough Square. The Doctor is said to have been a regular patron, and the chair from which is he alleged to have held court occupies a place of honour, beneath his portrait. A steel grating protects the front doorstep, worn into a bowl-shape by the countless feet which have stepped over the threshold. The restaurant is particularly famous for its steak and kidney pie and its roast beef, served by smartly uniformed waiters. The floors are covered with sawdust and the atmosphere – if it were not for the many foreign tourists – is such that at any moment one expects Doctor Johnson to step through the door and take his customary seat.

One lunchtime, a camera-laden American with literary pretensions walked in and began to inspect the place. As he walked through the bars, he was accosted by a conman who took it upon himself to give the tourist a free conducted tour. He casually mentioned that the sawdust covering the floor was the same stuff that Doctor Johnson himself had trod. It was swept up every night after last orders, taken away and fumigated, and relaid the next morning. The American suggested he would like some as a souvenir to take back home and put in his den. That, said the conman, was quite out of the question. If every visitor went away with some of it, the priceless sawdust would all soon be gone. Over a drink the trickster reopened the subject of the sawdust and said that as a special favour he would see what could be done, and if he was successful he would call round at the American's hotel next morning. He could not, of course, promise anything definite. But next morning he arrived at the hotel with a small bag containing a few pounds of sawdust, and made his victim give him a solemn promise that he would never divulge his source. A sizeable sum of money changed hands, and the American returned home, presumably blissfully unaware that he had been hoodwinked, that the whole story was rubbish and the famous doctor had no association with the sawdust at all. The conman had simply called at the nearest pet shop and bought sawdust destined for a cat's toilet.

While I have admitted to a grudging respect for some conmen's antics, there have been others which I considered utterly despicable. A journalist friend of mine was putting up a conman with a view to writing about his activities, and one day he saw the man carefully stacking up a pile of small envelopes. He had had these personally printed for a totally spurious charity, and his intention was to carry out a door-to-door delivery, and collect them, containing donations, later in the evening. His horrified host forbade it, pointing out that he would never be able to look his neighbours in the face if he knew they had been conned. His admonition fell on deaf ears; when he returned home later that evening he saw his guest counting out a pile of notes and silver on his dining-room table. He was appalled and exploded with rage, telling his guest in no uncertain manner that he was to return the money immediately. The conman was genuinely surprised at his reaction and could not understand his anger – charity, as far as he was concerned, began at home.

One man – I will call him John Smith – whom I got to know well, specialised in death-cell letters. To his utter chagrin his lucrative source of income virtually disappeared with the abolition of capital punishment. To look at he resembled a vicar who did not enjoy a very good living, but to whom money was unimportant; his reward, if any, was in heaven.

To be fair to him, however, if it hadn't been for newspapers he would not have had a market. As soon as he got wind of a juicy murder that would capture the imagination of the public, and many did in those days, Smith would attend the committal proceedings in the Magistrates Court, which were then fully reported, and build up a dossier on those accused. Then he would start to write to them. His letters rarely differed, which was understandable, for until he had seen them in the dock they had been unknown to him. He would say something like, 'You may not remember me, but I shall never forget how kind you were to me … ' It invariably worked – they would reply saying that they remembered him well. Sometimes he would pose as a clergyman, saying he would like to join the accused in prayer, and an invitation to do so often followed; perhaps in the loneliness of the remand cell any helping hand was gratefully grasped. On one occasion, Smith wrote to a doctor who was awaiting trial for murder, expressing confidence in his innocence and assuring the doctor how he would never forget how he had turned out in the foulest weather and saved the life of his (non-existent) daughter. The accused man wrote back saying he vividly recalled the totally imagined incident, and would welcome a visit.

His tactics seldom varied; once he had got his foot in the cell door a correspondence began which continued throughout the trial proper. And no one waited more anxiously for the jury's verdict than the spurious pen pal. An acquittal was a setback; if the accused was found guilty he was in business. Letters from the death cell were worth a lot of money. He would hold a Dutch auction in the nearest pub and sell the letters to the highest bidder. Their value depended not only on their content, but also how close the condemned man was to the hangman's noose. A last letter was worth its weight in gold.

Although the Old Bailey was John Smith's favourite hunting or haunting ground, he was prepared to travel all over the British Isles to visit the men and women with whom he had established a rapport. Once, when he had posed as a clergyman in order to facilitate visits, he was sitting on a railway platform in Scotland waiting for a train to take him back to London when a crocodile of schoolboys passed, and in deference raised their caps. He grabbed the last boy in the line, soundly cuffed him, and said, 'Don't take the piss!', whereupon the boy burst into tears and said, 'We are taught to respect the cloth, sir.' 'I gave him five bob and patted his head. I'd forgotten I still had my dog collar on,' he told me.

One night, I was sitting at home watching a television discussion about the rights and wrongs of capital punishment. It was heavily slanted in favour of abolition, which I did not mind as I hated the awful ritual of the judge putting on the black cap and intoning the most dreadful words that any man or woman can possibly hear. Even more, I hated those mornings outside prisons with a crowd of ghouls or well-intentioned abolitionists singing 'Abide With Me' and waiting for a notice to be placed on the prison gate announcing that the sentence had been carried out.

Suddenly, the vague figure of a man in silhouette and totally unidentifiable appeared on the screen and was introduced by the interviewer as someone who had endured the agonies of the death cell and had lived in the shadow of the hangman before being granted a reprieve. I listened quite unmoved as a voice described in the most harrowing terms the mental and physical anguish an innocent man went through who had been condemned for a murder he did not commit. It deserved an Oscar. I had immediately recognised the voice of Fleet Street's most celebrated letter-writer. Violence was not his game, but the opportunity to earn a fat fee was too tempting for Smith to miss. He saw nothing immoral in his masquerade, or in conning the producer, who could so easily have checked out his story – though no doubt Smith had done his homework and come up with a plausible story.

One of the most outrageous and audacious confidence tricksters I encountered was 'Sir Sidney Rawlinson Cain, Bart', who looked the part but wasn't. He wore impeccably tailored Savile Row suits with an Old Etonian tie, and was seldom seen without a red carnation in his buttonhole. Short, dapper, with patent-leather hair and a truly charming manner, especially with the ladies, his speciality was defrauding rich elderly women. Although he was often caught, he really was a leopard, clinging to his bogus title, and revelling in his newspaper title of 'self-styled king of the conmen'.

His favourite ploy was to charm his way into the heart of a rich, and usually much older, woman, and propose marriage. Once accepted, he would reveal his murky past – sometimes by engineering his own exposure in the Press – and would then suggest to the horrified family that hard cash might encourage him to ditch her and save the family from disgrace.

There was, however, one exposure that he did not welcome; this was when Charles Manifold, one of the *People*'s top investigative reporters, uncovered him as he was planning to pull off the greatest coup of his career. Charles – who certainly saw nothing charming in 'Sir' Sidney, but had to admit he had the qualities of a rubber ball – had been trying to track him down since he had gone to ground after having defrauded and left a woman who owned a Chelsea hotel. To Charles's surprise, however, Cain one day called at the *People* office, asking to see the Editor; Charles went down to interview him and straight away he began to question Cain

about the hotel owner. 'That's nothing,' said Sidney. 'I am
about to pull off my biggest coup and you will have it
exclusively. You must not ruin it.' And he confided that the
lady in question not only had a Rolls which he used but also a
Jaguar; and she would receive £250,000 of shares as a wedding
settlement.

Charles told me, 'He knew he couldn't hope to bribe me,
but he was smart enough to know I would fall for a better
story. "I'm going to marry a Wills heiress. She's outside in the
Rolls," he said. He brought her in and we took a picture of
the happy couple.'

She was sixty-year-old Mrs Doris Maude de Winton Haag,
widowed daughter of Sir Ernest Wills, the tobacco
millionaire. Sidney told Charles that the wedding was due to
take place at Chelsea Register Office on the coming Monday.
'It was now Thursday,' Charles told me, 'and Cain planned to
meet the family before the wedding, and he said that if I did
not publish anything I would get a hundred pounds and the
exclusive story by exposing him after the wedding.'

Apart from not being interested in the proposition, a
Monday story was the worst possible thing for *The People*
which would not publish for another week. Nevertheless,
Charles pretended to agree; but then he went to see the family
at their Wiltshire house.

Although Sir Ernest was ill in bed, a confrontation was
agreed to at which Major George Wills, his son, would be
present. Charles handed over the dossier and file of cuttings
which he had brought with him, and told them that Cain had
served terms of imprisonment for defrauding women while
posing as a baronet.

Next day, just before tea, 'Sir' Sidney arrived, driving the
Rolls with his bride-to-be beside him. They were escorted
into the sixteenth-century hall bedecked with suits of armour,
swords and guns, and Cain, sporting his red carnation, seated
himself before a roaring log fire. Charles was concealed
behind the curtains. Then Sir Sidney was presented with the
incriminating file of cuttings. Mrs Haag read them too and
called off the wedding.

At that point Charles stepped dramatically from the
curtains. 'You bastard!' Cain shouted.

Major Wills said to him, 'I think you had better leave this minute.'

After phoning over his story, Charles and his photographer headed back to town, and on the road they passed a dejected-looking 'Sir' Sidney, lugging a heavy suitcase.

'I stopped and offered him a lift and he said he needed a drink, and he did,' said Charles. 'We stopped at a pub and he straightened his Old Etonian tie and went up to the bar and ordered fifty Benson and Hedges cigarettes, a snob smoke in those days. He had bounced back immediately.'

The entire story – apart from 'Sir' Sidney's remark which questioned Charles's legitimacy – appeared in the paper.

When I next encountered Cain the experience had not deterred him. He was still posing as a baronet and still using the same name, and he was still concentrating on elderly ladies with money.

Our paths continued to cross; on one occasion he told me that he was going to sue a newspaper for calling him a conman. He was now going straight and it was unfair not to allow a man to live down his past. I pointed out that it was a description he had done a lot to encourage, and in any case he was still posing as a baronet. But that did not deter him from threatening legal action. The newspaper in question knew it was being conned, but it was easier and cheaper to give him some money – the chances are that Cain would not have gone ahead if he had been told to clear off, but it wasn't worth the risk.

The course of true love never sailed smoothly for 'Sir' Sidney; not long afterwards, his name was again headline news. It was announced that 'the self-styled knight Sir Sidney Rawlinson Cain' was to marry the wealthy Marquise Diana de Visdelou-Guimbeau in Alderney. The Press descended on the island, and 'Sir' Sidney was given a real rough ride. 'Casanova Cain', they called him, 'the rogue with a brogue', as they recalled his past escapades in colourful detail. The bride-to-be's family, in the form of her sister Mrs Olga Smith, a daughter of the late Sir Harry North, arrived on the island with a whole series of objections, determined to see that the wedding did not take place. Apart from his previous convictions, there were other reasons, she said, why the marriage was not suitable.

When legal objections failed, she pleaded with her sister to change her mind but again met with no success. 'All she would say was that she was deeply in love,' complained Mrs Smith.

Cain, however, was confident and buoyant: 'I can't see how the wedding can be stopped. I know I'm called a conman. But I don't care. I'm in love for the very first time and this wedding is going to take place. Time will tell. And not the sort of time I've done before.'

Meanwhile, the Marquise skilfully fended off questioners. 'I cannot tell you anything about a legacy that I am supposed to be getting.'

But Mrs Smith eventually managed to get the ceremony postponed while the legal objections were being studied. 'Sir' Sidney was not too downcast, and after downing a large Scotch he went into the hotel ballroom where he delivered an impromptu rendering of 'Everybody loves my baby'. He apologised for his croaky voice – 'Too many Coronas, old boy' – and as no one considered it worthy of applause he clapped himself, ending his rendition with an elegant bow.

'What an awful exhibition. And that man wants to marry my sister,' Mrs Smith remarked, and pleaded with Diana: 'If only for the sake of your two lovely children, Oriana and Barbara, you must not marry this awful man.'

Her concern was understandable, for Cain had only recently been released from a Guernsey prison on a false pretences charge. 'He is nauseating, disgusting,' she said to reporters. 'Diana is the only one of the family I have left. She must not marry that man.'

Her entreaties fell on deaf ears. Diana was in love, and if the mention of a legacy made the reporters prick up their ears it sounded no warning bells for the Marquise. Nor had the stories in the London newspapers when they arrived on the island. One reporter noted that Cain had bought a new shirt for the called-off wedding. 'Not that he was out of pocket. He sent his latest love by taxi to buy it for him with her very own money. But he is used to that sort of thing. Used too, to a premature puncturing of romances in which the woman does the paying.'

Rarely have reporters had such a field day, uninhibited as they were by the fear of a libel writ.

Mrs Smith had finally to concede defeat when she was told that there were no legal grounds for objecting to the marriage, and the couple were married a few hours later in the home of a milk-bar owner. It may not have been the most decorous wedding of the year, but it was certainly the most rumbustious. Sidney took a drink before the ceremony, and urged Diana to have a second, but she declined: 'I want to say my marriage lines properly.'

Throughout the short ceremony, the couple – Sidney holding on to a big cigar – stumbled over their words and the Registrar had to keep repeating them. When they came to the end, Sidney was not asked to put a ring on her finger. 'What about the ring?' he asked, but the Registrar remained silent, and Diana took over, murmuring, 'Put it on now, Sidney.' It was golden copy for the reporters, but even they were beginning to feel it had gone too far.

The Marquise's two daughters, who had been standing at the back of the room, then came forward and presented her with a silver horseshoe and a wedding card.

The crowd outside pronounced it 'The craziest wedding ever.'

A reception was held, in carnival atmosphere, in the Grand Hotel, while, in her room in the same building, Mrs Smith wept.

In spite of the unorthodoxy, everyone sincerely wished the newly-weds a happy future, and prayed that Sidney would mend his ways. Three months later the couple were again headline news. Mrs Cain, who had piled up substantial debts, was a virtual prisoner on the island, her creditors having threatened to obtain a court order if she attempted to leave. She admitted the debts, but assured everyone that as soon as her cousin's will was settled, everything would be paid. Meanwhile, her husband was on the mainland trying to sort things out.

'Sir' Sidney was tracked down to the best hotel in Chester, where he was lunching with friends, and there he assured enquirers that all would be sorted out without any trouble. 'I don't really want this debt business to come out now. It's going to muck up all my plans.' It sounded ominous.

Months later the couple were again in the news, with

reports that her two daughters were being held hostage in Alderney until the money the Cains owed was paid. The Cains themselves were on the mainland at the time, having left the two girls behind in the home of the milk-bar owner where they had married.

Sidney and his wife kicked up a fuss, claiming that the children were being forcibly restrained from joining them … but like everything else involving Cain there was another side to the story. The children didn't want to leave; it was, they claimed, the only home they had ever known.

A year later Cain, still posing as a baronet, was standing in the dock at Chester Assizes, accused of obtaining money by false pretences from an hotel owner in Wales where he had posed as a wealthy stockbroker. 'For the few days they were in my hotel they lived a rich, idle life, with breakfast in bed every day,' the hotelier told the court. 'He was a very entertaining person. Very extravagant and very generous.'

Sentencing him to three years' imprisonment, the judge said, 'You are a fraudulent rascal, preying on the public in your craving for pleasure.'

Several years elapsed without my seeing or hearing his name, and I sincerely hoped he had seen what judges are so fond of describing as 'the error of his ways'. But it was too much to hope for. Staring at me over breakfast one morning was the familiar name: at the age of sixty-two, Sidney stood in the dock at Manchester Crown Court accused of fraud. He pleaded guilty to obtaining credit totalling £83 2s 9d by fraud from a hospital where, posing as 'Sir' Sidney Cain, he had occupied a private room for two weeks, and, the court was informed had each day sent out for two bottles of whisky.

He also asked for eighteen other offences of false pretences and fraud involving £1,275 to be taken into consideration.

The court was told, in addition, that he had served prison sentences in England, Eire, Guernsey and Denmark for fraud and false pretences. He had certainly cast his net wide.

In a plea of mitigation, his counsel said, 'This old reprobate comes of a good family. He looks like a baronet and talks like a baronet, and for twenty years or more his friends have referred to him as "Sir Sidney".' His wife, the Marquise de Visdelou-Guimbeau, was ill, the court was also told.

Because he sympathised with him over the sickness of his wife, and because Sidney had not been in trouble for six years, the judge decided to give him one last chance. He sentenced him to two years suspended for three years. There was one condition: he must drop his bogus baronetcy.

'If people come up to you and say "Hello, Sir Sidney. Here's five pounds", it is your duty to say, "No, I don't want it. I am not Sir Sidney." ' And, added the judge, 'Don't run away using this fantastic pretence you have been using for so long. Have the strength to resist the temptation of living in a fantasy world.'

Outside the court Sidney said, 'Call me anything you like, but don't call me "Sir Sidney". This is the first time I have ever had a chance and I intend to take it.'

He obviously meant it because I've not heard his name since. He really was an enigma. He had genuine charm and could be delightful company, but he truly believed that he was a smart operator – he was anything but that; he invariably got caught.

I like to think it had a fairy-tale ending with them both living happily for a long time afterwards. Without doubt, he was a rogue, but he was a beguiling one, and a newspaper reporter has no right to sit in judgement over others.

If he has to be judged, let it be by his peers.

15

TROUBLE IN ADEN

When I first tentatively touched the hem of fame as a foreign reporter it was with a story that I knew I *had* to write, but one which I honestly wished I had never got. From the start I knew it spelled trouble, and there is nothing worse than being thousands of miles away from the office when a major row erupts. Isolated, shunned by the people who have been upset by your story, you are inundated with a flood of cables demanding explanations and verification for what you've written, when you only have the vaguest idea of what is going on back in London. The reasons for their misgivings seep through only gradually, like coffee dripping through a filter, because communications are affected by several hours' time difference. You know damn well that you are right but feel pretty helpless when you learn that official sources back home are denying the story and a Minister has told the House it isn't true.

One lunchtime on a bitterly cold December day, I was enjoying a well-earned day off with a pint in my hand in my local pub when the landlord told me I was wanted on the telephone. It was my wife, who said the office wanted to contact me urgently. I phoned through with that butterfly feeling of 'What have I done wrong now?' It was the *Express*'s Foreign Editor, who said, somewhat tersely, 'Pack a bag and get in as quickly as possible.'

I went home, packed a suitcase, put on a suit, a heavy overcoat, gloves and a trilby. It was the kind of day when monkeys stayed indoors.

When I got to the office I was told I was going to Aden, the military, naval and airforce base that was then the gateway to

India and the Far East. My heart did not exactly soar at the prospect, for I had been there twice before – once going out East during the war, and again coming back when it was over. Then the lower deck had described it as 'the arsehole of the Empire', an opinion I fervently shared. It is an extinct volcano, arid, unattractive, oven-hot and overpopulated with millions of drowsy flies.

Discontented service families, mainly RAF wives, had written to the paper expressing dismay and disgust at the accommodation they were forced to live in, and urging the office to do something about it as no one else seemed to care. This had reached the ears of Marshal of the RAF Lord Tedder – no longer serving, but holding his rank for life – who was planning to fly out and investigate.

An hour later I was at London Airport, waiting to board a Britannia aircraft known as 'the whispering giant'. It was a long tiring flight in those days, and when I stepped out of the aircraft at Aden it was as if someone had just opened a furnace door: the heat literally hit me and the whole barren landscape seemed to be dancing and shimmering in the heat haze. I attracted a lot of attention from people on the runway who were wearing shorts and shirts, whereas I was wearing a suit and my thick winter coat and carrying my portable typewriter. I went straight to the Crescent Hotel, had a shower and went to work immediately. A few hours later I was sitting bathed in sweat with a towel round my midriff typing out my first story: 'I flew to Aden today – a 4,000-mile hop from London – to see the slums in which many British service families live … '

It appeared next morning under my by-line alongside my photograph. In the adjoining column was a photograph of René MacColl above his story from Delhi – he was touring India with President Eisenhower. Of course, I didn't see it until much later, but I had got alongside one of the immortals.

It was a good, tight story, full of facts and figures and interviews which confirmed all that had been alleged. I had gone on a tour of the area with an Air Ministry official who was most co-operative. And at the end of the tour I was able to write: 'After only a few hours here I have seen enough to convince me that drastic action is needed.' I also wrote that,

although Lord Tedder's visit was welcomed, it was tempered
by scepticism. 'We want action, not pious platitudes,' was a
quote I obtained from one RAF officer.

I saw families living in areas surrounded by incredible
squalor. Goats trotted in and out of doors, and wives were
forced off the pavements by cattle with enormous humps. On
all sides they were surrounded by Arab shanties made of
animal skins and branches, and everywhere they were
pestered by terribly deformed boys and girls begging for
money; some of the streets resembled nothing more than
open toilets, and the stench was awful. The service flats –
approved by the authorities – which cost about £40 a month,
were overcrowded, with no air-conditioning and with the
most primitive toilet facilities. At Khormaksar Barracks, the
main RAF base, overcrowding was so acute that men were
living on balconies with just a bed and a wardrobe.

My guide assured me that the senior officers were bending
over backwards to find a solution, but were hindered by a
flourishing black market which sent rents soaring – I found a
sergeant, with eighteen years' service, living with his family in
a dingy hotel room for which they were charged £100 a
month. 'I couldn't manage if my wife didn't go out to work,'
he told me.

It had been a hard but fruitful day, and my story wasn't too
bad for starters.

The next day I wrote that Air Marshal Sir Hubert Patch,
commanding the British Forces in the Arabian peninsula, was
flying to London for 'routine' talks. The appalling slum
conditions in which so many service families were living was
not on his agenda. I spent the day again visiting service
families, and gathered a great deal more material. There was a
woman paying £24 a week for a windowless room which she
shared with her husband and three children. She said of her
two-month-old baby: 'He has not seen the light of day since
we left hospital. How can I take him out in this area? We are
sick to death of it. The RAF led us to believe we would be out
of this place by October.'

There were several more similar interviews. I was entitled
to feel a bit smug. I had accomplished all I had been sent out
to do, but I sensed there were even better stories to come. I

was right – but, oh, how I regretted it for the next couple of days.

I went next day to see the Air Commodore, who was responsible for Service Housing in Aden. I expected a few comforting comments and would have been more than happy to have got a few quotes on the lines of 'Everything will be done to look into your revelations.'

The Air Commodore instead spoke his mind. 'I am fed up with bellyaching service families here. Families living in the conditions you state are doing it through choice. It is nothing to do with me.

'If they cannot wait in their slums at home until they get proper service accommodation, I can't help it. If they insist on coming to the slums here, I cannot stop them.' And he added, 'If they choose to live like that, it is not our concern.'

The speaker was one of the Air Force's most distinguished and gallant officers – he had been a wartime Pathfinder and a post-war commander in the A-bomb tests – and I sensed that although I was on to a big story I was also looking down into the jaws of trouble. There was no stopping him, however, and no doubt he was doing his utmost to improve conditions and possibly resented outsiders dropping in uninvited and making suggestions. Furthermore, the intense heat often made one's temper fray at the edges. He made it clear, too, that he didn't think Air Marshal Tedder's visit would be all that helpful. Lady Tedder had distorted the position: 'Her husband is coming here merely to try to force us to open Malcolm Clubs.' (These were clubs in which Lady Tedder had a considerable interest.)

The Air Commodore went on to say that he and his staff were doing everything humanly possibly to put up new houses and flats, and they wanted to be left alone to get on with the task. Nagging at the back of my mind was that someone had once told me that he was a friend of Sir Max Aitken from his own RAF days. That knowledge did not help.

When I supplied the Air Commodore with details of the complaints I had heard and of promises for accommodation that had not been fulfilled, he replied, 'They are liars,' adding, 'We want fighting men out here, not bellyaching families.'

I was provided with a detailed account of the housing position regarding the fifteen hundred families on the base, and figures for those living in official quarters and those in 'approved hirings', but I knew that the story lay in the comments of the Air Commodore.

I returned to my room and began to transcribe my notes. All the time, I had a sinking feeling that trouble was in the offing, but knew it would be a betrayal of my trust if I did not file it. Typing a long cable is hard work and not conducive to fluency; punctuation is a real chore, for you have to type out the words 'comma', 'quote', 'unquote', 'para', 'colon', and so on. So concerned was I, that, when I had finished my very long cable, I went back and showed it to the Air Ministry official responsible for Press matters. He read it and made no comment other than, 'If that's what he said ... ' and shrugged.

I had tried to do the decent thing and flash the warning lights, for I knew that the story would create a big stir; senior officers are not expected to talk like that about the men they command or the women who are married to them. I transmitted my story and returned to the hotel to wait for the first cable to arrive, for not until then would I have any idea of how much impact my piece had made. But I knew it would get a good show. When the cable arrived it was full of congratulations, and informed me that I had got the front-page splash, which was everybody's idea of Utopia on the *Express*.

The story covered a great deal of the front page, and, inside, in the Opinion column under 'Action This Day', it said, 'Memo to the Air Minister, Mr George Ward: Read Alfred Draper's despatch from Aden on page one today.' It then went on to demand the recall of the Air Commodore.

Then the cables which I had been dreading began to arrive. My story had been denied in Parliament. Had I a shorthand note of the interview? What was I going to do about the allegation that I had misreported the gallant officer? I did have my notebook, but that wasn't a great deal of help four thousand miles away from the office. My head was well and truly on the block. But I knew I had not fabricated anything, and I cabled back that I stood by everything I had written.

Mr Ward, I was then informed, had told the House: 'I have

now received a full report of the interview, and I am satisfied
that the officer was misreported.' He went on to assure the
House that he had the fullest confidence in the officer who
had done so much for servicemen and their wives.

More cables arrived, demanding further evidence about the
interview; I had a sinking feeling that no one believed my
version, and I broke out in a cold sweat that had nothing to
do with the temperature. I decided to go fishing and let the
whole thing sort itself out. I bought a cheap hand line and sat
on one of the oil pipes at the end of the harbour to try and
forget my bleak-looking future. Suddenly I was almost
hauled into the water; I had something so monstrous on the
hook I just could not handle it. Several Arabs came to my
assistance and we finally landed a giant sting ray that must
have measured nine feet across. Normally I would have been
elated, but my thoughts were elsewhere. The Arabs drove a
stake through the fish and walked away, leaving it pinned to
the sand. No one wanted it. I felt akin to the fish.

In the meantime, a continuous stream of servicemen and
their wives called at the hotel to provide me with further
information. This was most useful, as the *News Chronicle* had
flown out a reporter to shoot down my stories. I referred him
to the callers. Fortunately, we were old friends, and he did
not think it was his job to scupper me for the benefit of the
Air Ministry. There were two callers who meant more to me
than any others, army officers I had got to know who said
they had overheard my interview with the Air Commodore
and were prepared to say so if they were subpoenaed. It was a
brave thing to do because officers were reluctant to drink
with me in the Crescent, fearing guilt by association. I knew
then that I had nothing to worry about, and cabled the news
to the office. I felt I was now in the clear, but it was not a
happy time. Clubs which had previously welcomed me now
gave me the cold shoulder; I was not the type of person to be
seen with.

Meanwhile, I waited for the debate in the House; it
produced a headline that spread right across the front page:
'RAF orders clean up'.

A vast sum was to be spent on providing new homes. The
first paragraph stated: 'Five big moves to improve living

conditions in Aden were announced following *Daily Express* disclosures.' The Air Ministry was to spend the money on pre-fab buildings, made in Nottingham and assembled in Aden, as quarters, officers' messes and clubs – part of a £10,000,000 development project.

The debate in the House was a heated one, during which Mr Ward came under severe criticism. But he justified all I had written by giving details of what was to be done without delay. He would not, however, comment on my interview with the Air Commodore – he had asked for a report and had yet to receive it.

That really was the end of the affair and no one was more relieved than I was. I was told to head for home, as no doubt I would like to be there for Christmas.

My stint in Aden was not all personal worry and despondency, however. A reporter has to learn to be resilient and carry on as if he hasn't a worry in the world.

While the pressure was at its greatest, my mind was taken off my own problems by a telephone call from the Foreign Desk asking me to obtain by fair or foul means an interview with a young serviceman who had been sentenced to life imprisonment for the rape of a Somali girl. The telephone call underlined the sensitive nature of the inquiry; clearly, the Foreign Desk did not want to put anything in words in case the cable was read by some interested party. It seemed that there was mounting unease in London that the man would be made to carry out his sentence in conditions totally unsuitable for a white person, but such was the atmosphere in Aden at that time that it was considered undiplomatic to make a direct approach asking for him to be transferred to an English prison – which would suggest that a white man was entitled to different treatment from a native. Apart from that, the actual crime had aroused extremely strong feelings locally. My instructions were to get into the prison without mentioning the serviceman, and in some way contrive to get an interview with him.

I soon realised the depth of feeling it had aroused when I spoke to some local journalists who were harshly critical of the manner in which British newspapers had covered the trial,

protesting at the inadequate coverage in London. Their own
papers had gone into the most lurid and explicit details of the
crime and they saw the sparseness of the British coverage as a
deliberate attempt to minimise the offence. I tried in vain to
point out that there was no question of a cover-up: our papers
just did not go into the medical evidence in minute detail.
Grisly descriptions of an attempt to penetrate a girl whose
vagina had been sewn up according to tribal custom, or of
spermatozoa and so on, was hardly breakfast reading.

Warned off trying to ask for an interview, I sought
permission instead to write a colour piece about Aden's
humane prison conditions. The result was a conducted tour of
a grim building that made Dartmoor look like a rest home. I
was escorted around by an immaculately uniformed official
with a swagger stick who resembled a regimental sergeant-
major, and before we set off, was told that on no account was
I to try to talk to him unless he spoke to me first.

I suppose that, to natives accustomed to the primitive living
conditions in Aden – some actually lived in caves dug into the
surrounding hillside – the prison was relatively comfortable,
but to a European they were unbearable. Some of the cells
were no more than iron cages in the middle of the sun-baked
courtyard. The heat was intolerable, and, from what I could
see, little attempt was made to segregate prisoners. In one
large walled cell I saw three naked men, clearly mentally
deranged, being calmed down by fire hoses. An elderly Sikh,
who was awaiting execution, stood ram-rod stiff and whipped
off a salute that would have scored full marks on an Aldershot
parade ground. 'God bless Queen Victoria,' he called out to
my astonishment. I was even shown the execution shed, and
had the trap demonstrated. 'Just like Pentonville. Only three
at a time,' said my guide and held up three fingers in case I
had missed the point.

I also saw several men and women without hands, and was
told they were thieves who had been punished according to
Islamic law for offences committed outside the colony. When
I remarked that, although it effectively prevented further
theft, it seemed very barbaric, I was told it was not meant as a
deterrent but as a means of identifying a thief.

Most of the prisoners seemed quite happy, and I was told

that those who could afford it were able to purchase their meals from outside.

As I passed one particular open-air cell I had no difficulty in spotting the crew-cut serviceman. He was the only white man I had seen. I paused there and remarked to my guide that the *Daily Express*'s readers would be impressed by the enlightened manner in which the prison was run, and as we turned to move away the soldier called out, 'You from the *Express*? Can I talk to you?'

I looked at my guide and he nodded his approval. I had not, he agreed, attempted to speak to him first, so I had not broken our verbal agreement.

I had a long chat with the young man who told me how harsh he found the routine, and expressed the wish to be sent home to serve his sentence. Not long afterwards I learned that he had been sent to a prison in England.

When I walked into the office on my return, the Editor took me for a drink in the Press Club, and laid on his own car to take me home. Referring to the Air Ministry affair, he assured me that at no time had he lost confidence in me. I refrained from mentioning the fusillade of telegrams he had sent me.

When I called on my mother she said, 'Are you still on the *Express*? I never see your name these days.'

And when I reported back for duty I was put on the dog watch, the 9 p.m. to 4.30 a.m. shift which everybody hated. The *Express* never allowed you to become swollen-headed.

16

ILLEGAL IMMIGRANTS

Reporters live in fear and hope of a telegram from the Editor. If it was one of congratulations you felt you had suddenly grown ten foot tall, if it was a stiff rebuke you felt almost suicidal. Editors and proprietors had that kind of effect on reporters – you lived for the newspaper and life was very much like being in the ranks of the Grand Old Duke of York: when you were up you were cloud-floating, but when you were down you felt you were on the way out.

One telegram I shall never forget was addressed to 'Arthur Draper, Royal Hotel, Winchester.' It was not an ordinary telegram but a greetings one in colour, depicting Britain's wild animal and bird life: 'My warmest congratulations to you and Jack Hill on the splendid story and pictures in this morning's paper – Derek Marks.'

The fact that the Editor had sent it to 'Arthur' Draper didn't blunt the thrill of smug satisfaction, although I did momentarily wonder what his reaction would have been if I had got his christian name wrong. An indication of my unreliability? A black mark on my record for not even being able to get a name right? Reporters have been sacked for much less.

I am only reminded of the story because today I'm not even sure there was a *story*, although this one occupied the front page with inch-high headlines and a picture spread across six columns. It began in the Editor's office with the kind of briefing that every reporter dreams about but knows will never materialise. I was summoned into Derek's presence to find Harry Chapman Pincher reclining languidly in one of the armchairs. Chapman Pincher, the Defence Correspondent of

181

the *Daily Express*, and a most remarkable man, had no equal in his own particular sphere, defence, in which he produced exclusive after exclusive, many of which were embarrassing to the government of the day and often had successive Prime Ministers tearing their hair in frustration. Very much a loner, throughout the many years I knew him I never saw him in a Fleet Street pub. When Harry said he had received a tip-off, it was accepted without question as genuine; his contacts numbered generals, attorney-generals, Ministers and Heads of State.

On this particular occasion he had received from a prison source information to the effect that a prisoner with a twinge of conscience had confessed that some Pakistani illegal immigrants had been murdered and robbed by the people who had brought them into the country. As a result a massive search was about to be launched to recover their bodies. The facts were vague but Chapman had been told that the digging would be centred around the Kingsworthy area in Hampshire, which was fringed with dense woods and not far from the New Forest. Chapman Pincher could be compared to a Chief Constable in so far as he issued instructions but did not pound a beat. That was the role of the general reporter. In this case, I was detailed as the PC Plod.

I certainly did not quibble with that, for my brief was a reporter's dream. I was told to pack my fishing rods and drive with my wife to a hotel which had a private stretch of water, book in and pose as a fisherman, catch as many trout as I could, and await further instructions. The dream quickly faded, for not only was the hotel fully booked but the cost of fishing the exclusive water was astronomical; so we drove off to Winchester where, if we couldn't have fishing, we could have comfort and good food. I waited for more news, but none came, so I contacted Jack Hill, the *Express* man who covered the south coast of England, and one of the most astute and tenacious reporters around, whose contacts covered a very wide sphere, including quite obviously top police officers in Hampshire. He made very discreet inquiries, carefully putting out feelers, so as not to alert the opposition that we might be on to something big. Everywhere he encountered a blank impenetrable wall of silence. But silence can often be most eloquent; although it didn't leave us any wiser, it at least alerted us to the fact that something was going on that they did not want the Press to get wind of. We split a large area between us and began to cover it with immense care, driving along rutted roads that would have made hard going for tanks, through densely wooded areas, along river banks, startling the occasional deer as we did so. When we eventually met at our rendezvous, we had to report total failure. We decided to have a beer and a snack and discuss our next move, and were driving through the picture-postcard village of Farleigh Wallop, four miles south of the A30 Great West Road at Basingstoke, when suddenly we struck gold. In a field owned by farmer Ernest Hooper, we saw a dozen police officers stripped to the waist in jeans and Wellington boots, feverishly digging up a large area of ground. A radio van and nine police cars were lined up round the perimeter, and beside a hedge was a plastic bucket filled with rubber gloves. Toiling away with his men was Detective Chief Superintendent Cyril Holdaway, head of Hampshire CID. Astonishing as the scene was, none of the villagers seemed to find it of any interest, continuing to go about their work as if it was an everyday occurrence in Farleigh Wallop.

I had a recently purchased camera in the car, but I was not at all sure how to work it, so I took a series of pictures, varying the shutter speed and the focal depth in the hope that at least one of them would be fit to print. Jack, about as capable with a camera as I was, took over and finished off the reel. Having obtained, we hoped, evidence of their presence, we appeared from behind the hedge and approached Mr Holdaway and asked him what he was doing. His cautious reply was an exercise in ambiguity. 'I am here with a team of officers. Acting on information, we are searching for buried property. I will say no more.' And he did not through the four hours they remained digging. Farmer Hooper had fared no better: 'The police said something was buried. I asked what, but they said they were sorry, they could not tell me.'

As the dreamy summer's day drew to an end, the policemen tossed their tools in the back of a lorry, put on their shirts and called it a day. 'We have finished for tonight,' announced Mr Holdaway, and expanded enough to say they had not been looking for bodies. It sounded to us a most unconvincing assurance – if it had been stolen property, surely they would have used metal detectors? But we were more than satisfied; every denial only served to strengthen our story.

Jack raced into Southampton and had the film developed, and there were a couple of beauties, so sharp that individual blades of grass were visible. The pictures were put on the next train to London where a motor-cycle despatch rider was waiting at the station to take them to the office.

The next day the picture and story had a front-page splash position with a joint by-line. It was, of course, a one-day exclusive. Early in the morning an impressive corps of reporters and photographers besieged Police Headquarters, and Mr Holdaway held a conference at which he made no attempt to hide his displeasure. A full inquiry had been ordered into how news of the hush-hush dig had become known. Of course he wanted to know the source of information, and I was relieved to be able to tell him that I did not know. I took the brunt of his anger, not through any sense of chivalry, but because Jack had to live and work in the area and could not afford to alienate one of his most important contacts. I did not mind being in bad odour, it might be years before I set foot on his patch again.

Although we got nothing but more denials, Jack and I were able to phone over another front-page story. But it had run its course, no more digging was contemplated, and I returned to the office. The mysterious affair at Farleigh Wallop had all the ingredients for an Agatha Christie thriller – certainly several missing bodies that were never accounted for. To this day, neither Jack nor I know if there was any truth in the tip-off. Had the man in prison given the police the wrong location? I can never drive that way without casting a glance at the fields and wondering whether or not a mass grave lies beneath the turf.

It doesn't take much in Fleet Street to become the acknowledged expert on a subject, and the saga of Farleigh Wallop made me one on illegal immigrants. I was despatched to Folkstone where three Pakistanis were languishing in jail after being smuggled ashore at mist-shrouded St Mary's Bay.

It would, I was assured, enable me to crack the smuggling
ring which was causing so much concern in Parliament. The
story had none of the drama of the alleged murder and
robbery at Farleigh Wallop. True it appeared on the front
page, but in the much-coveted slot always reserved for a
light-hearted piece.

As the boat ground on to the shingle, the three men had
stepped ashore unseen and been told to make their way to the
nearest railway station. There they sat on a bench and waited
and waited for the train to take them to a new life in
Wolverhampton. After several hours, one of them knocked
on the door of a nearby cottage and asked in faltering English,
'Next train, please?'

'Easter,' the householder replied, and showed them the
board on the platform, which they could not read: *Hythe and
Dymchurch Railway. The world's smallest public railway.*

'Naturally I was suspicious. Everybody knows the
miniature railway only runs in the summer,' he told me later.

One of them then asked, 'Bus?', and he directed them to
the nearest stop and went off to telephone the police.

After I had telephoned my copy, the News Editor merely
said, 'Come back.' He made it sound as if I was responsible
for the fiasco.

17

FOREIGN-WISE

When reporters were in remote spots, far away from the office, the cable was often the sole means of sending copy, and the really top-class man's first task on arrival was to establish his lines of communication. The best story in the world is worthless if it does not reach the office. The cable was also the only avenue for the Foreign Desk to pass on instructions, and these had the effect on reporters that a telegram has on the average family: they are opened with great trepidation.

Don Seaman, who received more than most of us, summed it up with these words: 'Cables! They were hero-grams to some, the bum's rush to others. A good one made you feel ten feet tall, while a rocket drove the recipient to contemplate suicide. Failure to receive any kind of cable whatever good or bad – could almost drive you round the bend.'

It became something of a tradition for Foreign Editors to vie with each other in sending cables that were witty and renowned for their brevity. Many have passed into Fleet Street folklore.

No one ever received instructions to 'go to Cairo' – it would be 'Cairo-wise soonest'. And they were often baffling in their complexity. I was in Ethiopia when I received a cable reading: 'Terretsia-bound-soonest'. I pondered for hours over its hidden meaning; obviously I could not display my ignorance by sending a cable asking the Foreign Editor what the heck he meant. So I just forgot about it pending clarification. It never came. Weeks later when I was back in the office I asked the sender what it meant, and he replied, 'I was just going out for lunch in the Italian restaurant' – a popular 'noshery' not far from the *Express*.

Neither was anyone ever told to get a move on. Donald Seaman was ordered to 'De-digitate-soonest'. Unknown to him, Prince Philip had made headlines at home by telling the heads of British industry, 'Pull your finger out'.

There was one celebrated foreign correspondent who stubbornly refused to use cable-ese and in consequence cost his office a small fortune by sending everything full-out. Eventually he received a final ultimatum and he conformed, but just once, 'Upstick job arsewise,' he replied.

One classic exchange began with a reporter who was short of money and cabled, 'Unfinanced require funds.' The reply came back, 'Unexpenses-unfunds,' to which he responded, 'Unfunded unstory,' and was warned, 'Unstory-unjob.'

The quest for brevity often had unexpected and hilarious results, as when one of the *Express*'s best women reporters received a cable informing her that a Royal Navy submarine had 'upturned' at a naval base, miles from where she was staying in Cyprus, and motored at breakneck speed half-way across the island to the scene of the disaster, only to find that the Foreign Desk had simply been telling her that the submarine had turned up.

John Weaver, an Australian and one of the *Express*'s young men being groomed for stardom, was in the Congo working alongside John Ridley, one of the *Daily Telegraph*'s most experienced foreign men, who spent much of his time covering events in Africa, which he disliked intensely. Ridley had been there for two years and was longing for London and his favourite seat in the King and Keys, when he received a cable: 'Return home soonest.'

'He threw a terrific party,' recalled John Weaver, 'and we then took him to the airport where we intended to put him aboard. I asked him for a memento of our friendship, and he said, "You can have the cable recalling me." I smoothed it out and realised he had misread Tome, in Togoland, for home. He went asbolutely spare.'

Brian Freemantle, who was on the *Express* in my time, before moving to become a distinguished foreign reporter with the *Daily Mail* (he later left Fleet Street to become a best-selling author, and creator of the successful Charlie

Muffin series), treasures a cable he received from two friends on the *Express* with whom he had worked for many years. He was in Vietnam at the time when Kissinger was believed to have negotiated a peace settlement, and was on Highway One when he and several newsmen were caught in an ambush which pinned them down in a ditch for some considerable time until they were able to escape one by one to a safe spot down the road. Brian was the last out, on the pillion of a South Vietnamese Honda, and as he arrived at the safety line he realised that his face was a mask of blood and the photographers were taking a series of pictures. In diving for cover into the ditch he had plunged into a bamboo thicket and a sharp piece of splintered bamboo had punctured a small blood vessel in the side of his head, but everyone assumed he had been shot.

'When I got back to Saigon I realised the *Mail* were going to have a photograph of me apparently hurt, when I wasn't really. So to cover the picture, I put in about para 17 that I had been nicked. David English, the Editor, wasn't in the office for the first edition and the Back Bench got very excited with the picture and rejigged my piece, and led the paper with "*Mail* man wounded in Vietnam". When David got in he asked whereabouts in the story I had mentioned being hurt, and when they said paragraph 17, he said I was such an egotist that if it had been serious I would have introed with it myself, and so he put the piece back as written and knocked out the headline. I knew nothing about this, of course, until the following day when David Eliades and John Moger, on the *Express* Foreign Desk, sent me a cable, through UPI to ensure everyone in Saigon would read it: "*Mail* earlies have you wounded. *Mail* lates have you unwounded. Congratulations your miracle recovery. Presume next dateline Lourdes." '

Brian later became the *Mail*'s Foreign Editor, and discovered that foreign reporters have an uncanny knack of getting their own back on the poacher turned gamekeeper. John Edwards, one of the paper's finest writers of colour pieces, was in Saigon on a particularly quiet day, and began to telex a story. Brian thought he should do it a different way and interrupted John's filing to 'talk' to him on the telex. They argued for some time with John wanting to do it *his* way and Brian *insisting* that it should be done *his*.

'John was furious and took with him the hugely long cable traffic when he went to the Continental Hotel for a drink. There he met the *New York Times* man and showed him the cable. The next day the *New York Times* ran about 2,000 words on the lines: "Vietnam was itself quiet yesterday, but intensive battles were being fought on other fronts ... " and carried most of the cable exchanges.'

Certainly, editors sitting in their London offices, were not always right. Even the legendary Lord Northcliffe, who permitted no human error in others, was capable of the most astonishing blunders. One day 'The Chief', as he was known, met Charlie Hands, one of his star men, on the stairs of Carmelite House and said, 'Charlie, leave tomorrow for New York. Instructions will follow.'

Hands reported to the head of the New York Bureau who promptly sent him to an hotel with instructions to call in daily until Northcliffe sent his instructions. He stayed there for three months without any communication from 'The Chief' until the *Mail*'s Editor arrived on one of his periodic visits. 'What on earth are you doing here, Charlie?' he enquired.

'Mostly I play billiards, sir,' Charlie replied, and explained that he was still awaiting instructions. The Editor cabled Northcliffe and received the following reply: 'Sorry, forgot about Hands; send him home.'

I was once despatched at very short notice to Athens to cover the 'Murder on the Orient Express', and told that it might mean waiting for several days for a British student and a Swedish girl, suspected of being involved in the death of a fellow hitch-hiker – whose battered body had been found near the track of the famous Orient Express sixty-five miles from Istanbul – to turn up in Athens. I booked in at the best hotel and planned a sight-seeing itinerary, but I had only been in Athens a few hours when I was put in touch with the students, who had been contacted by the British Embassy as soon as they arrived in the capital and told of the death of their travelling companion. It turned out that they did not even know he had been killed, and inquiries revealed that he had been accidentally killed when trying to stow away in a goods van, and had either fallen off or been struck by a bridge.

Although I sent a story about the murder-that-never-was

and it made a page lead, it was a bit of an anti-climax and not at all the Agatha Christie riddle the Foreign Editor was sure it would be. I was told to return home without delay in a manner implying that I had deliberately misled the office in order to enjoy a trip abroad.

That night I was mugged and robbed, and it was only through meeting an *Express* woman reporter who was in Athens on honeymoon that I was able to borrow some cash and make it to the airport. There I encountered one of those strokes of luck which Beaverbrook insisted did not exist. I bumped into Betty Ambatielos, a London school teacher, who had fought for years to secure the release of her husband Tony who was serving a life sentence in prison on the small Greek island of Aegina. A former leader of the Greek Seamen's Union, he had been sentenced to death, later reduced to life imprisonment, for his activities with Communist guerrillas in the Greek Civil War, and I had met Betty a number of times in London, where for seventeen years she had campaigned to get him freed, insisting that he had been unfairly imprisoned. She told me that she had been informed he was to be freed and had only had time hastily to pack a bag before catching a plane to Athens.

I travelled with her to the island where I interviewed Tony and witnessed the reunion of a couple who had not seen each other for many years. 'You can pack your things,' she told him. 'You're coming home today.'

It was a moving story, with pictures, that made a page spread. After I had phoned it over, I spoke to the Foreign Editor who said, '*That* was the real story I had sent you out on.'

Understandably, no Foreign Editor ever admits that his news sense might be suspect, or that his judgement of distances at fault.

Arthur Brittenden told me of how he received a cable when he was in Africa telling him to go to Lambarene to interview the oil heiress Olga Deterding, who was working in Albert Schweitzer's leper colony.

'I was a long way away – I suspect someone in London had looked at a map and seen I was within three inches of the place – and it took me several days to get there. The last part

of the journey was by river in a boat, which I had to hire and
have rowed by several Africans. As we approached the
landing stage at Lambarene a group of people came down to
it, among them Schweitzer. I stepped ashore and told him I
had come to talk to Olga Deterding about her work with him.
He said, "No. Impossible. You must leave." '

Arthur, a most tenacious and persuasive man, talked and
argued in an attempt to convince Schweitzer that the publicity
would be beneficial to his work, but the doctor was adamant.

'I realised I was not going to get anywhere, as he indicated
he was not prepared to talk any further and was leaving. I
stepped back into the boat, and as I did so, Schweitzer
signalled to one of his helpers who handed him a canvas bag
which he passed to me. "I am sorry for you," he said. As I
was rowed away I opened the bag. Inside it were a dozen
bananas.'

Arthur's story in the *Sunday Express* of his hazardous
journey and how he did not interview Olga Deterding
remains a classic, and an example to the aspiring newcomer of
how to turn a failure into a triumph.

Another hazard in foreign reporting is the informant – the
worth of his tips has to be very carefully assessed, for they can
be a minefield, to be negotiated with utmost caution.

In 1953, Mohammed Mossadegh, the Persian politician
who nationalised the British oil refinery in Abadan, was
overthrown by a Royalist uprising. Arthur Cook, one of the
paper's top foreign men, was given a tip-off that he had been
arrested and sentenced to death. He cabled the story which
made the front page. But no other paper followed it up, and
Arthur received a barbed cable from the Foreign Desk: 'Your
exclusive still exclusive. Why?'

Cook, who had the utmost confidence in his informant,
stuck to his story, and the cables flew back and forth until
Arthur stated, with an assurance he did not feel, 'Mossadegh
definitely hangs tomorrow', to which the reply was, 'Either
Mossadegh hangs tomorrow or you do.' The politician was
released after a relatively short spell in prison. Every foreign
reporter sympathised with Arthur.

When I was in Aden a local newspaperman called on me at
the Crescent Hotel with what he called 'a world exclusive'.

The King of the Yemen had been killed in a riding accident, and this could result in a bloody uprising between opposing factions. His description of the fatal fall was vivid and most convincing. I was tempted to cable the story, but had second thoughts and decided I would sit on it until I could check it out. The next morning my informant called and asked if I had sent my 'world exclusive', and I said I had. 'Good,' he said. 'Although he is not dead, just hurt. But he could have been killed.' To him there was very little difference in the two stories.

When I last met Brian Freemantle, he told me of how the *Washington Post*, a very influential newspaper – as Nixon found to his cost – ran a whole page on 'The Faker of Fleet Street'. This man was a regular contributor to newspapers, including the *Daily Mail*; unfortunately most of his stories were made up.

One of his allegations was that President Carter, in order to hype up his fading presidential image, was growing an Abraham Lincoln beard. The exclusive story in the *Mail* was relayed back to America, where a White House official vehemently denied it; nevertheless, on the first day of a scheduled appearance by Carter there was a horde of photographers waiting to capture the bearded President. He appeared – clean-shaven.

When the *Mail* demanded to know what had happened to the beard, their informant calmly explained that the President had been caught out by the *Mail*'s exclusive, and had shaved it off rather than admit that the newspaper had such incredible sources in the White House.

Contrary to the commonly held belief, newsmen do have integrity and a sense of professional honour. Apart from a few rare exceptions, they bear no malice when they are scooped, as everyone is sooner or later, and they are the first to applaud the successes of their competitors.

That does not mean, however, that they do not grasp the opportunity to 'screw' the opposition when they inadvertently hand them their own exclusive on a plate. When I was working on the *Mail* I was sent to Copenhagen on what everyone secretly admitted, but would not say openly, was a wild-goose chase. It was what was known in newspaper jargon as 'going through the motions', but was in fact an insurance policy adopted by all Foreign Editors to protect themselves from criticism for failing to have the foresight to 'buy up' the story before a rival. By sending a reporter they could excuse themselves by saying that the reporter had fallen down on the job, as he was almost certainly bound to do.

The story was a good one: a thirty-three-year-old Royal Marine, who had been captured in the Korean War, had refused to be repatriated when it ended, and, listed as a deserter, was returning home after twelve years, with his French-Chinese wife and two-year-old son. He had been branded a Communist, and accused of visiting Moscow and saying a lot of indiscreet things. It was the ideal opportunity for many questions to be asked and answered. The trouble was that he had been bought up by the *Express*, which had chartered a private aircraft to fly him home, while two of the paper's top reporters were on the scene to make sure the marine did not utter a word to anyone else.

One of these reporters was my valued friend Cyril Aynsley, who had covered the Korean War with such distinction, and knew more about the story than anyone else. I turned up at Copenhagen Airport, feeling like an uninvited guest and well aware that two such experienced old hands would never allow me even to ask him the time. The marine was whipped away into a private room, and I had as much hope of a story as I had of entering Fort Knox. Then, to my astonishment, I was asked to look after their precious property and his family while they went off to get a bite to eat. Whilst I did not get a great amount from the marine, I got enough to write a front-page story that took the edge off the *Express*'s scoop, and gave the impression that the *Mail* considered that that was all the story was worth.

In inviting me to look after their charges, Cyril and his colleague had been under the misapprehension that I was still on the *Express* and had been sent out to give them a helping hand. When I disillusioned them they were naturally aggrieved, but it was a short-lived anger and we were still able to have a drink together.

With people moving from one newspaper to another quite frequently, such blunders were not all that rare. Brian Park, who left the *Express* to become Chief Reporter of the *Daily Mail*, must be credited as the man who pulled off the great scoop against his old paper.

It was at that time when attempts were being made to deport the Great Train Robber, Ronald Biggs, back to England from Brazil where he had fled after his daring escape from Wandsworth Prison. He had been tracked down, and arrangements had been made for a Scotland Yard detective to fly out and arrest him.

Brian was at Lisbon Airport waiting to fly home, when Sir David English, his Editor, asked him if he would mind returning via Brazil as he wanted him to do what he could to sabotage the *Express* which had Biggs under wraps. Sir David, an ex-*Express* hand himself, was not torn between conflicting loyalties – off with the old, on with the new, is the name of the game in Fleet Street.

Brian duly booked aboard the first available flight and then sat in the airport, fuming as the aircraft was delayed by several hours because of an engine fault. In the restaurant he got into conversation with a Brazilian who was returning home on the same flight, and they renewed their acquaintance during the flight, exchanging names and addresses before parting at Rio de Janeiro. Soon afterwards, the Fleet Street contingent of reporters and photographers descended on the city, all with the same brief – to cock-up the *Express* venture. It was a period of great frustration and confusion. Brian had a tip that Biggs and his minders were in Brasilia, in the Amazon area, but when he got there he found they had returned to Rio.

'Back in Rio a large number of us were in a bar in Copacabana Beach and deciding it was a pointless needle in a haystack situation, because the *Express* had gone to ground in one of the world's most heavily populated cities and nobody – including the authorities – was offering the slighest clue. I suddenly thought of the man I had met aboard the aircraft and decided to give him a ring and explain my difficulty. To my surprise, he asked where I was and would I stay by the phone for the next half-hour. Even more amazingly, he was back on to me to say he had managed to discover from a distant relative in the local police the address at which the *Express* were holed up.'

Within half an hour the Brazilian had turned up to drive Brian and his photographer, Geoff, 'Chalkie' White, to the secret address.

'While they remained in the car I went up to the relevant floor, identified the apartment and put my ear to the judas shutter in the middle of the door. To my intense delight I heard the voice of Michael O'Flaherty, one of the *Express* team, and some mumbled words which I thought came from Biggs and his then heavily pregnant girlfriend, who was largely responsible for Biggs's continued residence in the country.'

Brian returned to the car and explained to his friend that the *Express* were hardly likely to admit him if he knocked on the door, but might let the Brazilian in. Sportingly, the gentleman agreed to go along with the plan, and while Brian and White stood unseen at either side of the door, he knocked. As soon as the door opened, Brian and Geoff were inside. White fired off a flashgun and got a picture of Biggs and his girlfriend before they could be whisked out of sight. O'Flaherty, alone in the room with the man who had first tipped off the *Express* about Biggs's whereabouts, bellowed at him to 'Go and get Bill and the boys from the pub', and then turned his attention to ejecting White. 'In the utter chaos, I stepped behind some curtains on the balcony and stayed put,' recalled Brian.

A few minutes later the *Express* team returned and forcibly ejected the *Mail*'s cameraman. One can imagine the feelings of the *Express* team, for thousands of pounds had been invested in the enterprise.

Still behind the balcony curtains, Brian listened to the inevitable inquest before stepping out and remarking that it was good to see them all. Bill Lovelace, the *Express*'s chief photographer, congratulated him and said it must have been a hell of a job tracking them down. Brian, with great aplomb, said he had heard all he needed to and had to be off to phone his copy, but that he would meet them for a drink after.

'I believe it just caught our last edition and then, as it was no skin off my nose, I phoned the rest of the mob at Copacabana Beach. The remainder of the night was sheer circus, with television crews clamouring outside the flats, with the whole place lit up and startled Brazilians screaming their heads off from the windows of the surrounding flats. In the end, the police were called to restore order. I did manage to have a drink with Bill and his team and, as usual, we all agreed everything was permissible – and possible – in love and war, although Bill reckoned there would be quite an inquest when his office heard what had happened.'

There was one thing (other than actually stealing copy) however, that no one would ever tolerate and that was sabotaging an opposition man's copy. It happened to me once in Africa when I was stranded in a remote spot with no cabling facilities and no seat on the only plane out. I handed my copy to another reporter who promised to file it for me. It was a first-rate story which had been obtained under conditions of great discomfort and difficulty. He sent the copy all right, but a page at a time with a day's break between each page and in reverse order. For some time he was boycotted by the rest of the Fleet Street corps.

But my misfortunes were minuscule next to those which befell Stephen Harper, one of the best men in a team of unmatchable foreign correspondents the *Express* had in my days.

In 1959 Steve was sent to the Everest region, on Nepal's frontier with Tibet, to cover the first All-Women's Himalayan expedition. They aimed to reach the summit of Cho Oyu, a 26,750-foot-high sister peak to Everest. Steve had trained as hard as an Olympic athlete for the job and was incredibly fit for what amounted to his own mini-expedition. He followed the progress of the women with his own Sherpa porters, who worked in pairs to run his cables to the post office in Katmandu, for transmission to London. The journey, over mountain tracks that would have tested a goat, normally took twenty-six days, but his messengers did it in six to eight. To encourage even better results, he offered a bonus payment for every day they cut off the journey to the post office.

He was in the Sherpa village of Namche Bazar when he

heard rumours of fatalities on Cho Oyu after severe
blizzards, but two women, who were brought down with
altitude sickness, told him that all twelve women were safe,
although two, who had been at a high camp, had returned to
Base Camp to sit out the bad weather. The rumours, they
assured him, sprang from the death of a Sherpa porter in an
avalanche.

The runners he despatched with the story reached
Katmandu in a record five days, but as Harper was departing
for the women's Base Camp, four days' climb above Namche
Bazar, one of the two women recuperating from altitude
sickness confessed that they had lied to him; in fact, two
women – the French expedition leader and a Belgian woman
were missing. They had kept it from him so that the news
could reach their families before they read about it in the
Express.

Harper set off in pursuit of the expedition's own runners,
who had started several hours earlier with the official news of
the two deaths, and caught up with them on the banks of
Dudh Kosi river, where they waited while he typed out a
story giving details of the tragedy. He then promised them an
even bigger bonus for every day they cut off their journey.
What he did not find out until much later was that two men,
supposedly hunting the legendary yeti, were sending stories
to the *Daily Mail*'s New Delhi stringer who was waiting at an
Indian frontier town where the Sun Kosi river flowed into
India. It had all been masterminded in the London office by
Ralph Izaard who had covered the 1953 Everest expedition.

The result was that the *Mail* had a story that beat Steve's by
a day. To this day he does not know if it was based on
rumours that were rife in Namche or whether one of the yeti
hunters, camped across the route of his runners, had
intercepted them with the detailed story of the two deaths.
What he does know is that a deliberate attempt was made to
get his runners drunk on whisky.

Steve had climbed higher than any reporter had climbed
before, and, while covering the story, had performed feats of
incredible endurance. He had covered the journey to Namche
Bazar in twenty-three days, three less than the normal
trekking time, and had made the trip from there to Katmandu

in eight. But it had all counted for nothing. His own detailed story about the disaster had arrived too late for the *Express*'s last edition, while the *Mail* contained a story, very sketchy, but nevertheless a story. Even worse it was a Saturday, so the *Express* was unable to recoup. The *Sunday Express* had it on the front page.

Steve was able to follow up his original story with a series of page-one splashes which included lots of pictures. But the *Mail* had stolen the initial impact, and he was in the office doghouse for quite a while, until he re-established his reputation in the Congo.

Fortunately, reporters have the ability to laugh at themselves, and the most often recounted stories were those which never appeared in print. One veteran foreign correspondent had a weakness for nubile African girls and on one occasion, quite unknown to him, his amatory encounter was being listened to by a colleague with his ear glued to the wall. When the copulating ended the eavesdropper heard the rustle of money and the off-hand remark, 'Here, buy yourself a new hut.' In no time the story was going the rounds of the Fleet Street pubs. The reporter in question was never sure whether it was a remark he had to live up to or live down.

John Weaver, who was often under fire when covering events in distant trouble spots, was proud of the fact that 'I was the only man to have a woman shot from under me.' It was no idle boast. He was in Cyprus at the time when the island was a hotbed of violence, with General Grivas and Archbishop Makarios campaigning for union with Greece.

One evening he invited a young policewoman out to dinner and took her back to his hotel in the MG sports car he had rented at the paper's expense, with the intention of taking her to his room. But as he approached the hotel he spotted several policemen – among them Joe Mouncey, who helped send Myra Hindley to prison for the Moors Murders and later played a big role in the hunt for the Yorkshire Ripper, who was there investigating the murder of Britons by terrorists. Not wishing to embarrass the girl, John suggested that they should make love in the car. In the confined space of a sports car it required the ability of a contortionist. Unfortunately, an elbow or a knee, he was never quite sure, hit the horn button which woke up two Turkish policemen, who were supposed to be guarding the hotel, and they promptly opened fire on the car. Luckily no one was hurt.

18

SCRUPLES

There is a fine line between what might be called acceptable and unacceptable behaviour among rival newsmen. As I remarked in the last chapter, most reporters bear no malice when scooped, but there are occasions which stick in the memory. I will, for instance, never forget the way in which Randolph Churchill got Derek Marks to spike an exclusive story of mine. It happened at the time when there was immense speculation as to who would succeed Sir Anthony Eden, who had resigned the Premiership for reasons of ill health. There had been several secret meetings at which the long knives had been sharpened, but the general feeling in the office was that the job would go to Mr R.A.B. Butler.

I was given the unenviable job of door-stepping Number 10 Downing Street and listing the comings and goings of the various Cabinet Ministers – a thankless task as it would not produce a single line for the next morning's paper. But I was in good company, and we broke our boring vigil by standing in for each other while we nipped off for a drink.

Mr Butler, the hot favourite, emerged from Number 10 and walked through a narrow passage that led to Horse Guards Parade, and most of the reporters set off in pursuit. Almost immediately afterwards, Harold Macmillan appeared and began to walk down Downing Street. It occurred to me that if you have just become Prime Minister you do not slip out through the back, so I followed Mr Macmillan and caught up with him as he was being met by his wife, Lady Dorothy. But he refused to answer any of the questions fired at him. I continued to follow when everyone else had given up, and at the entrance to Whitehall I asked him on the spur of the moment: 'May I congratulate you, sir?' I cannot recall his exact words, but they were in the affirmative and that was good enough for me. I returned to the office and informed the Editor that Macmillan was the next Prime Minister, and when I told him my story, Derek was sure that I was right.

No one knew the political scene better than Derek, and he proposed to make the story the front-page splash. That is, until Sir Winston's son Randolph Churchill, who wrote for the *Evening Standard*, appeared in the Big Room and assured him that it was Mr Butler. With his political pedigree, he was above contradiction. Derek took his advice and my story was spiked. Next day the first edition of the *Evening Standard* carried a by-line story by Churchill, exclusively announcing that Macmillan was the man. He had known, I suspect, that my story was correct, and he was going to make sure he was not pipped at the post. A picture appeared in the *Express* showing me talking to Mr Macmillan, which brought the rebuke from Derek Marks: 'Do you always keep your hands in your pocket when talking to eminent men?'

Newspapermen may always have been ruthless when it came to beating the opposition, but one thing most of them had in common was a deep respect for the people who read their work. Apart from a few exceptions, they never tried deliberately to deceive them. Unfortunately, it is the black sheep that the public have wrongly assumed to be in the majority, and this has accounted for the mistrust so many people have for the Press. Sadly there is some justification today, for there are newspapers that flagrantly fabricate stories and show no remorse when they are exposed, and consequently give strength to the public's mistrust.

I can remember, when I was still in Fleet Street, the look of sheer incredulity that appeared on the face of my friends when I told them that I knew many newspapermen who would have resigned rather than betray their professional trust. For the doubters, the Press will always have the attributes of the harlot – power without responsibility, as Stanley Baldwin put it. Yet no newspaperman starts out with the wrong intentions, but, with dismissal held over their heads like the Sword of Damocles, some succumb. William Blake could have been thinking of them when he wrote 'Every harlot was a virgin once.'

But many more remained virgo intacta.

Cyril Aynsley, who was shot down over France and spent most of the war in a POW camp, and looks more like a diplomat than the average person's image of a reporter, is a man of immense integrity who just would not be bullied or panicked into writing a story if he was not sure of his facts. And he was prepared to risk his job for that principle. He was one of a large party of reporters gathered at an African airport to meet Dag Hammarskjöld, the Swedish Secretary-General of the UN, who was flying in from the Congo after a peace mission. His arrival was of world-wide importance, but by midnight he had not yet appeared although the rumour got around that he had in fact landed. Pressed for time, most of them cabled their offices with the news of his safe arrival, and one actually attributed some 'safe' and innocuous quotes to the peacemaker. All, that is, except Cyril. The Foreign Desk contacted him urgently, wanting to know why he had not filed, and he replied that he had been unable to confirm it. In fact, Hammarskjöld's body was lying in the wreckage of his plane. It was a hollow triumph for Cyril; no one ever remembers stories that were never written. But his colleagues admired him for his guts. It is so easy to acquiese.

Donald Seaman was my closest friend on the *Express*, and, although he covered stories and wars in many parts of the world, I never knew him to 'fly a kite'. He left The Street many years ago to write very successful books from his cliff-top eyrie on the Dodman in Cornwall. Few men chalked up so many triumphs as Don, yet one story sticks in his mind and continues to torment him. It was an untrue one which he had not written, but which appeared under his by-line. It illustrates once again the perils that often confront the reporter when abroad. It began on the final night of the British evacuation from Suez, forty-eight hours before Christmas in 1956. The Army and Press corps had withdrawn to an ever-shrinking perimeter, awaiting shipment to Famagusta in HMS *Manxman*, one of the Navy's fastest ships. Tension was high, as Lieutenant-General Hugh Stockwell, the Commander-in-Chief, was threatening to delay the withdrawal unless the Egyptians returned a young infantry officer, Lieutenant Moorhouse, who had been kidnapped by a commando snatch group in Port Said. A last-ditch search of the shanty-town area, where he was thought to be being held had failed to find him, and Stockwell was digging his heels in. Owing to the conditions there was only one transmitter available, so all correspondents were limited to a fifty-word cable: a most inadequate number with which to chronicle the death throes of a once proud part of the Empire. Furthermore, each reporter was given a deadline they had to meet. As it was Saturday, Don filed his meagre wordage to the *Sunday Express*. By agreement, the final messages were to be left to the three agency men, and it was further agreed that every office was free to pool their material.

Stockwell was still insisting on the return of the young lieutenant, when a Norwegian UN officer appeared at the barbed-wire fence enclosing the perimeter and asked to speak to the General. In the hearing of the reporters, he said he had just left Moorhouse who, although still in Egyptian hands, was safe and well. For prestige reasons, his captors intended to hold him until the ship sailed. Then he would be repatriated.

Two of the agency men got their copy away while the third waited until the very last minute. Knowing that radio silence would be maintained during the passage to Cyprus, he deliberately delayed filing, aware that this would be the last message. He cabled an exclusive that he was the only reporter who had managed to interview the soldier, and inserted a quote that urged his parents to keep some champagne on ice for his return by Christmas.

He genuinely believed that the young soldier was alive – had he not heard the Norwegian say so? In fact, Moorhouse had been killed by his captors; they had bundled him into a trunk the night of the abortive search and left him to suffocate. The man the Norwegian had seen was someone dressed up to look like Moorhouse.

When Don reached Malta he found the agency copy had been married into his own story, and he was credited with being the only reporter to have seen the soldier before leaving Suez. The other papers attributed the story to the agency.

Don prepared for a Christmas break as no paper was due out till Boxing Day, forgetting that the Scottish *Daily Express* came out as usual. He was awakened around midnight by the

Editor of the Scottish *Daily Express* who told him that doubts had arisen as to whether the young soldier was alive, and since he had spoken to him would he dictate a few words to reassure the anxious family.

Recalling it many years later, Don said bitterly, 'Well, how do you explain away a mistake like that? I'm afraid I chickened out and explained the situation to the Editor, and left it to him. I was wrong, and ever since I have bitterly regretted that I did not act as my conscience dictated there and then, which was to travel to Yorkshire myself – Christmas or no Christmas – and explain to the kid's family what had happened. There was no excuse for the agency man's conduct, although I accept completely he had no idea of the trouble he might be causing – never mind grief – by his action. He wasn't the first to be tempted by the craving for a scoop into dishonesty, and I doubt very much if he'll be the last. But I still feel bad about it. "Ashamed" I think is the right word.'

It takes a great reporter and an even bigger man to be conscience-stricken by an incident so many years afterwards and which most people would have forgotten.

But I can honestly say that through my years in Fleet Street I met more Cyrils and Dons than I did those who jettisoned their integrity for the sake of a transient moment of triumph. I like to think Disraeli got it right when he told the House of Commons, 'I am myself a gentleman of the Press, and I bear no other scutcheon.'

When I was on the *Daily Express* I did myself deliberately fabricate the news – only twice, and each time it was with the full approval of the Editor. I don't mind admitting it, for there was nothing dishonest about them, and, although one was an abuse of a proprietor's responsibilities, the second time was quite enterprising.

Just before Lord Beaverbrook died, his countryman Lord Thomson of Fleet had given a splendid dinner in honour of his eighty-fifth birthday, and Sir Max Aitken wanted to pay a similar tribute to Lord Thomson on the occasion of his eightieth birthday. He also had the idea that, as the hundreds of guests were dining, each would receive, hot from the presses, the First Edition containing a detailed report of the dinner. The trouble was that it meant the report had to be written before they had even taken their places at the dining tables.

I was given the job of writing it – a daunting prospect, for it occurred to me that if something untowards happened, such as the principal guest meeting with an accident on the way to the Dorchester in Park Lane, I could be in real trouble. It was not a fanciful apphrehension, for I recalled a friend who worked on a magazine who told me of a really traumatic experience. Few readers realise that magazines are often prepared weeks in advance, and at the time they were preparing this particular edition, the man who contributed the regular horoscope column was off sick with a very minor ailment. The person deputising for him consulted the stars, and was able to console readers that he would shortly be back. Unfortunately, the regular man died a couple of days before the issue hit the news stands. Not only did the magazine look foolish, but the reputation of the man who had consulted the stars took a fearful denting. Naturally I did not relish the idea of being known as the author of a piece about the man who did not come to dinner.

All togged up in my Moss Bros hired dinner jacket, I sat down at my typewriter, and began to write against the clock. All I had to go on were the cuttings the library had on Lord Thomson, a copy of *Who's Who*, and a menu with a Giles cartoon showing a smiling Lord Thomson in yachting cap surrounded by tiny paper boats made from some of the two hundred newspapers he owned. A cake with a single candle said, 'Roy-boy. Many happy returns'. Fortunately, the menu contained a guest list. One thing worried me, though, and that was that I had been told it was his Lordship's eightieth birthday, while by my calculations he was only seventy-eight, I therefore left his age out, telling the Back Bench I thought someone had slipped up when planning the event.

The pages were ripped out of my machine as soon as they were finished and by the time I had tapped out 'Ends', I was bathed in perspiration. Then I caught a taxi to the Dorchester for the job of up-dating the story as the evening progressed. I dashed in as the guests – literally hundreds – were taking their places, and asked where my table was. I was escorted to one behind a pillar. It had to be the Press table; I could just about see the top table, and if I craned my head hear what was being said. I heaved a visible sigh of relief when Lord Thomson arrived and was photographed with Sir Max. At least they had made it.

When the special First Edition was brought in and circulated round the tables, I grabbed mine with a shaking hand. What I had written would happen had. Under a bold headline and a big by-line was my story: 'They came in their hundreds to The Dorchester Hotel, London, last night to honour a Toronto barber's son who became a legend in his own lifetime – Lord Thomson.'

I looked around for the people I had said were there ... Ted Heath, the Prime Minister; Harold Wilson, Leader of the Opposition, and anybody else I could recognise. They were all there.

The band of the Royal Marines played what I had said they would, as the guests tucked into the meal I had said they enjoyed so much. The story filled three complete columns, most of it details of Lord Thomson's life culled from the cuttings.

I can't say I enjoyed the food or drink myself, for the simple reason I did not have much of it. Every few minutes I had to get up and race to the telephone to bring the story up to date. I only had a sip of the Bollinger champagne and a nibble of the fillet of salmon cooked in white wine, for when I got back to the table the next course, roast saddle of lamb with rosemary, haricot beans, courgettes and new potatoes, had already been served along with the Château Grand Laros 1961 St Julien. That suffered the same fate.

Not only was I hungry but I was thirsty, so I nipped out and had a beer in the bar. Cyril Aynsley, who took a good shorthand note, took over.

Lord Thomson made a brilliant speech, so did Ted Heath. But my to-ing and fro-ing to the telephone went on as I continued to add the odd touch of colour. I even missed out on the cheese course which was Cricket Malherbie, produced at Lord Beaverbrook's farm in the West Country. It is a famous cheese which has won many awards, but what was resting on my plate looked very much like ordinary mousetrap. My waiter had pulled a fast one: he presumably thought that such a rare delight would be wasted on me.

I wondered, when it was all over and the guests had departed clutching their still ink-wet editions, if any of them realised the story had been written long before they had left their homes. It seemed to me at the time that it was not the function of one newspaper to go to so much trouble to flatter another newspaper's proprietor. Why could he not have waited for the tribute to have taken place first, like any ordinary reader was expected to? It was a gimmick which did not enhance the *Express*'s proud reputation. It was an abuse of an owner's responsibility. But I had dutifully sung for my supper, even if I did not get much, and I have no right to object at this stage. Clearly my own sense of values was more elastic in those days.

The next occasion I was called on to repeat the performance was when Sir Francis Chichester was nearing the end of his epic single-handed sailing trip round the world. But it was justifiable and showed newspaper enterprise and team work at its best.

The *Express* had an enormous team covering the event which had captured the imagination of the entire country. An elderly man who had been written off as a cancer victim, had not only defied the doctors, he had defied the perils of some of the most inhospitable seas in the world. And the paper was going to do him proud. There were reporters and photographers following *Gipsy Moth IV* in specially chartered ships and boats. Money was no object, and we even hired the motor vessel *Queen of the Isles*. We were also patrolling the sky in RAF Transport Command aircraft, and there were more men in our own specially chartered plane. Others had smaller craft, and reporters were posted at strategic points along the coastline where beacons burned brightly, last lighted to warn Sir Francis Drake of the arrival of the Spanish Armada.

Half a million visitors and 10,000 cars had descended on Plymouth, and as all accommodation had long since been gobbled up, thousands were forced to sleep in the open or in their cars. The *Express* virtually took over a guest house near the Hoe, which guaranteed we had a telephone, on which we kept the line open to the office.

On the Saturday, the *Sunday Express* managed to get a

front-page splash out of Sir Francis's progress by steaming alongside his small yacht and receiving relayed messages from the escorting naval vessels. Then he was almost becalmed, and it was feared his arrival would be delayed until late Monday or even Tuesday. He had been at sea for 118 days, and we who were waiting in Plymouth were biting our nails for some hours. The famous naval town had planned a hero's welcome, and if he arrived at the wrong time the evening papers would scoop the pool. Apart from that, ITV, which had put a camera crew aboard *Gipsy Moth*, was in a position to transmit live pictures, an ominous reminder that an enterprising challenger had arrived on the scene to question the hitherto acknowledged supremacy of Fleet Street.

I was given the job of writing the front-page splash for the first edition, which would go to bed long before Sir Francis entered the harbour, as the West Country edition was printed in London and had to travel down by train. I was working in harness with Mike Charleston, the *Express*'s Plymouth man, who was reporting direct from sea. All I had to go on was the official programme. I hammered out the story and phoned it over, and told the office to have it set but to hold on to it until I gave the go ahead. I kept my fingers crossed as I walked down to the Hoe to see how things were shaping. Our greatest fear was that he would be forced to anchor offshore for the night, then my story would be spiked. An equally grave fear was that his yacht would be sunk by one of the hundreds of big ships and smaller craft which were milling around it blowing sirens and tooting klaxons.

Then I heard the welcoming boom of the gun on the breakwater fort and saw the signal flag ZU, meaning welcome, hoisted on a halyard, and I knew the 35-foot ketch had crossed the official finishing line. It was 8.56 p.m., and the precise time was the only addition I made to the story. The first edition had a big photograph of Sir Francis on the front page – it was taken in London by a photographer watching television.

It had been a race against time, for us as well as for Sir Francis, as it was getting dark and any further delays would have almost certainly ruled out the possibility of him making harbour that night. The front-page headline proclaimed: 'By the skin of his teeth,' but it referred more to our efforts than his.

It was a brilliant piece of team work, and we wondered if any of our readers realised how we had got an edition beat.

From then on it was a process of up-dating the story, and soon every member of the team was busy filing copy. We darted from place to place to cover every angle; sometimes we phoned over no more than a paragraph, but the flow was continuous. By the time the last edition went to bed, the story filled the front page and spread over to pages 5, 6, 11 and 12.

There was an amusing side to the story which our office and readers never learned about – we made sure of that. Too late in the day, we discovered a television crew had been filming us at work for a documentary depicting how Fleet Street had covered the event. If we had been told, we would have co-operated wholeheartedly and would have presented ourselves in the manner our offices expected. But concealed mikes and cameras had been employed to catch us as we really were, and that was not very flattering. Several of us bundled into a car and made a very strong protest at the studio and sought an assurance that certain bits would be eliminated. One of them was a 'bugged' incident in an hotel bar, where a senior *Express* man ordered a vast round of drinks saying, 'Have this one on Beaverbrook Newspapers.' Others had been filmed and recorded using words that would have made a Billingsgate fish porter blush. One of the *Telegraph*'s top reporters was filmed dictating copy and using phrases, not for inclusion in his copy, which were entirely out of keeping for a newspaper read by gaitered bishops and others who thought the use of the word 'damn' was a passport to perdition.

We watched the programme with great trepidation, and rose at the end heaving profound sighs of relief. While we had not emerged as boys taking their First Communion, neither had we been depicted as the uncouth louts we often were. Our sworn opponents had embraced us and adopted our motto – 'Dog doesn't eat dog'.

19

THE GREAT HAMSTER
JAIL BREAK

One of the strangest and most hilarious stories I covered for the *Express* was blazoned all over the front page under a massive three-decker headline, 'The Great Hamster Jail Break'. It ran for three days and was described as the most astonishing story to come out of prison. That certainly was no overstatement. It had all the ingredients for a Peter Sellers comedy. And it dropped into my lap by sheer chance. Security in Britain's prisons was attracting a great deal of public interest at the time, and I had become acquainted with a well-known underworld figure while looking for background material from people who had seen the inside of a cell in a maximum security unit. We were having a drink from his well-stocked trolley in his ostentatiously furnished council flat when he suddenly asked me if I was interested in buying an exclusive story. The sum he mentioned was far too big for me to make an on-the-spot decision, and I explained that I would have to obtain the Editor's permission, but before I did that I needed to know what he was selling.

He could see the point of that, and he rapidly outlined the story: a major break-out, complete with fast getaway cars, had been planned at Durham Jail's maximum-security E-wing, but months of work on a tunnel had been ruined by a premature escape bid by three men who couldn't wait any longer. That hardly seemed worth the kind of money he was talking about until he produced a pile of letters smuggled out by one of the ringleaders. It made the Wooden Horse sound like a clumsy effort. The letters were all written in the underworld vernacular, gave a day-to-day progress report, and contained rough drawings of the work carried out, and the tools they had made to achieve the break-out from the 'escape-proof' jail. But what really sold the story to me was the fact that they had used a pet hamster with a length of string tied to a hind leg to measure the length of their tunnel.

I hailed a taxi and went straight in to the Editor and outlined the story. He conferred with one of his executives, a rather flamboyant Australian, who talked about 'writing sticks' instead of pencils, and 'talking trumpets' for telephones, and 'wheels' when he meant a motor car. Anyone who talked like that could not resist urging the Editor to buy the story. An hour later I was on my way back to the flat in the office 'wheels' with an envelope bulging with crisp new fivers. I handed over the cash, and the letters and drawings were passed over. The pile of notes was lying on the table when there was a thunderous knock on the door and one of the men present in the room announced it was the police. No one made any attempt to conceal the cash, so I kicked it under the settee before heading for the door like a scalded cat. If it was a raid I did not want to have to do any explaining. The office would certainly wash their hands of me. (As it turned out, 'the Bill' had just dropped in for a drink.)

When I got back to the office I was able to peruse the letters at leisure, and I realised that every pound had been well spent. The centre for the break-out was the shower room in E-Wing, where the escapers used to spend three hours at a time taking Turkish baths. It was not an obsession with cleanliness, but because the steam was so dense it provided a smoke screen for their activities and prevented the warders seeing what was going on. Apart from that, it helped the men to slim: 'It would be awful getting stuck in the hole,' as the letter-writer remarked.

The debris from the tunnel and the wall they had to breach was thrown out of the cell windows on to a convenient pile of rubble made by workmen digging new drains. All the tools were fashioned and tempered in the prison's machine and blacksmith's shop, and the sewing room was used to make rope and sheet ladders which were tested on a device in the gym. A lamp to illuminate the tunnel was made from a tin, with a rag dipped in machine-oil for a wick.

But it was the letters which made the story, written as they were in the vein of a second-rate gangster novel. They were so unconsciously funny that Giles used the hamster for his cartoon that day.

We made a right fuss of the hamster (poor sod). He lives on the fat of the land. He will look like a cow if we give him much more milk … We are working on the hole in twos. Two in the shower and two outside on the weights making a lot of noise. It is hell in the showers because we have the five showers full on pouring out hot water for two hours at a time. I do not think it could be any hotter in hell. But we have got to do it to get lots of steam up so if any of the screws look in they can't see a thing. We have lost a few pounds in weight, but we love it.

To cover the noise of the digging, some of the plotters took up weight-lifting, and puzzled the warders by the way they kept dropping the weights. The gaps made by removed bricks were covered with papier maché painted to resemble the real thing. On one occasion one of the prisoner's feet were actually sticking out of the hole they had dug, but the warder did not notice. And on another a warder inadvertently helped them by accidentally knocking a hole in the wall, which turned out to be hollow, with a rawlplug tool.

We bag the sand up in small bags and put it down the toilet. We have all made out that we have the runs because we are in and out of the toilet all day. The digging is tough. If we do get out we deserve a medal each.

One of the most difficult tasks was to smuggle the handmade tools into the shower room, because a prison officer with a metal detector body-scanned everyone leaving the workshop.

One of the chaps says, 'How about trying the metal flask we have our tea in?' We looked at each other and one of the cons says: 'I have a good chance because I always come out with something funny when they run the machine over me.' So we try a small nut and bolt in the flask. It works, and we have a right old laugh about it because I was saying to the one who was going over me with the machine: 'You better open the flask and take the file out.' He just gives me a smile.

As the weeks passed and the work progressed the plotters were confident of success. 'We are all talking like Hank Jansen and Mickey Spillane. It's sweet death or glory. We are all willing to take our chance at the wall and God help anyone who tries to stop us.' And as the final stages were approached, they became positively buoyant:

We might have triple sets of bars in our cells (the third electrified) and alarms on our doors. But, boy, what a shock the screws will have when we go. We can just see their faces now. How many heads will roll – starting from the top and slowly working down to the screws. We'll give them maximum-security block!

Clearly there were some old scores to be settled when they did get out: 'There will be quite a few out there in London in a panic when it comes over the telly in the pubs and clubs.' That the letters could be smuggled out may have been a public scandal, but they made lively reading, and the language used was a greater indictment of inefficiency than any outraged editorial.

I have sent a plan of our way out. Once outside the shower the walls are only a few yards away. We have the rope and bits of iron put together to make a ladder. The cars and clothes and other gear will be waiting in the court car park outside.

Even so, the writer suffered twinges of conscience about the fate of the Assistant Governor when the break-out succeeded:

He is really a great chap and helps us all he can. I could not help thinking what would happen to him when we go. I know I am on the wrong side of the fence to him, but if I was to see him outside I would offer him a drink; that is the sort of chap he is. (I am not going soft in my old age).

The final letter read:

It is all easy work from now on. Only a few feet to go. We really had a right go today. We have had no more trouble with the papier maché falling out. We have ten bricks filling in the front of the hole and the papier maché over it. I don't mind saying it, it looks really good. Let's hope it works when we get to the wall and in one of them fast cars without any fireworks going off. First one over gets the prize for not helping the others (it's a joke man).

The plotters had been working for three months, but it all came to nothing when three of them couldn't wait one day longer. I was glad it had failed, for the men included some of Britain's most dangerous prisoners, and no one knows what mayhem they would have created on the run. In any case, I only got the story because it failed. Most of the three-day serial had been written for me by one of the ringleaders, but I still shudder when I recall the pay-off sentence inserted by a sub-editor who got carried away: 'The best-laid plans of hamsters and men had gone agley again.'

I had a letter from Derek Marks next day: 'Dear Alf, I am most grateful to you for your part in obtaining the Durham Jailbreak story and I am awarding you an immediate bonus of £20.'

My expenses for that week included one item, 'Payment for information ... ' which made my bonus seem like a tip. I used it to buy paint for the outside of the house, and I looked on my children's hamster with newfound respect.

But did the exposure ruffle any feathers in high quarters? A statement from the Inspector of Prisons read: 'I am satisfied that the prison is adequately staffed, but there are alterations that need to be made.'

I covered many famous jailbreaks, and, apart from two of them, I had no sympathy for the people who 'went over the wall', no matter how much ingenuity and skill they employed. Most of them deserved to be behind bars, and I saw nothing Houdini-like in their antics. Whatever social reformers and penologists may claim, most of us crime reporters honestly believed that there were professional criminals who would never see the error of their ways. Crime does not pay may be a commonly expressed assertion, but it is no more than wishful thinking. Crime does pay, and handsomely, for a minimum of effort – and most crooks, whether they have escaped, or have served their time, cannot wait to resume their chosen profession.

Alfred Hinds was one of the exceptions. His numerous escapes, were all aimed at clearing his name, and he was genuinely entitled to the *Express*'s description of 'the escaper extraordinary'. He was jailed for twelve years for his part in what became known as the Maples robbery, and spent ten years and 227 days in prison before clearing his name.

I covered some of his break-outs and got to know him reasonably well, and became convinced he had been wrongfully imprisoned. It wasn't just the sheer tenacity with which he pursued his claim, but the brilliance he displayed in court as his own advocate; and he made no secret of the fact that he had a criminal record. But on other occasions, when caught, he accepted his punishment; he would not give up over the Maples case.

He did not look like the master criminal he was alleged to be. He had a gnomish face, thinning hair, and thick glasses, which gave him a scholarly appearance. He was certainly one of the brainiest men I have met, and later in life he became a member of Mensa. He also had an acute sense of humour, and even when he spoke ill of anyone it was with a twinkle. On one occasion he recounted to me how, when he was on remand in prison awaiting trial for the Maples robbery, he learned that it had been postponed, and that Lord Goddard, the Lord Chief Justice, was interrupting his holiday in France personally to try the case.

A prison officer read about it in the newspaper and said to me, 'Have you read the news?'

'No,' I replied.

'Lord Goddard is taking your case.'

'That's what I want,' I told him. In my innocence I thought the head of the judiciary would give the matter a fair hearing.

'Take my advice and go sick.' And he warned me to watch the judge and see when he started picking his nose. 'He does that as soon as he's decided a man is guilty.'

When the jury had been sworn in and Christmas Humphreys opened the case for the Crown, I noticed that Goddard was picking his nose.

Hinds related it to me in a light-hearted manner, but I could sense that he felt he had been the victim of a miscarriage of justice. He was sentenced to twelve years' preventive detention. He appealed but it was disallowed, and from that moment onwards he never ceased to fight against what he considered a police frame-up. He had hundreds of pamphlets secretly printed, urging a review of his case, which were sent to MPs and other influential persons. But when his efforts to have his case reviewed failed, he decided to escape.

The first of many was from Nottingham Prison, although he claimed he did not break out but merely walked out, which was not a criminal offence but simply a breach of prison rules. He went to Ireland and continued to argue his case, always supported by his wife Lila. As a skilled carpenter and a competent car mechanic, he had no difficulty in finding work in the Republic, and every moment of his spare time was spent attending law lectures at Trinity College and building up a private library of legal books.

Hinds remained at liberty for eight months before he was arrested by the Irish police and handed over to Scotland Yard and returned to prison.

With his law books available to him in his cell, he continued his fight. It is too long and complicated to go into in detail, but suffice it to say that he had studied enough to obtain a hearing at the Law Courts in the Strand – from which he also escaped by means of an audacious plan, which earned him the grudging respect of millions. He eluded the two prison officers meant to be guarding him by slipping a padlock through two screw-eyes which had been attached to a toilet door and locking them inside. I was one of the team which covered the hue and cry which ensued. He did not get far, however; he was arrested at Bristol Airport on his way back to Dublin.

Now rated a security risk, he was transferred to Chelmsford and it was not long before I was there covering his next escape. He again reached Dublin where he adopted the name of William Herbert Bishop. The second name was chosen because it was the Christian name of Bert Sparks, the detective he claimed had framed him. Once back in Dublin he continued his legal battle during the twenty months he remained at liberty. But he was arrested in Belfast for smuggling cars across the border and knew that, once his fingerprints were taken, his true identity would be revealed.

Lila, his wife, had meanwhile arrived, escorted by *News of the World* reporters who were anxious to buy his story. I travelled over at the same time, but was never permitted to get close to her, and as soon as they arrived in Dublin a waiting taxi whisked them away. I set off in pursuit, but soon lost them. However, I was travelling in a taxi from the same company, and over the wireless system I heard their driver request assistance as they had broken down. I promptly told my driver to ask them where they were and tell them we would arrive within minutes. Unsuspectingly, their driver obliged, and I persuaded the *News of the World* team that it was a waste of time trying to throw me off – I would track them down wherever they went.

At their hotel I was introduced to Lila, and managed to convince the *News of the World* men that it was in their best interest to let me talk to her every day – if I did a regular story it could only arouse greater interest in the story they were planning.

Hinds was sentenced to six months for the car-smuggling, during which time he continued to argue his innocence in the Maples case. He also played for time against being handed over to Scotland Yard, but even his knowledge of the law could not stave off the inevitable, and he was handed over to a Yard detective at the expiration of his sentence. He then refused to board the aircraft on the grounds that he was too ill to travel, and the pilot acquiesed. But it was only a temporary delay, and he was soon returned to Pentonville Prison.

In December 1960 he made the first of a number of appearances before the Appeals Committee of the House of Lords, where he conducted his own case with a brilliance that was admitted by many legal experts. They were all to no avail, however.

He was then transferred to Parkhurst on the Isle of Wight, where one day he was listening to a radio interview with Detective Superintendent Sparks, now retired, in which the former police officer said he had written a series of articles for the *Sunday Pictorial*, one of which would tell how he had outwitted Alfred Hinds.

Hinds's legal studies had not been in vain, for he recalled that a man named Glinski, who had been involved in the Jack Spot case and been acquitted, had subsequently sued Sparks for perjury, in a case which was settled out of court. Hinds managed to get a copy of the *Sunday Pictorial* and sued for libel. It was a long case, which amounted to a re-trial of the Maples robbery. Hinds, brilliantly represented by Mr James Comyn, won and was awarded £1,300 damages. The jury found he had not taken part in the Maples robbery.

I later saw Hinds several times at his home in Leyton, East London, where he and Lila talked at great length about the long struggle to clear his name. He bore very little malice, and I believed him when he said he had no desire for revenge against Sparks. He told me he was planning to write a book which he proposed to call *Contempt of Court*, I thought that the title was his personal opinion of English law. It was not. It was only when I read his book that I discovered it was an exposure of the country's judicial system. 'My quarrel,' he wrote, 'is with many of the men who have elected to dispense justice. I believe they have by the way they have dealt with me in so many of my cases, shown themselves guilty, in the broader, non-legal sense of the phrase, of contempt of court.' Soon afterwards I lost touch with Hinds, but I heard that he had become an extremely successful business man.

I do not know enough about the law to accept or reject Hinds's strictures. I only know I admired his fight to clear his name. But I do remember an American, at a meeting of international lawyers, who said to me with a wry smile that he had once asked a London taxi driver to take him to the Royal Courts of Justice. 'Where's that, guv?' asked the cabbie. 'In the Strand,' replied the lawyer. 'Oh – you mean the Law Courts.'

The other exception was Goldie, a huge eagle who twice escaped from his cage at the London Zoo, made headlines all over the world, and captured the hearts of millions of people. The bird was attributed with human qualities because of the way he managed to elude every capture attempt. Hundreds of people gathered daily in Regents Park to watch his antics, and for twelve days he put on a magnificent show, dive-bombing his old cage to pay court to his mate Regina, and showing a total disdain for the experts who pronounced he would be better off behind bars perched above a chunk of butcher's meat, instead of spreading his wings above London's chimney pots and dining on the plentiful ducks in the Park's boating lake.

The most ingenious ideas were introduced to put him back behind bars, including the appearance of a pet golden eagle named Random, owned by a gentleman from Hampshire. The idea was that Random, who had acquired a reputation as something of a Mick MacManus of the eagle world, would be staked at the base of a tree and given a dead hare to peck at. Concealed above him was a spring-loaded net. In theory, Goldie would join him for lunch, and Random would then fasten on to him and force a submission. Goldie stayed up in the higher branches of a tall tree, surveying the set-up, and decided not to enter the arena – as far as he was concerned it was a fixed fight.

The Zoo was inundated with callers making suggestions, which included helicopters dropping nets over the tree he perched in, and attaching a steak to a balloon filled with gas which would knock Goldie out when he grabbed the meat and punctured the balloon.

I covered the story for the *Express*, and had a side-bet with the *Mirror* man as to who could get the most number of clichés into his story. We both did well, but he conceded I had earned the pint when I ended another day of freedom with 'It had been a hard day's flight.' Nothing he wrote was as abysmally corny.

To everyone's regret, the show came to an end when the curtain was rung down with Goldie's capture. I visited him in his cage where he sat immobile and inscrutable on a wooden pole, which I was assured was far better than any lofty oak. He did not seem to agree.

Of course, when Goldie did a repeat performance I was sent hot-foot to Regent's Park as I qualified as the paper's eagle expert.

Again the Zoo switchboard was jammed with calls from places as far away as Japan, America and Australia: 'It's been like a Test Match with people ringing up and asking for the latest score,' an official told me.

The escape was also raised in the House of Commons, where a pompous MP wanted to know what the Minister of Works was going to do about helping in Goldie's recapture, seeing that the bird was occupying a royal park.

When Goldie was finally recaptured he was put into a maximum-security cage with double doors. As far as I was concerned he should have been rewarded, not punished, and encouraged to fly the coop at regular intervals. He became such a national hero that turnstiles at the Zoo clicked like typewriters.

20

THE KRAY TWINS

Dartmoor is no place to be at any time, least of all December, but that is where I found myself just before Christmas 1966. Below the title on the front page of that morning's *Daily Express* was the weather forecast: 'a foggy start and generally dull', and the Met Office was right; the mist was so thick and swirling that the beam of my car's headlights just bounced off it. But my problems were nothing compared with those of the hundreds of commandos, prison officers, policemen and helicopter pilots who were scouring the barren moors for one of the country's most violent criminals, who had escaped from the famous prison. His name was Frank Ellis Mitchell, and he had been sentenced to life imprisonment for robbery with violence. At his trial, the thirty-seven-year-old, sometimes referred to as 'the mad axeman', had warned: 'I am sane. No prison will ever hold me. I will die first.'

And now he had proved it was no idle boast. He had escaped from Rampton, the prison for the criminally insane, in 1957, and while on the run had kept a young couple and their baby hostage in their home, for which he was sentenced on his recapture. He was also sentenced to nine years for attempting to murder a man, and to the 'cat' for attacking warders. He was sent to Broadmoor, another maximum-security prison for the criminally insane, but eighteen months later he escaped. When he was again recaptured he was sent to Dartmoor, the granite fortress built by Napoleonic prisoners-of-war. People had been known to break out, but they seldom remained at liberty for long: the inhospitable moor usually forced them to give themselves up. But Mitchell seemed to have vanished into the enveloping mist. What

aroused countrywide indignation was the disclosure that he
had slipped away during a sudden hailstorm while on a
working party sent out to repair fences. With his record it
seemed unbelievable that he should have been allowed out. As
soon as he disappeared messages were broadcast: 'This man is
extremely dangerous', and people in the area were advised to
lock and bolt their doors and keep their children indoors.

Yet the Home Office, with remarkable complacency,
confirmed that he had been working outside for two years.
'The stage at which a prisoner is considered for outside work
is considered in the light of all the available circumstances,
including both his past history and his present behaviour,'
said a spokesman. Dartmoor staff had repeatedly protested,
but had been overruled.

Mitchell – a Goliath of a man, well over six foot tall, with
the physique of a Charles Atlas – was a keep-fit fanatic who
could lift two men in his hands. As the team of reporters
joined in the hunt, we debated among ourselves what we
would do if we encountered him; the unanimous decision was
to beat a hasty retreat. Some of us had covered his previous
escapes and knew better than to consider him harmless.

As the search dragged on an incredible story emerged of
what Mitchell had been allowed to do. The wife of a farmer
related to us how scared she was when Mitchell and his fellow
convicts dropped in for tea, but when she had protested she
had been assured that he was as 'harmless as a kitten'. We also
discovered that he had been in the habit of popping in to the
Peter Tavy Inn for lunch and cider. For recreation he used to
ride the wild Dartmoor ponies. And such was the fear other
prisoners had of him that he had been able to recruit his own
retinue of servants – one to clean his shoes, another to tidy his
cell, and another to massage his muscles. He was also supplied
with plenty of 'snout' (tobacco) and had his own radio. It
also emerged that he had been in the habit of lifting up
warders to demonstrate his strength, yet no disciplinary
action had ever been taken. To add to the public unease, when
I interviewed a friend of Mitchell's who had recently been
released from the prison, he said, 'I knew Frank was going to
escape. He told me.'

The next day it was announced that a member of the

Mountbatten jail-security team had begun a separate inquiry into Mitchell's escape and the disclosures about his privileged treatment. (The Mountbatten inquiry had been ordered following the escape from prison of the spy George Blake in circumstances which have never been satisfactorily explained but which revealed an astonishing laxity in prison security.)

I wrote for the *Express* a front-page splash which could not have filled Mr Robert Mark, then Chief Constable of Leicester, and later Commissioner for the Metropolitan Police, with much confidence. Below the headline announcing the inquiry there was another which said, 'And the pantomime season opens one week early.' It was not a flippant observation. Mitchell had been allowed to do just as he pleased. I wrote about the taxi driver from Mary Tavy who had driven Mitchell to a pet shop in Tavistock to buy a budgerigar. The landlord of a public house, the Elephant's Nest, had booked him over the telephone to collect a customer neither realised that this customer was a convict with a long history of violence. 'When I picked him up he was very apologetic for being late,' the driver told me. 'He was out of breath and explained he had been running.'

In Tavistock Mitchell bought the bird for 30 shillings and put it into a cardboard box. The fare was 12 shillings, to which Mitchell added 5 shillings as a tip. 'He said he had a gang of men working for him at Baggator, digging trenches. I asked him if he was working for a farmer. He said no, it was more secure – he had a Government contract.'

It was from the working party there that he later escaped.

The stories that were emerging were so incredible that one tended to forget just how dangerous he was, but I felt that they were far more likely to achieve a tightening-up of security than anything else. As more details were unearthed about Mitchell's mode of life, the demands for the Home Secretary's resignation increased. A Commons motion tabled by prominent Tory backbenchers recommended that he 'should resign his office forthwith'. Of course, he did not.

When I went to the Elephant's Nest, the landlord's wife told me 'He drank a lot and always took a lot away with him – orders for £10, £12, £14. He was a big spender – and I have lost a good customer.' And at another pub he drank cider, cherry brandy and orange curaçao, and took away bottles of gin, whisky, vodka and cartons of cigarettes.

The Governor commented ruefully, 'I wish I had time to get away for a drink.'

It could have served as a pilot script for *Porridge*, the television series which became a top hit many years later with its send-up of prison life.

Naturally, a scapegoat had to be found, and he was an ex-Governor of the prison who had retired and was living in New Zealand. The *Express* interviewed him at his home where he sorrowfully accepted the time-honoured system that someone, preferably half the world away, should be left holding the baby.

The hunt meanwhile had produced some important clues. Mitchell's prison clothing was found behind a hedge, and it was discovered that he had been picked up by a car, and that he was armed with a knife.

During our own investigations, we discovered that two East Enders some time previously had called at a public house on the Moor, and from the rough-and-ready descriptions we were given we were pretty sure they were the notorious Kray twins, then the acknowledged bosses of London's underworld. Arrangements were made for photographs to be rushed down to us by train to confirm our suspicions. Naturally we were unable to name them publicly, but Percy Hoskins and I went as far as was legally possible. We wrote that Mitchell was being harboured by two hoodlums. To dot the Is and cross the Ts we added, 'The place is within a square mile of Hackney town hall in Mare Street.' That was the heart of Kray territory. Ronnie Kray had first met Mitchell in prison, and after his release used to write to Mitchell and to send him presents, and regularly visited him with Reggie.

Mitchell never lived to regret his escape from Dartmoor. He was murdered, but his body was never found and no one was convicted of his murder. Reggie and Ronnie admitted to helping him to escape and harbouring him, but strenuously denied having anything to do with his alleged murder.

As I write I have in front of me a long letter written by a man who worked for The Firm, as the Krays' criminal empire came to be called. It begins:

Alf,
Here is the true story on everything that Mitchell said and
the things he would do on his last 12 days before he was
murdered. I would like to no [sic] if you could use it as a
true story on your paper.

I was never able to use it, but it did confirm something I
was told: that Mitchell was 'sprung' so that he could enjoy
just Christmas at liberty. Trouble began when he refused to
return after he had sent a series of letters to the Press pleading
to be given a date for his release. It had also been arranged for
him to telephone Tom Tullett of the *Mirror* to say he was
going to give himself up. He never did.
During the time he was hidden away, I learnt, Mitchell
became more and more morose, and a girl was laid on to keep
him company. One night a van arrived to drive Mitchell into
the country. The letter ends with:

A few minutes later, the few people left standing in the hall
hear gunshots. [The girl] screams, 'They have shot him.
They have shot him.' 'Has Mitchell got a gun with him?'
—— cries out. 'I don't think so,' says [the girl], her voice
breaking. They ran to the window and saw the van
disappear into the distance. The End.

The mystery of what happened to Mitchell's body and who
pulled the trigger will for ever remain unsolved.

On Tuesday 4 March 1969 I was sitting at the reporters' table
in Court Number One at the Old Bailey when the jury
returned and announced they had found the Kray twins
guilty of the murders of George Cornell, another gangster,
and Jack 'The Hat' McVitie, a small-time crook. Their elder
brother Charlie was convicted as an accessory to the murder
of McVitie by helping to dispose of his body which was never
found.
Massive sentences were passed on them and on several
other members of The Firm, and the vast empire of crime
which the Krays had ruled over for years was toppled.
Philip Finn, another *Express* reporter, and I went over to
the Magpie and Stump and celebrated, for it had ended for us
months of background research into the lives of the identical

twins who boasted they were above the law. We were mightily relieved, for we knew that if the Krays had walked out free men they would not have overlooked the attention we had given to their activities. But we were not alone in feeling a deep sense of relief. There were many people who had been given round-the-clock police protection for fear that the Krays would have had them silenced.

Since my novitiate days on the *Daily Herald*, I had known that the Kray twins considered themselves the unchallenged bosses of London's underworld. It was a knowledge shared by everyone who covered the crime beat. There were other well-known criminals in that twilight fraternity, but they had no desire to be heralded as gangsters, and, as far as the public was concerned, they tried to maintain a low profile, and waxed indignant whenever anyone suggested they were anything but hard-working businessmen intent on earning an honest crust. Reggie and Ronnie Kray, on the other hand, flaunted their villainy, and it always amazed reporters that they managed to survive so long. It was openly rumoured that they had a number of policemen on their payroll, which explained their apparent immunity.

They began as rather brash small-time crooks, their activities giving little indication that one day they would rule a vast criminal organisation engaged in the most sophisticated crimes. They themselves, however, were semi-illiterate, and relied entirely on violence to achieve their aims. And when it came to that, they had no equals; a man who jokingly remarked that Ronnie was putting on weight was razor-slashed so badly that he needed seventy stitches to repair the damage. A member of The Firm admitted to having witnessed beatings that were totally unnecessary, even by gangland standards, and razor-slashings administered for the sheer hell of it.

Even at the zenith of their power, when they had amassed a vast fortune and had a country house and luxury flats in town, they preferred to spend most of their time in the East End where they were born and raised. They lived in a dreary terrace house in Vallance Road in the sprawling slum area of Bethnal Green. It was known as 'Fort Vallance' – Ronnie had visions of turning it into an impregnable stronghold similar to the one in the film *Scarface* – and its exterior was extremely misleading: inside it resembled a Mayfair apartment; outside it stood a large American limousine grinning chromium. There they were looked after by their adoring mother, Violet, who referred to them as 'my lovely boys', even at the height of their infamy.

From early childhood they were inseparable, and at school no one dared to cross them – their motto was: 'Fight one, fight us both'. They had reputations for being useful scrappers, thanks to the tuition they got from their grandfather Cannonball Lee, an old-time boxing pro. (When I met him, in his nineties and near blind, he did little but boast of his prowess with his mitts.) When they were evacuated during the early days of the war, the twins revealed a sadistic streak that was never to desert them. One of their first known offences was to kill a pet cockerel for the fun of it. But, despite the threat of Hitler's bombers, they could not resist the lure of the East End and they saw the Blitz through from the shelter of nearby railways arches.

As teenage tearaways they frequently escaped punishment by exploiting their uncanny resemblance to each other, protesting, 'It wasn't me – it was him.'

They became talented boxers, and proof of their prowess were the hundreds of trophies which adorned the house in Vallance Road. They later turned professional, and, although they did not make the big time, their record was quite impressive. But as far as they were concerned, it was not a noble art and the Marquis of Queensberry did not exist. In any case, they soon realised there were easier pickings to be had than the meagre purses they fought for. They did not drift into crime, neither were they lured into it. It was their vocation. After a spell in the Army – much of it in detention for violence – they took jobs for which they were amply qualified: bouncers in a night club. Soon afterwards they branched out and muscled their way into the protection racket, and also began to 'cut' themselves into businesses others had established. Cut had more than one connotation for them.

In gangland vernacular, in which he revelled, Ronnie first

had his 'collar felt' when he walked into a pub and stabbed a
man with a bayonet. He was jailed for three years, but in
prison it soon became apparent that he was mentally unstable
and he was transferred to a mental hospital. He was not there
long. One day Reggie paid him a visit, and it was Ronnie who
walked out at the end. When his brother was well clear,
Reggie disclosed his identity. Ronnie claimed he had escaped
to prove his sanity, but when he gave himself up he was sent
back to hospital. When he was released the twins went into
organised crime on a big scale. In addition to the protection
racket, they opened the Double R Club, whose sign was their
intermingled initials.

By then they were the undisputed bosses of the East End,
but they wanted something more in keeping with the image
they had of themselves. With the aid of Peter Rachman,
whose terrorising of tenants introduced a new word into the
English language, they bought their way into fashionable
Esmerelda's Barn, a gambling club in Knightsbridge
frequented by rich, titled and famous people. They claimed
among their acquaintances Lord Boothby, Lord Effingham,
Judy Garland, Jackie Collins, Sybil Burton, Sophie Tucker,
Joe Louis and other famous boxers and sportsmen. They
cultivated celebrities like squirrels garnering nuts, and were
photographed in dinner jackets dining with people like
Edmund Purdom, Adrienne Corri and Victor Spinelli – none
of whom seemed to mind being seen in the company of two
known gangsters. They were even invited to dine in the
House of Lords, and to visit the clubs of some of their most
distinguished customers. Not all the celebrities were used to
improve their image; some were cultivated for purely
business reasons. One was Tom Driberg, the Labour MP and
future Chairman of the Party, who could be relied upon to
put in a good word at the right places. Like Ronnie, he was a
homosexual, and Ronnie repaid by providing boys. Later,
they opened another club in the East End, The Kentucky,
which was intended to attract a better class of clientele than
the Double R.

By then they had enlisted the aid of two brilliant
businessmen and branched out into big crime, involving 'long
firm' frauds, blackmail, gambling, dealing in stolen American

securities. The twins were now fully entitled to the image they had bestowed on themselves: the vast network flourished because their brooding presence was always there to threaten violence to anyone who tried to muscle in. Their tentacles stretched out in all directions, and what they grabbed they held on to. And in spite of the fortune they were making, they could not resist getting that little extra, and even small-time crooks were forced to hand over a proportion of their loot. If payment was not forthcoming the twins resorted to 'debt collecting', which meant a severe beating.

Ronnie was now 'The Colonel'. There was little doubt that he was a dangerous psychopath, and when a fortune teller told him he was the reincarnation of Attila the Hun, far from being angry he was delighted. He was often fuddled with drink and the drugs he took to stabilise his mental condition, but only those closest to him knew that Ronnie was a human powder-keg. He was obsessed with guns and knives, and had a vast collection of swords, bayonets and kukris which he honed to razor-sharpness on his own grindstone. His personal armoury also included pistols, sawn-off shotguns, a Mauser and two machine-guns, and he would spend hours making dum-dum bullets; he also carried a sword-stick and an automatic in a shoulder holster. He planned to establish his own 'Murder Incorporated', and dreamed of having a fully equipped army he could summon up at a moment's notice. Foolishly, his family continued to protect him.

Esmerelda's Barn was a gold mine, but Ronnie exhausted its rich seams by driving off good customers and helping himself to too much money. At one stage it seemed as if their empire would be toppled. They were charged with demanding money with menaces from the owner of a Soho club. But they were acquitted, and threw a big celebration party at the club owned by the man they were accused of threatening and which they had taken over. They renamed it the El Morocco, and announced that 'From now on it's the quiet life for us'.

They did not mean a word of it, but they were determined to be more careful; they knew that Scotland Yard had been investigating their activities. One man who was particularly interested was Detective Chief Inspector Leonard Read, who had first encountered the twins when he was at Commercial

Street Police Station. Now at West End Central, he kept observation on the Soho club, watching the guests as they arrived. He was spotted, and invited in for a drink and handed a glass of champagne by Ronnie. Suddenly a flashbulb exploded. The picture of the policeman with the gangster appeared in the newspapers next day. Ronnie had deliberately fixed it to damage Read's reputation. Read was cleared of any suggestion of impropriety, and was promoted, but his investigation was halted as he was sent to help track down the Great Train Robbers. It was a photograph that Ronnie was bitterly to regret.

By then I had become personally involved with the Kray story. Fleet Street's antennae had picked up clear signals that Scotland Yard was not prepared to let the twins' rule remain unchallenged, and I was detailed to investigate their activities.

Public interest had been aroused by a story in the *Sunday Mirror*, which alleged that Scotland Yard had begun an inquiry into an alleged friendship between a well-known peer and a gangster. It all came to nothing when the peer, who had not been named, sued the paper and won susbstantial damages and an unqualified apology. He was Lord Boothby whom I got to know reasonably well, having obtained his confidence by urging the Editor to let me write a front-page story about his missing dog. It led to his pet's recovery, and Boothby was so grateful that I became one of the few reporters he would talk to.

Soon after their acquittal and acquisition of the El Morocco, Reggie married his childhood sweetheart, Frances Shea, and there were congratulatory telegrams from Lord Boothby, Judy Garland, Billy Daniels, and many others. Fashion photographer, David Bailey, resplendent in a velvet suit, took the pictures. The Krays were determined to improve their image, and even asked a well known publicist to project them in a more favourable light, but he declined. David Bailey was a little more accommodating and featured them in a glossy book of photographs titled *Box of Pin-Ups* which sold for 63 shillings – a lot of cash in those days.

It caused some embarrassment in high places, for included among the pin-ups was Lord Snowdon, Princess Margaret's husband.

The Bailey photograph, with a caption provided by Snowdon's friend John Wyndham, was also sold separately in card shops. Astonishingly it enjoyed considerable sales. The twins wallowed in it: they had been elevated into celebrities.

'The Kray twins,' read the caption, 'are an East End legend – their exploits have inspired almost as many stories (both false and true) as those of Frank and Jesse James. To be with them is to enter the atmosphere (laconic, lavish, dangerous) of an early Bogart movie. The Kray clan is large with connections throughout the sporting and show business world.'

Heads were shaken in disbelief in Scotland Yard and Fleet Street. How on earth could the public and so many public figures be so gullible? It was a façade that was not difficult to see behind. Frances Shea did with tragic results.

Reggie at one time seriously wanted to shed the violent tag and concentrate on earning money and settle down to a happy married life. But Ronnie would have none of that. He could not exist without violence or Reggie; their lives were inseparable. Frances Shea became more and more depressed with having to share her life with Ronnie, whose evil brooding presence ruined all chance of happiness. She claimed her marriage had never been consummated, and, after three attempts, committed suicide.

Reggie was heart-broken, and like so many men steeped in cruelty he revealed a maudlin streak that was quite nauseating. He wrote a 'poem' he had printed on a card bearing her photograph:

If I could climb upon a passing cloud,
That would drift your way
I would not ask for a more beautiful day.
Perhaps I would pass a rainbow,
With Nature's colours so beautifully aglow
If you were there at the Journey's End.
I would know, It was the beginning, not the end.

He insisted that she be buried in her wedding dress, but her parents made sure she wore other clothing so that as little as possible of the hated dress touched her skin. They blamed Reggie for her death.

By then the Krays were victims of the myth they had created about themselves. They were convinced they were above the law and would reign for ever. Their only serious rivals had been the Richardson brothers, but they and most of their gang were behind bars. Except, that is, for their chief lieutenant, George Cornell, who was hated by Ronnie not only for the possible threat he posed, but also because Cornell had once taunted him with being a 'fat poof'. On the evening of 6 March 1965, Cornell had the audacity to walk into the Blind Beggar, a public house in the heart of Kray territory and therefore out of bounds to him. When Ronnie was told of this affront, he left another pub he was drinking in, and headed for the Blind Beggar with one of his henchmen. While his accomplice fired two shots into the ceiling, Ronnie calmly shot Cornell above the right eye with his Mauser. When Reggie heard of the cold-blooded killings, he shrugged and said, 'Ronnie does some funny things.'

It was not long before everyone in the East End and Fleet Street knew who had killed Cornell, but the police were hamstrung: no one in the pub had seen or heard a thing. Soon after the shooting I sat in the bar not far from where Cornell died and was amazed that a Kray could command such silence. No one knew what I was talking about. The only positive reaction I got was from a regular who advised me to change my seat. 'Bloke had a nasty accident there. Ceiling fell on him.'

As well as for personal reasons, particularly the taunt about his homosexuality, Ronnie had killed Cornell with the deliberate aim of demonstrating to London's underworld that he was beyond the law and would murder anyone who stood in his path. When months passed and no one was arrested, it seemed as if he had proved his point. He was so proud of what he had done that he kept goading Reggie and asking him when he was going to do *his* murder.

Unknown to the twins, Scotland Yard was determined to bring them to justice, and a team of top detectives was set up under Commander John du Rose with that specific objective. He chose as his chief investigator Leonard 'Nipper' Read who had by now rapidly risen to the rank of Detective Chief Superintendent and had established a brilliant reputation for solving big crimes. Nipper, who had had to cheat in order to beat the Met's minimum height requirement, was a former lightweight champion of the Metropolitan Police, and had acquired his nickname through his speed and dexterity in the ring. He also had the qualities of a terrier: once he got his teeth in he would never let go. Although he would never admit it, he also had old scores to settle. He knew just what he was up against and was acutely aware that his activities, if not closely concealed, would soon reach the ears of the Krays. So he and his team were established in Tintagel House on Albert Embankment, far away from Scotland Yard.

It was at this stage that Phil Finn, a roly-poly fellow who is now one of the most celebrated reporters covering the American scene, and I teamed up. Our job was to unearth everything we could about the Krays and build up a massive dossier of background material, only to be used when and if they were convicted. Our investigations gave us a glimpse of London's underworld, for we visited sleazy clubs and mingled with known criminals in the pubs the Krays frequented; and we also shared the plushier side of life, as enjoyed by the celebrities the twins so assiduously cultivated. All along, Phil and I were worried that our efforts would never see the light of day; the Krays seemed so confident they would slip the hook.

There were moments of personal danger too, and on one occasion I was personally grateful for the intervention of Harry Clement, then a detective sergeant in Nipper's team, who thwarted an attempt by a Kray supporter to frame me. (Harry later became a detective chief superintendent, with a remarkable record for bravery and detective skill.)

I soon met Nipper and several members of his team, among them Frank Cater, who was to become head of the Flying Squad. As the investigation progressed, I knew that the Krays' days were numbered. Nipper, aware that conventional methods would not bring them to justice, resorted to using spies and informants in his quest for evidence. He even posed as a clergyman when visiting men in prison who were prepared to talk. Policewomen were disguised as charladies, and members of the gang were shadowed round the clock and constant surveillance kept on their homes.

The time arrived for Reggie to 'do his murder'. The selected victim was a smalltime hoodlum, Jack 'The Hat' McVitie – so called because his vanity made him wear a trilby at all times to hide his baldness – and one evening the Krays turned up 'mob handed' at a club they 'protected', with the intention of killing McVitie there. They were, however, dissuaded from doing so there, and took him to a basement flat, where Reggie tried to blow his brains out. But twice the gun misfired, and he tossed it aside in disgust and went to work with a carving knife handed to him by one of the gang. Urged on by Ronnie shouting, 'Don't stop. Kill him!', Reggie thrust the knife into McVitie's face, then into his stomach. He administered the *coup de grâce* by standing astride his victim and two-handedly forcing the knife through McVitie's throat with such force that it stuck into the floorboards.

The bloody corpse was wrapped in an eiderdown and driven away in a car. Charles, the twins' elder brother, was aroused from a deep sleep and given the job of disposing of the corpse, which he did with the assistance of another gang member. As with Mitchell, no trace of McVitie was ever found.

Confident that they had achieved their object of establishing their authority, the twins decided to maintain a low profile, and moved to the big country house they had bought in Suffolk. There they increased their charity work, with parties for old-age pensioners, and collections for medical research, handicapped children and orphans. They even bought a donkey named Figaro to give free rides to local children, with either Reggie or Ronnie leading the docile beast by the bridle. One local school received a crate of oranges every week, and the gifts continued until every class had received one. There seemed no end to their generosity, and on one occasion special prayers were offered in an East End church for the two generous young men who had provided the funds for a new roof. The vicar had struggled for years to raise the money, but a collection by the twins did it overnight. The vicar might not have been so moved if he had known of the unorthodox method they employed in their fund raising.

They performed a similar charitable act for a hospital for

handicapped children in Hertfordshire, where they arrived laden down with sweet, fruits and other gifts. They had stopped at numerous shops on the way to collect the gifts – but no money had changed hands: charity was on a pay-or-else basis.

The twins were of course aware that they were being investigated by a force of dedicated and incorruptible policemen and women, and even drew up plans to get rid of Nipper. (Ronnie had developed such a personal hatred, he had purchased a boa constrictor from Harrods pet department and named it Nipper.) Yet they remained contemptuous, confident that fear of reprisals would ensure that the wall of silence which surrounded their activities would never be breached. They did not know that Nipper and his men were gradually chipping away at the foundations. While Ronnie still sang 'Wild Colonial Boy' with tears streaming down his podgy cheeks, and Reggie continued to render 'Danny Boy' with equal emotion, people were beginning to come with evidence against them. At first it was a trickle, but Nipper knew that once he had enough to put the Krays behind bars the stream would become a flood. Every witness was given a written assurance that none of their evidence would be used until the Krays were under arrest.

Then, at dawn on 8 May 1968, squads of detectives – sixty-eight in all – made a series of surprise swoops in the East End. Reggie was found in bed with a girl, Ronnie with a boy. By the end of the morning the entire gang was behind bars. To avoid any intimidation of witnesses, some twenty-five people were taken off to police-rented hide-outs where they were given round-the-clock protection. Detectives set up a direct walkie-talkie link with local police stations, and a hot-line was linked with Tintagel House. The big break came when a young barmaid who, after months of living in fear because she had witnessed the Cornell killing, came forward and told the police what had happened.

In January of the next year, the three Kray brothers and eight of their henchmen appeared in the dock at the Old Bailey. It had already been dubbed 'The Trial of the Century', and I soon had every reason for believing it would live up to that description. As there were so many in the dock, it was decided to identify each of the accused by means of a number on a sheet of white cardboard which they hung round their neck. But they staged a protest in the cells, and refused to appear in the dock until their labels were removed. They were not animals, they protested.

The trial took place against unprecedented security. Police cars, filled with armed detectives, and a cavalcade of motor-cycle outriders, all with their headlights on and blue lights flashing, accompanied the van carrying the accused to the court. Police with walkie-talkie sets patrolled the streets outside, and there were guards vetting those who wished to enter the public gallery, while special passes were issued to members of the Press.

On day four of the trial, the *Express* hit upon a brilliant idea for presenting a pictorial view of the dramatic scene, and the artist Robb spent a day in the public gallery and then sketched from memory a scene never before recorded, because cameras are not allowed inside, and even sketches are forbidden. The drawing covered seven columns on the feature page, and I wrote the colour piece below it.

After a 39-day trial, the jury returned after an absence of six hours and 54 minutes with their verdict. Ronald Kray was the first to appear, and the jury unanimously found him guilty of the murder of Cornell and Jack McVitie. Reginald Kray was found guilty of murdering McVitie and of being an accessory to the Cornell killing by harbouring Cornell's murderers, and seven others were found guilty of the McVitie murder or of being accessory to it. They were all to be given heavy prison sentences. Another member of The Firm was also found guilty of the Cornell murder.

The costs were estimated at £150,000 – which would have to be quadrupled today. Twenty-three Counsel, including nine QCs had appeared, all on Legal Aid.

The next day, in sentencing the twins to life imprisonment with a recommendation that they serve a minimum of thirty years, Justice Melford Stevenson said, 'I am not going to waste words. In my view, society has earned a rest from your activities.'

The evening before the sentences were passed, Phil and I went back to the office to add the final touches to our background piece, then we retired to the Waldorf Hotel to while away the hours until the first editions appeared. We had what by any standards was a big show, but we were bitterly disappointed, for although the verdicts had been reached, the office lawyer had decided that as they would not be sentenced until the next morning some of our stuff would have to be spiked, and naturally it was what we considered the best material. But the one person no one ever argues with is the lawyer – his word is law.

I spent the evening drinking with pals from opposition papers who had also booked in at the Waldorf. But they were celebrating; their lawyers had not had the same qualms, and had decided that nothing could be written that could possibly damage the Kray twins.

I was cheered up by the delivery of a telegram from David English, the Associate Editor, always sympathetic to a reporter who feels that months and nights of hard work have been in vain: 'Yours was the best. At least a million people will agree today. So it was not in vain. Many thanks.'

He followed that up with a personal letter to Phil and myself which went a long way to appeasing us:

> It should have been all your material all the way and it wasn't for lack of trying on my part that it wasn't. But I suppose we should be grateful for what we got in the final result and I would just like to thank you for the terrific effort you put in. Glad you didn't commit suicide, although I know how you felt.

Keith Howard, my immediate boss, also wrote a long letter of condolence.

> I know the ending of it all must have been a bitter disappointment, but I would like you to know that this in no way reduces my regard for the completely unselfish way in which you dedicated yourself to this job. I know that a great deal of work was done in your own time, very much to the neglect of your home and family life.

I kept both letters, not to have framed and hung on the wall, but simply to remind me of the *esprit de corps* that existed among professionals. They shared my disappointment, because it is a newspaperman's job to get things in the paper and when he falls down he feels a deep sense of failure.

Of course it was soon forgotten. Soon afterwards I was back in the Isle of Wight, watching Reggie arrive by ferry to join the train robbers and other high-security-risk prisoners in Parkhurst.

Almost twenty years later, the twins continue to make headlines; Reggie from Parkhurst, and Ronnie from Broadmoor. Books have been written about them, and at the time of writing a film is being planned about their activities.

And they are not short of champions who think the time has come when they should be released on parole. The twins, they argue, are reformed characters and proof of that, they say, is the vast amount of charitable work they do from behind bars. Reggie paints pictures to raise money for liver transplants, while Ronnie makes gypsy caravans from matchsticks. They are allowed to meet occasionally, on compassionate grounds, for they cannot bear being apart for too long.

Ronnie thinks his sentence too harsh. 'They were ordinary murders. People from gangland. We didn't do any kids or old ladies.' But it is that total lack of remorse which convinces most people that they are better off where they are; by the first 'they', I mean the public.

Even after the trial, official requests were made that some of the witnesses should remain anonymous and faceless. Neither their names nor photographs should be published, and, in accordance with their own request, they should remain under police guard for many months. Some of the witnesses even expressed a desire to move to distant countries, change their names, and begin life afresh. Such was the fear the Kray twins instilled in people.

Rather more recently, I read of Reggie that he was lamenting that the streets of London were no longer safe to walk in ...

21

'IF YOU HATE THE BRITISH SOLDIERS ... '

Like many reporters on the *Daily Express*, I did several stints covering events in Northern Ireland, for very wisely the Editor decided that no one should spend too long there. Not only was it extremely dangerous with very long hours, but it was demoralising. Familiarity with the sight of young people killed and mutilated by an IRA bomb planted in a dance hall or public house does not breed indifference, but, rather, the opposite.

When I returned after one particularly harrowing spell, I was asked by a senior executive what the solution to the Ulster problem was, and I replied, 'You should have asked me that before I went.' It was not a glib response, but a sincerely held opinion. Before I went on my first assignment I was sure that the answer was a united Ireland. But my experiences in various parts of the province convinced me that that is something which will never be achieved. There are too many who genuinely hate and detest each other, and that is a stark reality which many people in this country refuse to grasp. I told the well-intentioned executive that the warring factions reminded me of neighbours who threw bricks through each other's windows shouting, 'Why don't you invite me in for tea?'

Thoroughly disappointed with my observation, he said to me, 'You're supposed to be an expert' – a comment that implied I had fallen down on the job.

In fact, I received more congratulations for what I wrote when in Ulster than on any other assignment. But I kept only

one, and that came from a totally unbiased person, Leonard
'Nipper' Read, the brilliant detective who brought the Kray
twins to justice. He was Chief Constable of Nottingham
when he wrote: 'Many congratulations. It really is splendid
stuff. I was particularly impressed by the quote, "There is an
awful lot of religion here but very little Christianity." ' It was
not a slick piece of journalese: it was what I believed then, and
still do. Some critics thought I had overstepped the line of
objectivity by letting personal observations creep into my
work, but in fact, the remark was made to me by a man who
warned me not to be misled by packed churches and pulpit
appeals – God's spokesmen often say one thing and mean
another.

John MacDonald, the Deputy Editor of the *Express*, an
extremely talented journalist with a fund of good ideas,
suggested that I should go to Belfast and live with the Army,
then write a feature to let the public see Northern Ireland
through the eyes of the average soldier. Few people in Britain
had any real idea of what they endured: all they saw were
depictions of paint-smeared soldiers stealthily creeping along
rubble-strewn streets.

I was appalled at the primitive conditions in which the
soldiers lived, and the thankless task they were carrying out
so uncomplainingly. There would have been a public uproar
here if civilians had been forced to live as they did.

I went out on an armoured-car patrol, led by Lieutenant
Richard Getting, and wondered why there was a piece of
angle-iron rising from the bonnet like a submarine's periscope
until he explained, 'That's to stop any of the lads being
decapitated.' One of the IRA's favourite tricks was to stretch
piano wire across the streets. It was the use of such cowardly
tactics that led the soldiers to talk contemptuously of the
so-called freedom fighters. To them, IRA stood for 'I ran
away'.

During the patrol we drove down Annalee Street, where
some small boys were kicking a ball against a wall. Nearby
was a dark red patch at which a rather mangy dog was
sniffing. It marked the spot where Private Stephen Keating
was gunned down a few hours earlier.

Stephen was just eighteen, and the thirteenth soldier to die that year. I decided that I would write a piece that made him more than a mere statistic. To me his death summed up the lunacy of the situation in Ulster. He was a Church of England lad who had been shot through the head by a sniper while protecting a row of Catholic houses in a predominantly Protestant area.

'His killing,' I wrote, 'made no sense to his comrades in the Lancashire Regiment. It did not make a lot of sense to the Catholics in the street. Without the troops, they knew their homes were in danger of being gutted.'

Even crazier was the fact that his death was being investigated by the CID as a murder. Everyone but the British Government thought there was a war going on. I asked Lieutenant Getting what he thought about the whole sorry mess, and he diplomatically replied, 'We are here to maintain law and order until a political solution is reached.'

And that remains the official attitude fifteen years and countless lives later. It is not shared by the ordinary soldier. One said to me at the time, 'We ought to pull out and let them sort it out for themselves. There's no ruddy solution. They don't want one.'

Stephen Keating was with a company based in Finiston County Primary School, where the living conditions made some jails look like three-star hotels. Barbed wire encircled the walls, the windows were sandbagged, it was as crowded as a cattle boat and as cold as charity. The furniture was tatty and frayed, issued by The Ministry of Public Blunders and Wonders – the soldier's name for the Ministry of the Environment. The soldiers were never allowed out to relax, and were issued with two pints of beer a day. They often worked 140 hours out of 164. But they still managed to joke: 'They won't let us out of school.'

Keating lived in a bunk-filled room still bearing the sign 'Woodwork Shop'. Nearly every bunk was occupied by a hollow-eyed sleeping soldier in full combat gear, with his boots on and rifle at hand. No talking was allowed in the dormitories because someone was always snatching forty winks. To doze off on patrol could be the signing of their own death warrant. The only place they could chat was in the mess where the television was never off; Westerns were the most popular – they revelled in the one kind of gunfire where no one really gets hurt.

The officers shared the same mess so that they could keep observation and spot anyone who might be cracking.

I met Paul Brady, a Catholic from Bootle, Keating's closest friend in the Army, who broke down and wept as he looked at the dead man's empty bunk. 'He was only a kid, here one minute, gone the next.' Paul was only nineteen.

It was a poignant moment for me and it summed up the futility of it all. 'I should have been with him but someone stood in for me. It could have been me. He was dead before he hit the ground.'

Major Brian Hollingsworth, who commanded the company, expressed the confusion that tormented the soldiers. Hated and vilified, shot at and spat at, they were still expected to answer every call for help. 'We've coped with flooded houses, trapped dogs, stolen bikes, domestic quarrels and chimney fires. We also have a number of craftsmen in the company who turn out and do repairs.'

The Army also provided what were called lollipop patrols, aimed at combating trouble when Roman Catholic children met Protestant children when school closed. Some soldiers had been shot keeping them apart. 'Yet we hear parents telling toddlers. "Don't talk to those murdering bastards." '

It was those soldiers who had turned out earlier to rescue maimed and injured Catholics and Protestants from the bomb-gutted Abercorn Restaurant. The story of the incident in which two died and 145 people were injured, appeared on an adjoining page under the by-line of my friend and colleague Frank Howitt.

A banner headline spanned the two stories: 'For God's Sake, Why?'

Later I was to be criticised for not being able to answer that question.

When I had finished my spell with the Army I asked one of the officers to ring for a taxi to take me back to my hotel. He looked at me in bewilderment – any taxi that turned up at the barracks, he explained, was likely to be riddled with bullets by snipers sited on nearby rooftops. But he would provide an armoured vehicle to take me back.

When we reached the hotel, two soldiers jumped out and surveyed the immediate vicinity, their cocked rifles at the ready. Nothing disturbed the silence and I went to the bar to have a stiff drink before I started writing my copy. Three men appeared as if from nowhere, and made it clear that I was a candidate for assassination. I was, they claimed, working for the Army, and proof of that was my arrival in an Army vehicle, and the fact that I sported a military tie. (It was in fact the tie of the Crime Writers' Association, a series of silver daggers on a maroon background.) Only the intervention of the proprietor and some colleagues saved me from being despatched to oblivion with a black hood over my head.

I returned to Belfast a few weeks later to write a feature on the first day of direct rule in Ulster. My piece began with a cynical sick joke which was going the rounds among visitors, telling of an air hostess who says to passengers, 'We are now approaching Belfast Airport. Please put your watches back 300 years.' Again it was not a trite or slick observation. It mirrored the despair that hit visitors between the eyes when they arrived in the bomb-scarred capital.

It was Good Friday when William Whitelaw began his first full day as Secretary of State for Ulster. A big man physically, he was faced with a mammoth task – to turn the clocks forward and get around to burying the past instead of the dead. But within a short time I encountered people on both sides of the religious divide who said that peace would be established 'over my dead body'.

Yet that day the churches of all denominations were offering up special prayers, prompting me to quote in my feature the words of the hotelier, which appealed so much to Nipper Read.

While a large proportion of the population were on their knees, there were others standing erect and shouting defiance; sadly they were the people who could make or mar any peaceful solution. And, on the Sunday, the Catholics marched through the streets celebrating the Easter Rising, their lapels sporting the white lilies commemorating those who died at the hands of British soldiers. Memories are long in Ireland, and for many Cromwell still lives.

Mr William Craig – Stormont MP before it was prorogued,

and a former Minister of State – made it clear he would have no truck with Mr Whitelaw. If Stormont was not restored he would take Ulster out of the United Kingdom. It illustrated one insurmountable hurdle: if you appeased one faction, you alienated the other.

Meanwhile, the chariots of wrath continued to career through the streets: stolen cars with lethal cargoes of high explosives packed into the boots. And they did not give a damn for anybody's religion when they exploded. Whole areas had been devastated, and I asked one Republican how, if they attained their objective, they could ever hope to pay for the rebuilding of the city. 'The British will have to do that – after all, it's their fault.'

On the Easter Monday, I went to Belfast's Andersonstown. Not a wise decision for a level-headed reporter, as it was a very pro-Republican area which could have been bodily transferred from Eire. Orange, white and green tricolours fluttered from the rooftops, and the kerbstones were daubed in the same colours. The walls were covered with anti-British slogans. But I felt honour-bound to go in order to write about Martha Crawford, a Catholic mother of ten children, who had died in the gutter with an IRA bullet in her skull. She had been caught in the cross-fire when gunmen opened fire on some British soldiers, having exposed herself when throwing two of her children to safety beneath a parked car. Having written at length about Private Keating, I felt that Martha Crawford deserved a similar epitaph.

I was apprehensive about calling at the small semi-detached home of her mourning husband, but he welcomed me in and was anxious to talk about the tragedy. A shattered and broken man, he could make no sense of the disaster which had befallen him and his family. He was so sick and tired of the violence that he had been planning to leave and start life afresh somewhere else.

He insisted on taking me into the front bedroom where Martha was lying in an open coffin, holding the rosary she was carrying when killed. He was pleased that the undertaker had skilfully concealed where the bullet had struck. The bath upstairs was filled with floral tributes.

I had to walk back to my hotel as no taxi drivers would

venture into Andersonstown, and was shadowed by two men, who warned me not to set foot in the place again. It was a foreign patch that would never be a part of the United Kingdom. And even the death of Martha Crawford would not alter that fact.

I passed several shops which contained Republican propaganda and lists of men and women who had died for the Cause. Murdered by the British. Some in fact had blown themselves up. There was no indication that Mrs Crawford's death was to be regretted. It was a mistake, and such things cannot be rectified.

A month later I was sent to Londonderry to 'do a Doctor Spock' on the children living in the no-go area. The idea was to find out how they reacted to a life spent under a canopy of violence and bigotry. It was the most depressing assignment I have ever undertaken. The children were being weaned on a diet that encouraged them to hate their neighbour, and the British in particular. But what I found so depressing was that they gloried in it. The hooded gunmen had replaced Batman as their idol. Before I was allowed to enter Derry – the prefix 'London' was taboo – I was vetted by Martin McGuinness, the baby-faced ex-butcher-boy who was Commander of Derry's Provisional IRA. He has since consistently denied he held such a position, but when I met him he made no secret of the fact that he ran the place. He provided me with a written pass which would ensure my safety. I only hoped that a rooftop sniper would be able to read it at long distance.

I went to St John's School, perched like a limpet on top of the Creggan Estate, where the children were performing a play before the governors. They were clear-eyed, freshly scrubbed, and looked positively cherubic in their costumes. But McGuinness and his followers had done their work well and thoroughly. Most of the children had been indoctrinated into the Cause. Small wonder that many, as soon as they were eight years old, enlisted in Fianna Eireann, which means Warriors of Ireland.

The five-to-eleven-year-olds scarcely gave a glance at the sandbagged army posts, fire-gutted cars and wrecked streets, and the slogan-daubed walls they had to pass on their way to school.

The play was performed in the assembly hall below murals of Snow White and her dwarfs. But the fairytale atmosphere was marred by the bullet marks which pocked the outside walls, and there were plugged bullet holes in the wall and door of the headmaster's study. The building lay below an Army observation post, which frequently came under fire from the Provos, and the soldiers were forced to respond. St John's was often caught in the middle. But, for children encouraged to believe they were enmeshed in a holy war, such disruptions were acceptable.

One teacher confided to me, 'My little boy can't read yet, but he can write the letters I-R-A.'

She went on to say, 'We were singing "Nick-Nack Paddy Wack" one day when the shooting started. A little boy said to me, "Teacher, your mouth is moving but nothing is coming out." I was petrified. All I could hear was the sound of pistols being cocked outside the door and the whine of bullets. The children hit the floor automatically.'

In England at that time the kids were singing, 'I'd Like to Teach the World to Sing'; in Londonderry they sang the same tune, but with different words:

> I'd like to join the IRA
> And furnish it with guns,
> With gelignite and dynamite ...

And their favourite chant was: 'If you hate the British soldiers / Clap your hands.'

As one approached this citadel of Republicanism, someone with a warped sense of values had painted in huge black letters on the white wall of a house: 'You are now entering Free Derry'.

For some reason or another my presence in the area was unwelcomed, and word reached me that I would be wise to leave. One of the teachers drove me, crouching on the back seat, out of the no-go area. A stone whistled past the car, and I saw a small boy laughing beneath a poster which declared, 'All British soldiers are bastards.'

Hate is the one lesson the children quickly learned.

I had been told to 'do a Doctor Spock' on the children of Londonderry, but that was impossible – the eminent

American was concerned with bringing up happy, well-mannered children who would be a credit to their parents and society. I simply wrote what I saw. What was needed was a miracle cure.

During my stay I visited a safe house, and met a self-confessed gunman who was drying his socks and underclothes in front of an electric fire. He told me at considerable length of the privation he had to endure in a life on the run. But I had no sympathy; he had chosen to hit and run, and a shortage of underpants was not too great a cross to bear.

When the time came for me to leave the city I called a taxi and when we were a few blocks away from the hotel a tremendous explosion reverberated through the air. The taxi driver said, 'There goes your hotel.' I did not ask him to turn back to see if he was right. One more gap in the rows of partially demolished houses would not even be noticed.

I made a final visit to Belfast, on my own initiative, to write about a man who, amid the wholesale bloodshed, was preoccupied with saving life. He was Professor Frank Pantridge, a former Japanese POW and holder of the Military Cross, who ran the Mobile Coronary Care Unit at the Royal Victoria Hospital, where, ironically, most of the victims of the violence end up. Even the wards did not provide a safe haven. Gunmen had been known to slink in to finish their half-completed work.

Pantridge pioneered the world's first mobile coronary unit and his contributions towards defeating the twentieth century's biggest single killer have been honoured by many countries. His research showed that many people died from heart attacks before they reached hospital, and he made an observation that was to revolutionise the treatment of heart attacks: 'Let's take the equipment outside where the risk is highest.'

At the time, Pantridge and his colleagues were working to perfect an all-purpose drug that could be housed in an automatic injector. This would be issued to high-risk people who could treat themselves at the onset of an attack.

It was the one Northern Ireland story out of a great many that I enjoyed writing. At least, it showed that there were still people in the strife-torn province who were more concerned with saving life than ending it. A wave of hope in an ocean of despair.

Meanwhile, the booby bombs and car bombs continued to explode, and one or two were far too close to me for comfort. When I returned home I woke up next morning to find myself covered from head to feet in a vicious rash. I suspected it was food poisoning and called in the family doctor. My morale took a nose-dive when he put it down to fear.

At least I had the choice of never going back, which was an option not open to the luckless people forced to live in that divided land.

Ulster sadly endorsed something I had witnessed many thousands of miles away during another civil war, namely that when the people of one nation take up arms against each other, it brings out the worst in men and unspeakable atrocities become the norm.

22

A BUCKET WITH A HOLE IN IT

I was standing outside a college of art somewhere in North London, covering a rather boring students' protest rally when my photographer, who had just made a check call to the office, passed on a message that I was urgently wanted by the Foreign Desk. Next day I was in Lagos, the capital of Nigeria, covering the civil war. Things happened quickly on the *Express* in those days.

When I telephoned the Foreign Desk, David English, then the Foreign Editor, told me to drop the students' story, go home, pack a suitcase and get to the office and bring myself up to date on the conflict between Federal Nigeria and breakaway Biafra. I photocopied scores of cuttings, which I read during the long flight, and by the time I arrived in Lagos I was reasonably knowledgeable about the war which had horrified the Western world by its ferocity and barbarity.

But in Lagos it was difficult to imagine that, up-country, thousands were being killed or were dying of starvation. The shops and restaurants were doing a thriving trade, football stadiums were so overfilled that the branches of nearby trees were festooned with human fruit, while at night there was no shortage of entertainment. But for the heat and the colourful dress of the Nigerians, it could have been a modern city anywhere.

I booked in at the Federal Palace Hotel, as good as any I have stayed in, where the numerous servants moved on castored feet, and there as a casino where wealthy Nigerians gambled with incredible recklessness. In the bar, American and European oil men drank cold beer as if the four-minute warning had just been sounded.

Within a short time, however, I saw that beneath the sophistication there still lay a primitive Africa. In the bar I got into conversation with an oil man who had just been to a football match with a Nigerian barrister who had qualified in London. Just before kick-off the two teams had been lined up and searched by the referee, the oil man told me, and he asked the lawyer to explain what was happening.

'He is looking for ju-ju charms. Can you believe that people could be so stupidly ignorant?' the lawyer said disdainfully.

'Why doesn't he just leave them? If everyone has a charm, then it works out even,' suggested the oil man.

'Oh, no! Some of them are more effective than others,' replied the lawyer.

I did not think it was a very sensible joke to crack; as a reporter I had learned to steer clear of remarks that were offensive to the people of a country you were a guest in. In fact, the oil man was recounting a true story. And I was to experience similar incidents myself during a long and tiring, and often frustrating stint. I also met many Britishers who told me, 'I have lived and worked with the natives half my life, and I know them.' That was true, but what they failed to appreciate was that *knowing* was not quite the same as *understanding*.

I encountered my first obstacle when I took my initial story to the cable office and asked for it to be sent 'Urgent Rates'. I returned an hour later; it was still lying in the tray, and when I remonstrated with the man in charge he pointed to the red stick-on label on the cable and said, 'See, it is urgent rates'. I had to pass over some money before it was actually despatched. To me, that was a bribe, to the assistant it was his due, and I quickly learned not to moralise. From the highest to the lowest, the back-hander was part of their way of life.

My arrival coincided with that of Lord Hunt and his three-man fact-finding team, accompanied by a crowd of reporters and television men. They had been invited by General Gowan, who was perturbed at the amount of favourable publicity the Biafran cause was getting while the Federal Government seemed to get all the bad. The task of the man who had planned the conquest of Everest was to advise the British Government how best to spend the £250,000 offered in aid to Nigeria. Within a short time he realised what an inadequate sum it was. It was, as I wrote, 'Rather like giving a man a bucket with a hole in it to bail out a sinking *Queen Mary*.'

But Lord Hunt began his work with typical tenacity and enthusiasm, although the enormity of the problem shocked and dismayed him. Everest had been a molehill in comparison. Hunt spoke with startling bluntness, announcing that he was not interested in politics, but was there as a humanitarian. Unless something was done quickly, he said, the world would be witnessing the death of one million people. And he made two urgent recommendations that should be dealt with immediately so that relief supplies could reach the starving: the provision of fleets of lorries, and the opening of two land corridors, one from Calabar, the other from Enugu. He also planned to visit Ikot Ekpene, recently taken by Federal troops, where nearly 100,000 refugees were in danger of extinction. And that was only one of about six hundred similar camps.

From my own inquiries, I had already formed the impression that there were a number of highly placed people in the Federal Government who were not at all interested in 'mercy corridors', or improving the lot of the starving – whose plight was a powerful weapon in bringing the war to a satisfactory end. Neither was Colonel Ojukwu, the Biafran leader, blameless. He had a high-powered publicity organisation in Geneva, which made available to Pressmen dossiers of the most horrifying photographs showing mutilated bodies, the victims of alleged atrocities, and starving pot-bellied babies – the innocent pawns of an despotic regime. It was difficult not to be moved by the stomach-churning pictures of piled-up charred corpses, gutted hospitals, and close-up shots of decapitated civilians. Nothing was left to the imagination. One caption read: 'Head chopped off with an axe. Stomach ripped open and intestines flowing out.'

They were aimed at influencing world opinion, but they were so chillingly gruesome they were self-defeating; there was little point in wiring them back to London as they would never be published. Put the average Britisher off his breakfast, and you have lost a reader.

As we were not allowed to accompany Lord Hunt, four of us – Norman Kirkham of the *Telegraph*, Ellis Plaice of the *Mirror*, Michael Leapman of the *Herald*, and myself – decided to make our own way to Ikot Ekpene. We packed haversacks with tins of sardines, corned beef and hard tack, some Scotch and cartons of cigarettes (for barter), and managed to scrounge a lift in an Army lorry. But we never made it. We were turned back by the Federal Government, which was not prepared to let us see for ourselves what happens when a nation is divided against itself.

On our return to Lagos we decided to head for Port Harcourt and make a personal appeal to Colonel Benjamin Adekunle, who was responsible for the area which included Ikot Ekpene. We managed to get permission to fly there in an aircraft which had served throughout the Second World War and later in the Berlin airlift, and was in imminent danger of falling apart. I very nearly did not make it, as I had left my passport and vaccination and inoculation certificates at the hotel for safe keeping, thinking I would not need them. At Lagos Airport I was refused permission to board until I produced evidence that I had had the necessary jabs. I pointed out that as I was not leaving the country I had not thought it necessary; in any case, my mere presence was proof that I had had them, otherwise I would not have been allowed to enter Nigeria in the first place. But such logic did not appeal to the official – written evidence was what he needed. In desperation I warned him of the dire consequences of his action, and told him, quite dishonestly, that General Gowan, head of the Federal Government, had personally given me permission to fly. And he was not the kind of man who would tolerate disobedience from a minor official. That was enough to make the official relent. But his reaction typified the attitude of many African officials who are forced to alter a decision. To save his face, he ordered someone to produce the necessary certificate, then rounded on him for writing down the wrong batch of vaccine.

We had to board the aircraft by means of a fork-lift truck and through a gap which had once housed a door – which had been blown away by anti-aircraft shells. Once aboard, we made ourselves comfortable on piles of blankets which had been presented by some women's organisation in England, and we had not been airborne long before Ellis discovered they were covering a lethal cargo of bombs, mortars and shells. 'Tex', the American pilot, daily risked his life for fat fees which would enable him to return to the States and open his own freight airline.

There were other passengers aboard, among them a cricket-loving Englishman who had been working at the oil port when it was overrun by Biafran troops and he was forced to evacuate at very short notice. He was returning, now it was retaken by Federal troops, to collect his prized set of *Wisden*.

The interior of the aircraft was marked with emblems recording every successful mission to Berlin, and the wings shook and buckled as if they would drop off in the turbulence; faulty indicator lights signalled the most odd messages, such as 'Fasten ... ' and 'Extinguish ... '. In front of the cockpit was an Elsan closet, fully exposed to our view, on which sat a Nigerian reading a copy of *Playboy*. When anti-aircraft guns opened fire an Army officer told us not to worry: 'They are ours.'

Shortly afterwards a tropical storm burst. It was the first and only time I had got wet sitting in an aircraft.

When we reached Port Harcourt, we were greeted by a reception committee of soldiers armed with all types of automatic weapons. Scattered around the perimeter in blazing heat, without shelter or medical attention, were large numbers of seriously wounded troops, who lay, docilely clutching shattered arms and legs, and moaning gently like whimpering dogs. A doctor examined some by poking a stick at their wounds. Those who did not scream were considered malingerers.

As we clambered out of the aircraft, we asked Tex what we should do next, and he replied, 'Run like ——, and follow me.' We did as he suggested, and as we took shelter behind some sandbags, he explained, 'They roll those mother-fucking bombs and shells down planks on to some sacks of straw, and they're all primed.'

We watched with our fingers to our ears as they rolled down, but fortunately nothing happened.

An officer relieved us of our cash and solemnly wrote in a

ledger what he had confiscated, assuring us it would be returned when we departed. We never saw him again.

Officers openly looted bungalows abandoned by European oil men, and there was a thriving black market in radios, refrigerators and air-conditioning units. Golf clubs were also highly prized as they made ideal swagger sticks. I saw an officer strutting around with a five iron, which he used as a weapon of chastisement. I relieved him of it and humorously, or so I thought, demonstrated its proper use with a practice swing before showing him the Vardon grip. He snatched it back and began savagely to beat a soldier over the head with it. 'That is how I use it,' he said.

Soon afterwards we went in a motorised dug-out canoe through part of the River States to see for ourselves the plight of the primitive villagers caught between two opposing sides in the fierce battle for the vital oil port. There was a hole near the propeller shaft and two soldiers had continuously to bail to keep us afloat. Accompanying us was an Army doctor who had qualified in London, and he assured us that there was no shortage of food, and that what we had heard of starving people should be taken with a pinch of salt. But as he was carrying enough food and equipment to withstand a long siege, we took his words with the recommended pinch.

As we chugged through the sluggish water, fringed by foul-smelling mangrove swamps, the air was filled with the sickly odour of decay and the water was rainbow-coloured with a film of oil. The retreating Biafrans had smashed the pipe-line, and thousands of gallons were seeping into the water. The surface was covered with the dead bodies of birds and fish, and we saw natives forlornly casting their nets for non-existent fish. I remarked to the doctor that some attempt should be made to get food to them, but he shrugged and said, 'They are fish eaters.' It was such an illogical remark I could not think of a reply. It must rank with the oft-quoted comment of Marie Antoinette's as one of the most callous ever uttered.

Later we visited a field hospital, the roof of which was lined with patient vultures; and when a doctor opened the door to one of the wards a whole horde of them tried to force their way in. He assured me that they were not vultures but turkeys. In the ward I was appalled at the sight that confronted me. Every bed seemed to be occupied by a man with a leg heavily encased in bandages, and suspended in the air to relieve the weight. A doctor explained that it was a common casualty, for when the soldiers were crawling through thick brush they often failed to put on the safety catches of their guns, which resulted in the man ahead being shot in the foot.

When we returned to Port Harcourt we were escorted to a bungalow that had once been occupied by European oil-executives, and was now pockmarked by bullets and shells. There was no light, no electricity, and no water, and it seemed to us that it was the habit of the soldiers to occupy a house until the toilet was overflowing, then move on to another.

Norman, who looks like a Guards officer in mufti, wrapped himself in a sheet so that he resembled a shroud-covered corpse, and promptly went to sleep on the floor. I found a bed with a mattresss encrusted with dried blood, and stayed wide awake, unable to avoid the attentions of the ravenous mosquitoes and sandflies. Norman awoke next morning looking as if he had spent the night at the Ritz; there was not a bite visible on him, whereas I was covered and my eyelids were glued together because of the voracious sandflies.

A sentry armed with a heavy-calibre automatic rifle sat cross-legged at the foot of my bed slumbering. Suddenly the silence of the night was broken by a drumroll of gunfire, in which our sentry joined with a blatant disregard for any target. It turned out to be a nightly occurrence, one man had accidentally fired and the rest simply joined in. The enemy was nowhere in sight, but the neatly laid-out rows of white-walled bungalows took another dreadful pounding.

The only really happy man was the oil-executive who appeared clutching his collection of *Wisden*, and bookends which were sets of miniature stumps, complete with removable bails and pea-sized balls. He had even been up to the cricket pitch and noticed the scoreboard had been untouched since the day they were forced to depart in a hurry.

The heat was insufferable and our throats felt like the

proverbial bottom of a parrot's cage, but we dared not drink the water so we drew lots to see who would have the dubious honour of calling on Sandhurst-trained Colonel Benjamin Adekunle, the 'Iron Man' of Nigeria's Federal Army, who was commanding the forces in the area, and ask for some beer. I was unlucky to be the envoy.

I had not met the man dubbed the 'Scorpion', but I had heard a lot about him. He ruled his men literally with a rod of iron, and had been known to thrash soldiers who let him down or had committed an offence. I was told a baseball bat was his favourite weapon.

I found him in an undamaged executive bungalow playing Monopoly with a group of officers and lady guests. I wondered if they were actually playing for Port Harcourt. He was slimly built and wearing a tailored tropical suit, and he became quite angry when I requested some beer. Eventually he relented and said, 'Four, only four,' holding up four fingers in case I had not heard him.

I took the bottles back to our bungalow where the sentry insisted on putting them in the fridge which was not working. He reappeared an hour later with four bottles of lukewarm, fizzy beer, insisting they *were* ice-cold as they had been in the refrigerator. That is not meant as a cruel jibe, but merely to emphasise what happens when a simple man is hauled out of his village, put into uniform, and encounters a civilisation he has never before experienced. He is told that a refrigerator makes things cold; whether it is working or not makes no difference.

Later that day, Adekunle agreed to see us, and as we drank his chilled beer we protested that our efforts to reach Ikot Ekpene had been deliberately thwarted.

'You are not going there,' he told us, 'neither is Hunt. Lord Hunt is a nice fellow. I have read his books. But if he wants to occupy his mind doing good let him go to Rhodesia where Africans are suffering far worse than here.'

He dismissed Lord Hunt's mission as a cheap publicity stunt. 'All this humanitarian rubbish is a bit late. Now that we are winning the war, misguided British humanitarians have suddenly found a conscience. Where was it when the war started?' They were harsh words and were unfair to Lord

Hunt, but there was more than a grain of truth in them if applied to some of our politicians.

Adekunle remained unmoved when we recounted the plight of some of the refugees we had seen. 'Too bad. One man could stop it all tomorrow: Colonel Ojukwu, the rebel leader.' And he went on to say, 'We are fighting a war of survival. We must win it militarily, economically and politically.'

And, rather pointedly, he reminded us that the Allies had demanded the unconditional surrender of Germany in the last war, and had not been diverted by the plight of German civilians.

It occurred to me as ironic that the three soldiers so committed to their cause – General Gowan, Adekunle and Colonel Ojukwu – had all been classmates at Sandhurst, and often mentioned those happy by-gone days.

While we were at Port Harcourt, Lord Hunt – who had been visiting some of the distressed areas – arrived in a private aircraft, accompanied by a corps of television and Press men, and paid a surprise call on Adekunle. He took the Colonel's rebuff with dignity: 'His view of the refugee problem is to finish the war. Being a soldier myself, I understand his point of view. A visit to Ikot Ekpene is not acceptable militarily.'

When the time came to leave, the four of us who had made our own way there found ourselves stuck. The plane that we had been promised to fly us back to Lagos was no longer available, as it was needed to fly out some wounded. We watched it take off; there was so much oil spouting from them that as the engines were started the entire fuselage was engulfed in flames. Unaware that it was a normal happening, one of us shouted 'Fire!' Immediately soldiers, some still holding their saline drips, jumped out and crashed on to the tarmac, where they lay writhing in agony. They were ignored; they had been given a chance to leave and had wasted it.

We trekked to the airport, where we requested passage aboard Lord Hunt's aircraft, but he apologised and said there simply wasn't room. That meant we had a whole string of stories we were unable to file.

Then it began to rain curtain rods, and soon the

dust-parched earth was a muddy quagmire. Norman and I, determined to leave, lay down under the undercarriage wheels and refused to budge until we were invited aboard. Lord Hunt finally relented, and when we had clambered aboard, dripping water like a couple of retrievers, he generously lent me a pair of dry trousers.

As the plane took off, I looked out and saw the wounded stoically enduring the torrential downpour, and waiting for the sound of engines that would signal the arrival of their own transport. No one knew when that would be. I also looked for the officer who had relieved us of our cash, but he had vanished.

The four of us were very relieved to get away from Port Harcourt. Ellis had an experience which I am extremely glad I did not share. He was asked to attend the execution of a young lieutenant as an official witness. The soldier had shot a prisoner within sight of a roving television camera crew, and the incident was seen by millions. His punishment, therefore, had to be witnessed by a similar audience.

Camera crews jockeyed for position as the man was tied to a tree and the firing squad fell in. Then a cameraman shouted: 'Hold it, hold it a minute.' He needed a fresh battery for his camera. Obligingly the execution was delayed.

Ellis made the entire front page of the *Daily Mirror*, and no single story did more to bring home the horrors of the conflict. It also revealed to us how it could destroy the values of men who lived by reporting it.

Soon afterwards, Nigeria offered to open a 'mercy corridor' for relief supplies, which would enable food and medicine to be driven in convoy from a point twenty-five miles south of Enugu, the former Biafran capital, to Agwu, where the rebels could take over. Biafra, however, was far from ready to accept.

It was all so confusing to us Pressmen, for while Britain was hammering away at the humanitarian aspect, there were still regular flights from England carrying arms and ammunition, and meanwhile food and medical supplies piled up as both sides haggled over the delivery routes. General Gowan feared that the food would be given to the Biafran army, while Ojukwu said that his followers would never touch food that had gone through Federal hands. It seemed that both sides were prepared to let hundreds of thousands die while they played their own little power games.

An RAF Hercules flew from England with a cargo of food, but it took six days for half of it to reach Enugu from Lagos. In the docks, warehouses were piled high with relief food, but no one made much effort to shift it. Some of it had been there so long it was rotting. One excuse was the shortage of transport, but twenty Bedford five-ton lorries and five Land-Rovers, which had been shipped from England, remained in the docks for several days awaiting customs clearance.

Three of us – myself, Norman and Ellis – sickened by the steady stream of excuses, set out to show that there were no real obstacles to getting supplies into Biafra. We flew to Enugu, then hitched a lift in an army lorry to the front. It was the most perilous of trips as we were in constant danger of being shot: our bodyguard had the unfortunate habit of dozing off in the lorry and letting the butt of his rifle, which had the safety-catch off, bump up and down on the floor. When it got too close to one of us, we gently pushed it away until it was endangering the 'opposition'.

When we arrived we managed to get hold of some transport, and drove along the mercy corridor between Enugu and Agwu, a distance of thirty-three miles, in just over an hour. Apart from the odd mortar hole and the patched up sabotage attempts, the road was perfect, although everyone had led us to believe it was impassable.

At the Red Cross hospital at Enugu we saw at first hand the high price the civilian population was paying in the civil war. Emaciated children, with legs like matchsticks, were dying as they lolled on their mothers' backs. A young nurse from London told us they were treating four hundred new patients every day. There were fourteen refugee centres in Enugu, but only two doctors, two nurses and some local helpers to treat them. Their task was made even harder by the mistrust some of the native women had of Western medicine. I saw several mothers daubing crude ju-ju patterns on dying children with wood dye. A doctor told me, 'When that magic doesn't work they bring the children to me; by then it's too late and they blame our medicine for the child's death.'

In a market-place people fought over blackened pieces of fish, while another man was selling rats for ten shillings each. Dogs were also in great demand, but more expensive.

We had taken a hoard of coins with us, as they were accepted by everyone, and we used them to buy what we were assured were bottles of fresh water, until Ellis noticed that our water boy was filling the bottles from a filthy ditch filled with corpses. After that we resorted to drinking locally brewed palm beer, lethal but safe. When the time came for us to leave we were only allowed through a military road block after we had bought a quantity of tickets for an army ball which had taken place two years previously.

The harrowing stories we wrote on our return to Lagos made no impression on either side, and more than a week later the road was still closed. General Gowan said he was determined to crush Biafra.

Soon afterwards we flew to Niamey, the capital of the Niger Republic, where Ojukwu had agreed to meet for peace talks. We saw him depart from the airport in an armed cavalcade, but kept discreetly out of sight – we had been told we would be shot if we tried to talk to him. Although we had been invited to the talks we were refused admittance.

Every room in Niamey worthy of that description was taken by the delegates and we were forced to book in to a tin-roofed shack in the compound of an hotel. The sun beating down on the corrugated iron turned it into a tandoori oven, and our discomfort was not eased by the bucket standing in the middle, which served as a toilet. Our only consolation for the high price we paid was the assurance that Graham Greene had stayed there while writing *A Burnt-Out Case*.

The peace talks broke up with Ojukwu agreeing to renew them in Ethiopia, but when they resumed in Addis Ababa, under the chairmanship of Emperor Haile Selassie, it soon became clear that little progress would be made. The Federal Government was in no mood for bargaining; nothing except an end to secession was acceptable. But Ojukwu was equally intransigent. He appeared in the magnificent Conference Hall, which the Emperor had built for the Organisation of African Unity, as tall and as handsome as Paul Robeson and wearing immaculate camouflage battle-dress and sporting a red cockade in his cap. He delivered an impassioned speech which included the words 'My people are the victims of systematic extermination in violation of the most solemn promises made to the nations of the world.'

It was a master political stroke – Ojukwu was quoting from the speech made by Haile Selassie to the League of Nations when Ethiopia was invaded by Italy. He then staged a dramatic walk-out and returned to Biafra – in a fit of pique, we were told, because General Gowan had not personally attended. At a later session the entire Biafran delegation stalked out of the Conference Hall, and I was threatened with expulsion for the story I wrote. It may have seemed flippant to the Africans, but to me it summed up the petty attitude that was being adopted while thousands died.

The Biafrans stormed out after waiting forty-five minutes for the Federal delegates to appear. But it was all a ghastly mistake, caused by the Ethiopian way of reckoning time from sunrise and not from midnight.

This is what I wrote which incurred so much official displeasure: 'The talks were scheduled for ten o'clock local time, which is 4 p.m. normal time. But the Biafrans mistook it for 10 a.m. – and turned up six hours early.

'Confusing? Remember the Coptic calendar has 13 months and it is still only 1960 here.' (It was 1968 everywhere else.) And I ended my story by saying that, with luck, the talks would resume in 1968 – Coptic calendar, of course.

As everyone feared, the talks collapsed and the fighting was renewed.

On our way back to Lagos we landed at Tome to refuel, and were allowed into the transit lounge where we were promptly arrested as illegal immigrants and marched off at gunpoint by some men in dark blue suits and sunglasses. We were relieved of our passports, but they were returned after we had contacted the British Consul and given a promise that we would not try and escape. In an hotel bar that only served two drinks, red cocktail and white cocktail – you ordered white if you wanted red – I spotted Tex, the American who had flown us to Port Harcourt. He was there to pick up a small aircraft which he was to fly back to Lagos for a private

customer. We explained our plight, and, at considerable risk
to himself, he agreed to take us with him, provided that we
turned up at the airport at the crack of dawn. He explained
that the airport did not officially open until nine o'clock, and
therefore no officials would be on duty. It was automatically
assumed that everyone would abide by the rules: to us it
seemed rather like telling jailbirds that there were no warders
around so escape was forbidden.

It was essential to nip away undetected, so we wheeled the
aircraft out of its hangar – it was too risky to start the engines
– and minutes later we took off. We hugged the coastline and
flew so low we were almost brushing the tops of the palm
trees. People appeared as if from nowhere to gaze at us, and
we were convinced it was the first aircraft they had seen. We
had to gain height as we approached Lagos, and when we
landed we pooled the price of our airlift, and Tex kindly gave
us a bill each for the whole amount. We felt we were entitled
to that perk.

Later there was an official protest that we had broken our
word as 'Gentlemen of the Press' that we would not escape.

As we drove back to our hotel, the lorries from England
were still in the docks, minus tyres and headlights which had
been looted.

I returned home before the peace settlement to find
London indulging in an orgy of sick jokes about the conflict.
I remember some: 'Heard what happened when Arsenal
played Biafra at football? – Arsenal ate, Biafra didn't.' And:
'Will you have a Biafran baby for Christmas? – No thanks,
we've got turkey.'

I wished I could have taken some of the people who
cracked them to the refugee camps, but on reflection I realised
the sick humour was a safety valve. The spectacle of
unrelenting suffering becomes unbearable and we tend to
embrace Eliot's words ' ... human kind / Cannot bear very
much reality', and so we hide behind a mask of flippancy.
Certainly it is a reporter's favourite barricade.

23

TRAITORS IN OUR MIDST

Fleet Street has always been a hotbed of gossip, but from my own experience, there was more than a grain of truth in what was being said. And nowhere was this truer than when it came to a scandal involving security. Usually the gossip was leaked by someone who was not always motivated by patriotism, but more from self-interest. Many years ago, when I was told the names of some well-known Labour politicians said to give greater allegiance to Russia than to their own country, I dismissed it as being purely malicious; yet I heard the allegations, unchecked and unchallenged, repeated by others.

Some time afterwards I was having a drink with a contact in the Special Branch, when the conversation got around to security; I raised the matter of the men whose loyalty had been called into question – 'It seems such common knowledge it amazes me you don't investigate some of the rumours.' His reply surprised me: 'It's not Socialist MPs we have to worry about, but some Conservatives.'

He may have meant to be facetious, but it made sense. If the ends justify the means, a person will do or be anything. In any case, nothing is beyond belief in the murky world of spies and counter-espionage. It has been alleged that Sir Roger Hollis, who was Director-General of MI5 during the period when the country was shocked by one security scandal after another, was a Russian agent. The evidence for that is certainly impressive, and the public's confidence is not boosted by a series of bland denials.

Reporters I worked with on numerous spy stories were of the unanimous opinion that claims that any revelations about

the Security Services were against the public interest were no
more than a cloak to hide the fact that the Services are not all
that efficient, and that they have been penetrated. Why
should the public not know what the Russians already know?

The public conception of the twilight world of secret agents
is largely based on the derring-do exploits of James Bond or
the more cerebral activities of George Smiley. Maybe their
counterparts do exist outside fiction, and if they do I for one
will be extremely relieved. From my own experience in
covering numerous spy stories, the real faceless men would
have trouble finding a haystack, let alone the needle. There
have been so many examples of inefficiency, incompetence
and cover-ups that it is astonishing so few heads have rolled.

I worked on a number of cases, including those of Burgess
and Maclean, Philby, the Portland spy ring, Vassall and
George Blake. All were marked by incredible incompetence.

Most of my assignments consisted of gathering background
material after someone had been arrested, and only to be used
in the event of a conviction. I found it difficult to believe that
reporters were able to unearth so much damning information
in a comparatively short time – information of which the
Security Services seemed unaware; if they weren't, they had
remained remarkably complacent. This led to the suspicion
that there were cover-ups. And certainly there were grounds
for this unease in the case of the runaway diplomats, Guy
Burgess and Donald Maclean. If Percy Hoskins had not
broken the story in the *Daily Express*, it is quite possible that
the whole thing would have been hushed up.

When they defected to Russia a scandal broke, the
reverberations of which have not yet been silenced. Fleet
Street revealed that both men were dedicated Communists
who had been recruited at Cambridge. Burgess was a
drunkard who flouted his homosexuality and made no bones
about his political leanings. Donald Maclean, who had been
First Secretary at the British Embassy in Washington, had
regularly supplied the Russians with top-secret information.
One would assume that anyone holding such a position of
trust would have had his character investigated. He too was
homosexual, and drank to excess, and had been sent home
from Cairo where he was Head of Chancery, after a series of

drunken orgies in which he became uncontrollably violent. A colleague who intervened to stop Maclean bludgeoning a night watchman with a rifle suffered a broken leg for his efforts. Maclean was mildly rebuked for his high spirits.

Eventually the two men came under suspicion, and as the net was closing they disappeared. Someone had clearly tipped them off. But who?

Fleet Street was in no doubt that it was Kim Philby, whose newspaper and Foreign Office appointments were a cloak for his high position in British Intelligence. But Fleet Street was hampered by the laws of libel, and it was not until Lieutenant-Colonel Marcus Lipton, Labour MP for Brixton, named him in the House of Commons that the Press could report it without any danger of being sued.

'Has the Prime Minister made up his mind,' asked Lipton, 'to cover up at all costs the dubious third-man activities of Mr Harold Philby, who was First Secretary at the Washington Embassy a little time ago, and is he determined to stifle all discussion on the very great matters which were evaded in the wretched White Paper, which is an insult to the intelligence of the country?' (The White Paper he referred to was the inquiry into the defection of Burgess and Maclean, which the Press considered a whitewash.)

Pressure continued for the disclosure of the so-called Third Man. Harold Macmillan, then Foreign Secretary, stoutly defended Philby in the House. He admitted that Philby was a friend of Burgess, and that Philby had had Communist associates in his university days, and that when that fact became known he was asked to resign from the Foreign Service. But: 'No evidence has been found to show that he was responsible for warning Burgess or Maclean. While in Government service he carried out his duties ably and conscientiously. I have no reason to conclude that Mr Philby has at any time betrayed the interests of this country, or to identify him with the so-called Third Man, if indeed there was one.'

Philby could not have believed his good luck, and he latched onto it by giving a Press conference in his mother's flat.

I was one of the crowd of reporters who crammed into the

small flat. If Philby was nervous he certainly did not show it. He was relaxed and fended off awkward questions by saying he was regrettably unable to answer them, much as he would like to, as he was restricted by the Official Secrets Act. He considered Mr Macmillan's fulsome tribute a complete vindication.

People who have subsequently written about the case have said that Fleet Street was convinced of his innocence. That certainly is not my recollection. It was generally considered yet another whitewash.

Incredibly, Philby was given work as a Middle East Correspondent on the personal recommendation of a prominent member of the Security Services, and was soon busy working for the Russians. I distinctly recall that a story circulated in Fleet Street that Philby was a double agent whose real allegiance was with Britain. That was sufficient to curb any further inquiries. One can only surmise from where it emanated.

A long time was to elapse before Philby defected to Moscow, and the whole truth was revealed, that he had been recruited at Cambridge and had been a dedicated spy ever since.

Only once during the seemingly never-ending saga did I ever get remotely involved in spying myself. I hired a flat to keep observation on another flat opposite, where Philby's third wife Eleanor was believed to be in hiding. I laid on a crate of beer and sat in a rocking chair with a pair of binoculars glued to my eyes waiting for her to appear.

When she first met Philby and became his mistress she had been married to an American newspaperman. Twice she had journeyed to Moscow at Philby's request. But twice she returned on her own accord when it became clear that he was taking a more than casual interest in Mrs Melinda Maclean, who had joined her husband in Moscow. Later Philby revealed how unscrupulous he was by stealing the wife of his old colleague and fellow traitor.

I had initially traced Mrs Philby to Dublin, where she had gone to live following her first return from Moscow. But it was a wasted journey as she refused to talk. There was never any question about her own loyalty, but it would have been interesting to have heard her talk of life with a traitor. When the *Express* later learned that she was in London, I was told to try again on the strength of a tip-off that she was living in the flat in Lambeth. If she *was* there she certainly kept her presence a secret, and I soon discovered that she was being looked after by people who were anxious to ensure the Press did not speak to her.

I sat glued to the window for several days, and had almost given up hope when Eleanor Philby came out, wearing dark glasses and a head scarf, which made positive identification very difficult.

As soon as I and photographer Terry Disney attempted to speak to her, she lashed out at us with her handbag. I did not blame her; she was entitled to a little privacy – but try telling that to an Editor. Terry, however, did manage to snatch a picture before she stopped a taxi. I set off in pursuit and followed her to the Empire Theatre in Leicester Square. The film was perhaps an unfortunate choice, but it at least gave me something to write about: it was *Ninotchka*, the Garbo comedy about a dedicated party official who defects to the West. My story made the front page even though Mrs Philby had not spoken a word.

It seemed that the Philby-Burgess-Maclean story would never end, and it was some considerable time later that mention was made of a 'Fourth Man'. He was eventually exposed as Sir Anthony Blunt, Surveyor of the Queen's Pictures, who was subsequently stripped of his knighthood. I had long since left the *Express*, but his exposure came as no surprise; I had suspected, as did many other journalists, that there had been another vast cover-up. Like so many of the traitors recruited at Cambridge, he was a homosexual and a dedicated Communist. Although he had been exposed some time before he was branded in public as a traitor, he had been promised immunity if he co-operated. If it had not been for Andrew Boyle's *The Climate of Treason*, he would still be enjoying that immunity.

My own suspicion was not born from hindsight. Years before Blunt's exposure, Donald Seaman, an authority on the Burgess-Maclean-Philby affair who had travelled all over the word in his quest for the truth, casually remarked to me that someone connected with the Royal pictures was deeply involved. Don never confided the source of his information, but clearly someone in the know had told him. Blunt was nevertheless able to enjoy his life of ease and luxury for many more years afterwards. Whenever reporters enquired of anyone connected with the Intelligence Services why such things were hushed up, those they asked would merely touch the side of their nose as if to imply a good deal had been made. The strength of the Secret Service is not only secrecy but silence. Unfortunately, it is also a convenient cover for its shortcomings.

Blunt was named by Mrs Thatcher in 1979, although he had made his confession in 1964, and the extent of his treachery was revealed when the Prime Minister disclosed that he had been recruited before the war, when he was a don at Cambridge, and had talent-spotted for the Russians. Later, when a member of the Security Service, he regularly passed on top-secret information. Like so many Communists I have met, he had no desire to share the life he advocated for others. He was an arrant snob whose own taste in art would have been branded as decadent in Russia.

The breaking of the Portland spy-ring was one of the major triumphs of our counter-espionage services, but it also revealed some blatant flaws in our security system. Things that should have aroused suspicion in anyone concerned with security were either totally ignored or their significance missed. I worked on this case from the start to the end, and found I had a certain respect for the Russian professionals who considered they were acting in the interest of their own country, but had nothing but contempt for the traitors who served them.

In March 1961, five people stood in the dock at the Old Bailey charged with offences under the Official Secrets Act. The master brain was a man known as Gordon Lonsdale, who called himself a Canadian but was in fact a professional Russian spy. He was a talented man with a pleasant personality, and had shown great acumen in running the business which was his cover. Helen and Peter Kroger also claimed to be Canadian, but were in fact Americans named

Cohen. They had been professionals for many years and were suspected of being involved with the Rosenbergs. Peter Kroger's cover was a rare-book business, which he too ran with considerable efficiency. They transmitted to Russia the information garnered by Lonsdale, and their neat bungalow home in Ruislip was full of the most complicated espionage equipment, including a powerful transmitter concealed beneath the floor.

Two traitors stood with them: Henry Houghton, a regular Navy man who had retired as a Master of Arms in 1945, and Ethel Gee, a civil servant clerk. Both worked in the highly secret Underwater Weapons Establishment at Portland Naval Base.

Before the arrests were made, Fleet Street had been alerted that a big spy scandal was in the offing, and teams of reporters began their own investigations. In Poole it was quickly established that Houghton and Gee were lovers, which was of no great concern to anyone; what was important to reporters, however, was the intense dislike Houghton aroused among those who knew him. He was a prodigious drunk who flashed his money around, and was quite obviously living on a far higher scale than his salary permitted. His wife had also reported him to his superior for being a security risk, and claimed that he had taken home secret documents. This was dismissed as mischief-making by a jealous woman. There were, though, other reports questioning his reliability. And most damaging of all was the disclosure that an adverse report had been submitted to the Admiralty when he was working in the Naval Attaché's Office in the British Embassy in Warsaw and he was sent back for drunkenness. Yet someone had considered him fit to work in the top-secret establishment at Portland.

Observation was kept on the two lovers for some time, and they were seen to meet Lonsdale regularly and pass over documents. They were actually arrested whilst doing this. The surveillance of Lonsdale led security men to the 'house of secrets' in Ruislip.

Houghton and Gee had been handsomely paid for their treachery, and in the case of Houghton there was no question that he spied purely through greed. Gee claimed she had done it through her love for him, but there were many who doubted this and believed her motivation might have been political.

At the Old Bailey, Lonsdale was sentenced to twenty-five years' imprisonment, which he took with remarkable aplomb. The Krogers received twenty years, and Houghton and Gee fifteen years.

Understandably there was grave public disquiet, and an inquiry was ordered, which disclosed very little, and although there was some tightening up, Fleet Street considered there to have been a cover-up.

The next time I saw the Krogers was in the first-class section of a BEA Trident which was flying them home to Poland. They had been released in return for Briton Gerald Brooke, who had been jailed in Russia for anti-Soviet activities. It had been known for some time that two spies were to be released, and I had had a frantic couple of weeks flitting from one prison to another, to try to keep a check on their movements as they were allowed to meet at regular intervals. There was a hectic car chase when they were eventually freed and given a first-class passage to Warsaw.

Bill Lovelace, one of the *Express*'s finest photographers, and I offered up a silent toast as we took our seats in the tourist section of the plane. We were the only Pressmen aboard, and we had achieved that by what I considered was a smart piece of work, as the Polish Consul in London had announced that no visas would be issued to journalists wishing to visit Poland during the next few days. But I had found that the plane was going to Copenhagen, so Bill and I booked to there. Before we boarded we were warned that no photographs would be allowed, but as we passed through the first-class compartment in order to reach our seats, Bill managed to snatch a picture of the Krogers holding hands. Before anyone could intervene he had tossed the film through the open door to George Stroud, who was standing on the tarmac. But our triumph was shortlived. The crowd of reporters and photographers who had been refused permission to board had tumbled to our trick, and kicked up hell, insisting the aircraft should be delayed until they too had purchased tickets to Copenhagen. To our dismay, they were allowed aboard.

Despite the protests of the stewards, we invaded the

first-class compartment *en masse* to interview the Krogers, who, considering the nine years they had spent in prison, looked remarkably fit and well. Only their clothes indicated that they had been out of touch with things for so long. They played to the gallery, even toasting each other in champagne. In a thick Brooklyn accent, Helen Kroger said. 'We love youse all. Cheers to the whole lot of you. Let us grow up and be friends, not enemies.'

They dined in style, on smoked salmon, poached breast of chicken and fresh fruit salad and cream, and wrote a message for me on the menu: 'All the best with cheers. Peter J. Kroger, Helen J. Kroger.'

Eventually the pilot left his flight deck to plead with us to return to our own compartment as the aircraft was flying in a perilous nose-down position. The free champagne, he assured us, would continue to flow in tourist. We had all we wanted, and the bribe was readily accepted.

Bill's five-inch deep picture spread across five columns of the front page of the *Express*, and my story filled two columns. But it wasn't the splash. That was reserved for the story of a riot at Parkhurst where long-term prisoners had gone on the rampage in protest at the Kroger's release.

There was no such resentment among the Pressmen. Swaps had been an integral part of the spy business. In any case, no one could help having a sneaking regard for the Krogers, who had acted throughout as the professionals they were.

Seven months later I was back in Portland. Ethel Gee had been released and was returning to her terraced home in Hambro Road. She was a complete contrast to Helen Kroger, looking grim and angry, and refusing to answer any questions. She got a very mixed reception from her neighbours. One shouted, 'Traitor', one said, 'My four children and I might not be here today if she had gone on selling her country,' while a pensioner said, 'The sooner she goes the better.' But one woman showed the British ability to forgive and forget: 'If she turned up for a cup of tea I would make her one.'

That same day Houghton was also released from Maidstone Prison in Kent. 'I love Ethel,' he said. 'It was not her fault. I conned her into it. I want to make it up to her when we are married.'

There was, however, an even more shattering spy case before the Krogers and Lonsdale were to be exchanged. And it was one which created a deep bitterness between Fleet Street and Downing Street which took years to repair.

24

SCANDALS AND SCOOPS

In October 1962, an Admiralty clerk named John Vassall was jailed for eighteen years for spying for the Russians, and it sparked off another row about the efficiency of our Security Services. Like Houghton, he should have come under suspicion much earlier on, as he certainly provided enough grounds. He made little attempt to hide his homosexuality – a security risk – and lived in a manner far more luxurious than his £700 a year salary justified. The rent of his flat in fashionable Dolphin Square was £500 a year, in addition to which he enjoyed expensive holidays abroad.

He claimed that he was blackmailed into working for the Russians when he was employed in the Naval Attaché's Office in the British Embassy in Moscow. A Russian on the Embassy staff took him to a homosexual party where he was photographed, and under threat of exposure he agreed to spy. There was no doubt that the story of the orgy was true, but few believed that was why he became a traitor. His motivation was sheer greed. He was certainly handsomely paid. A great asset, which the Russians were not slow to latch on to, was that he had been trained as a photographer in the RAF.

When he returned from Moscow, Vassall was positively vetted and given a job in the Admiralty where he had access to top-secret documents. He took many home, and photographed them with a camera provided by the Russians.

Vassall himself later wrote: 'The fact that an obvious homosexual should have been appointed to Moscow and allowed to remain there is a severe indictment on our Security Services and those responsible for them.' (These were dismissed as the words of a man writing for a fat cheque.)

I was then on the *Daily Mail*, and was one of the team detailed to build up a background dossier. It did not take us long to discover Vassall's high living and his kinkiness; he was known to buy women's clothing and was suspected of being a transvestite. Later, Fleet Street was accused of starting a witch hunt, but the inquiries into his private life were pursued in what was genuinely believed to be the national interest. It would be naive to pretend that our newspapers gave no thought to the fact that the story was a circulation booster, but they did also consider that they filled the role of watchdog. We reporters on the story, who provided the ammunition the leader writers fired from their editorial cannons, were not motivated by such high principles or base commercial interests; we were solely concerned with getting a good story, and not being scooped by our rivals, which would have resulted in the sack – a risk that nobody outside The Street seemed to be running. So we often pooled our information, on the basis that if swaps were permissible between Russia and Britain, there was no reason why we should not come to our own private arrangement. It was a high-risk agreement because we would have got the boot in any case if our bosses learnt of it. But they believed that newshounds always followed the same scent.

The day after Vassall was sentenced the newspapers printed all the background material they had so carefully built up over the past few months. Coming as it did so close after the Portland case, there were demands from Fleet Street that the First Lord of the Admiralty, Lord Carrington, should resign. There was no dispute that Lord Carrington was a very good First Lord and popular with the Royal Navy, but someone had to play the role of sacrificial lamb. It was, if I remember rightly, described as collective responsibility. Something with which Fleet Street was not unfamiliar: if a newspaper prints a serious libel the Editor is as responsible as the person who wrote it. There were also calls for the resignation of Vassall's immediate boss, Thomas Galbraith, the Civil Lord of the Admiralty. Some newspapers unwisely suggested that they were on far more friendly terms than their respective positions warranted. (There were some letters from Galbraith which, although perfectly innocent, did suggest they were perhaps too familiar.) There was also mounting pressure from the Labour opposition for an inquiry.

Harold Macmillan bowed to the pressure and a three-man tribunal of inquiry headed by Lord Radcliffe was set up. Fleet Street quickly formed the impression that the inquiry was not going to be about lax security but was to be a stick with which to beat the Press. Certainly, the manner in which it was conducted provided roots for that suspicion.

Lord Carrington and Mr Galbraith emerged with their reputations and honour untarnished. Which is more than could be said of Fleet Street. The newspapers' conviction that the dice had been loaded against them had some justification. Before appearing before the tribunal, possible witnesses were questioned by Treasury solicitors. Some had then to go before the tribunal, where they were first examined by their own Counsel, who had no real idea of what the tribunal had discussed in secret session, and so were quite ignorant of why their clients aroused so much interest. The Attorney-General, however, knew in advance what he was after. It seemed an odd procedure if the object was to obtain the truth and nothing but the truth. An analysis of the transcript revealed that conclusions were reached which were completely false and men were accused of writing things of which they were innocent. No one, it seemed, was aware that reporters did not write headlines or that sub-editors frequently inserted additional material into their copy.

I was one of those summoned to appear before the Treasury solicitors, regarding an article I had written about Nikolai Korovin, a Russian diplomat who was said to be the spy master who controlled not only Vassall, but Houghton and the traitor George Blake, from his luxury flat in Kensington. Korovin had hastily returned to Moscow and safety when the story broke.

My story seemed very innocuous at the time I wrote it, and whilst I had not made bricks without straw, there was a certain amount of deduction in it based mainly on what I had been told by personal contacts and much more knowledge-able colleagues. Any misgivings I may have had were dispelled by my boss saying, 'The Russians aren't going to deny it, Alf.' At that time, of course, no one envisaged a tribunal. I had no desire to go to prison for refusing to divulge my sources, and I was extremely anxious when I was told a very serious view was taken of what I had written. I approached a contact of mine, who was connected with the Office of the Director of Public Prosecutions and who I knew had some knowledge of what was going on behind the scenes, and confided my worries. He simply said, 'Tell them you made it up. They'll be delighted to hear that.'

Nothing, I told him, would induce me to make such an admission, but when I appeared before the serious-looking men sitting behind a huge table covered with newspaper cuttings, mine among them, my resolve vanished. In answer to their questions I said the article was based on intelligent speculation and cuttings from the library. I was dismissed and told I would not be required to appear before the tribunal.

Two reporters with whom I had worked on the story, Brendan Mulhulland of the *Mail*, and Reg 'Fireman' Foster of the *Daily Sketch*, were jailed for contempt of court for refusing to name the sources of their information to the tribunal. There might have been more, for no fewer than ten times the Attorney-General invited Lord Radcliffe to direct newspapermen to reveal their sources of information. Lord Radcliffe wisely decided that was not necessary.

Brendan's stint in prison was made less painful by the knowledge that his colleagues turned to and dug the garden of the new house he had just moved into. As one remarked, 'It was a bloody sight less mucky than the digging we've been doing.' He was referring to what had been unearthed during the story.

The public in general believed that the Press had got its deserved come-uppance for fabricating stories. I personally knew Brendan's and Reg's source of information for much that they had written, and if they had taken the easy way out and named him there would have been an even greater scandal.

The report when it eventually appeared was not without its criticism of the failures to detect security risks. But the strictures were lukewarm. As Dame Rebecca West put it, 'It might even be accused of pulling its punches, for the direst breaches of security were described in sentences which were each like a spoonful of blancmange.'

While the tribunal was carrying out its investigations, however, another and even bigger security row was about to explode. For some time it had been known in Fleet Street that Mr John Profumo, the Minister of War, was under a cloud.

I was deeply involved in what became known as the Profumo Affair, and experienced at first hand the hypocrisy of many newspaper readers. Fleet Street was again accused of muck-raking, yet I found that when anyone discovered I was on the story they could not resist asking me for more and more lurid details.

It began in a rather mundane manner which gave no indication of the enormous repercussions to come. In December 1962, following a tip-off from a homosexual who wrongly described himself as a journalist, I attended a Magistrates Court hearing at which a West Indian was accused of firing shots at his girlfriend, Christine Keeler. The informant was not the kind of person whose company I would have sought on a day off, but he had been reliable in the past, and had been responsible for the resignation of another Member of the Government. Even so, I failed to see why a lover's tiff between a white girl and a coloured man should set the Thames on fire. Then the informant began to drop names: Christine Keeler was also having an affair with Mr Profumo, and it was all going to come out. It did not immediately, but a snowball had been started that was to turn into an avalanche. Unknown to me, Profumo's association with Miss Keeler was already known in the office. Some time earlier an anonymous telephone caller had told George Wigg, the Labour Party's watchdog on security matters, to forget Vassall and concentrate on Profumo. There were suspicions that the caller was a Russian.

This much was common knowledge: Keeler was having an affair with Eugene Ivanov, the Assistant Naval Attaché at the Soviet Embassy in London, who was an active spy. She had been introduced to him by Stephen Ward, an osteopath and talented artist who was also a pimp for wealthy and highly placed persons who needed a little sexual *divertissement*. He was also a Communist sympathiser who somehow or other had obtained the use of a weekend cottage at Cliveden, the country home of Lord Astor. It was there in July 1961 that he had introduced a near-naked Keeler to Profumo at the swimming pool. The next day he met Ivanov at the same pool, and in a short time the Minister of War was sharing Keeler's favours with a known Russian spy. Some sources claimed she went straight from Ivanov's bed to Profumo's.

The atmosphere in The Street was one of mounting excitment, and there were frequent editorial conferences to discuss the implications of the growing disclosures. The sole interest of reporters was whether or not they would be assigned to the story – it was like an invitation to the circus at which tickets were limited. Someone had to do the weather and the runaway vicar and the Sunday school teacher. I was lucky to be one of the members of the team detailed to work on the story.

At that stage we had no idea that any serious question of security was involved. It was just a juicy scandal in which a Minister married to a famous actress had formed an indiscreet association with a nineteen-year-old girl who seemed to know a lot of people in what is loosely called society. As we made our inquiries it began to seem like a bedroom farce with a cast drawn from *Who's Who*. There was no shortage of people anxious to give juicy details of sex romps in high places, and names were bandied around in the most scurrilous manner until it reached a stage when it seemed unfashionable not to be the subject of rumours. I personally heard of distinguished politicians, famous film stars and other prominent people whose sexual peccadilloes were, to say the least, a trifle unorthodox. There was a queue of informants anxious to reveal the identity of the Minister who waited at table wearing nothing but a mask and maid's apron and carrying a notice: 'If my services don't please you, whip me.' The trouble was no one could agree on the same person.

If it had been confined purely to a question of morals it is unlikely that the Labour opposition would have pursued it with so much energy and enthusiasm, for they had their own cupboards they had no wish to see opened. But George Wigg had been told that Ivanov had asked Keeler to find out from Profumo the date on which nuclear rockets would be delivered to the West German Army. That provided the necessary grounds for having a bash at the Government; from being a scandal about sex it became a major security issue.

Profumo's name had not been mentioned in the newspapers because of the fear of libel, but enough hints had been dropped to make the public aware that a prominent Government Minister was involved in a scandal.

On 21 March 1963, the House began debating the Vassall Tribunal and the imprisonment of the two journalists. There was a lot of lofty talk about the freedom of the Press being in jeopardy, and the sacred right of journalists to protect their source of information. Reporters observing politicians riding to their rescue suspect an ulterior motive, but none of us was expecting the powder keg which was about to be ignited when George Wigg intervened and altered tack with an attack on the Government, which was thinly disguised as a criticism of Fleet Street:

'There is not an MP in this House, and I don't believe there is one person in that public gallery, who in the past few days has not heard rumour upon rumour that involved a member of the Government Front Bench.

'The Press have got as near as they could. They have shown themselves willing to strike, and this comes about because of the Vassall Tribunal, because in actual fact these great Press lords – these men who control the great instruments of power – have not got the guts to discharge the duty which they are now claiming for themselves.

'Therefore I am going to use the privilege of the House of Commons and I am going to ask the Home Secretary to come to that despatch box tonight. He knows the rumours to which I refer. They relate to Miss Christine Keeler and Miss Davies and the shooting by a West Indian.' He wanted a Select Committe set up so that the rumours could be investigated and the honour of the Minister could be freed by innuendo. It was not as high-minded as it sounded because it was known that a letter existed in which Profumo had addressed Keeler as 'Darling'.

Mr Henry Brooke, the Home Secretary, declined to oblige, but during the debate the mysterious disappearance of Miss Keeler was raised. She had been due to give evidence at the

Old Bailey trial of Jamaican John Edgecombe, who in her absence was jailed for seven years for having a pistol with intent to endanger life.

The next day Mr Profumo made a personal statement to the House, which meant he could not be questioned about it, in which he denied any impropriety in his friendship with Miss Keeler. 'I shall not hesitate to issue writs for libel and slander if scandalous allegations are made or repeated outside this House,' he said.

Voices in Fleet Street's pubs were particularly muted that evening, although everyone knew he was lying and it was only a question of time before he would have to confess and resign.

Profumo also took the opportunity indignantly to deny that he was in any way responsible for her failure to appear in court. Nevertheless she had vanished, and, understandably, a great many people wanted to know why she had been allowed to go anywhere without disclosing her intentions to the police.

The discovery of Miss Keeler by the *Daily Express*, and her subsequent return to London, had the flavour of a Keystone Kops comedy about it, and as with so many other Fleet Street stories the unwritten story-behind-the-story would have made much better reading.

An *Express* team of reporters and photographers was formed with specific instructions to track her down. The first lead came from a Madrid free-lance who said she was in hiding in a small cottage in Altea, but by the time reporter Frank Howitt and photographer Harry Dempster arrived on the scene she had left for Madrid with a Spanish bullfighter. Christine certainly enjoyed variety. Frank and Harry made a tour of all the Madrid night spots but were handicapped by the fact that they had no idea what she looked like. When they booked in to the Hilton Hotel after their futile search, Christine was actually having a drink at the bar, but she went unnoticed. Next morning Frank rang a contact at the British Embassy and asked him if he would help in finding Keeler. He got a call back some time afterwards telling him that she had been arrested in the Hilton and was now in a police station and due to report to the Embassy later in the day.

Wisely he did not inform the office, whose money he had been spending with lavish abandon, of the true facts.

'I went to the Embassy and actually signed for her,' Frank told me. 'She had left her passport in Altea and I had to give a written undertaking that I would collect it and get her out of the country as soon as possible.'

Pat Chapman, a former *Express* man, who now worked in Madrid and was a stringer for the paper, agreed to let them use his flat, and they kept Keeler there for a couple of days. It was not long, however, before someone tipped off the Madrid newspapers, and the top-floor flat came under siege. An enterprising photographer from *Paris-Match* managed to get on to the roof with the intention of snatching a picture of Keeler when she appeared on the balcony. Unfortunately for him but not the *Express*, he fell off, broke his leg and smashed his camera.

Frank and Harry spirited her away in the middle of the night, collected her passport, and arranged to fly to London from Valencia. They stopped overnight in an hotel in Denia, but the owner tipped off the Spanish Press, and once again they were under siege. They fled from the hotel in a large American limousine, which was the pride and joy of the local taxi driver, but during the hectic ride through orange groves, pursued by a convoy of Spaniards, it broke an axle and shed a wheel. As the driver wept tears of anguish, Christine calmly sat in the back putting on her make-up; it was five in the morning. When reinforcements arrived in the bulky form of Rodney Hallworth, another *Express* reporter, Frank and Harry were busy bombarding the Spaniards with oranges to stop them taking photographs. Hallworth set off to find fresh transport. The only taxis he could hire were two old Model-T Fords. When they had finally shaken off their pursuers, they settled to write the story and wire the pictures. The front-page splash was: 'Christine at Last' under a 'World Exclusive' tag.

By then Lord Beaverbrook was concerned that the *Express* might get into serious trouble for having kept a missing witness away from court, and Frank received orders for them to return immediately to London via Paris, where Christine was to be made available to the assembled world's Press. At

Orly, one French photographer grabbed her by the hair and screwed it into a tight bun until the tears poured from her eyes, which provided *the* picture *he* wanted. A similar scene was enacted at Heathrow.

Keeler was ordered to forfeit her £40 recognisance for failing to appear at the Old Bailey. But what she had been paid by the *Express* made that a pretty painless punishment.

Tom Mangold, now a distinguished member of the BBC's Panorama team, returned around the same time with Mandy Rice-Davies, who had been holidaying in Majorca. Interest in her had increased with the revelation that she had also been the mistress of Peter Rachman, the notorious landlord. Now that a property racketeer was added to the high jinks at Cliveden, Fleet Street was prepared for anything. And it was not disappointed.

Like Topsy, the story growed and growed. It was like a play to which, as soon as an ending appeared in sight, a fresh act was added.

For days on end I door-stepped the flat Keeler shared with Mandy Rice-Davies, and also did my stint outside Profumo's house opposite Regent's Park. One evening, when I was in her flat, Mandy calmly stripped naked in order to change for a dinner engagement. She had a most wonderful body, and, unlike some, I would not have been ashamed to admit to having bedded her. I did not. Being a reporter and naturally suspicious, I feared that she might want to compromise me so as to make anything I wrote worthless. So I told her I was queer. She did not say anything except to ask me to help zip her dress up. Looking back, I do not believe Mandy cared tuppence about the gossip and rumour. She was a young girl who was having a good time, and she certainly was not overawed by the sudden notoriety she had acquired. At one stage when she was called upon to give evidence she calmly retorted, 'Well, he would, wouldn't he?' when she was reminded that a prominent public figure had strenuously denied an allegation she had made. I got the impression that Mandy was genuinely puzzled at the interest shown in her and Christine's activities.

At the height of the story Lord Beaverbrook discussed it with Chapman Pincher, who probably knew more about it than anyone else on the paper. Chapman Pincher later wrote of Beaverbrook, 'Shaking his fist, he cried, "Why in God's name should a great political party tear itself to rags and tatters just because a minister's fucked a woman?" ' It was a typical Beaverbrook reaction. His newspapers had been as diligent as others in pursuing the story, but when it looked like becoming an avalanche which would sweep away the Tory party, he wanted to run with the hare and abandon the hunt.

Dr Stephen Ward was soon to stand in the dock at the Old Bailey, charged with five vice offences. Several people decided it was an appropriate moment to maintain what is called today a low profile. They had no wish to appear as witnesses in which stories of flagellation and perversions were to figure so prominently. The public may have expressed abhorrence at so much dirty linen being aired, but the trial attracted the biggest crowd ever seen outside the famous court. Christine was pelted with eggs as an indication of their disapproval; nevertheless they battled for seats in the public gallery. Fashionably dressed women avoided the crush by being allocated seats in the reserved section.

Ward may have been an unsavoury character who meddled in security matters which he would have been well advised to leave alone, but he was hardly the Svengali he was made out to be. Christine and Mandy were scarcely innocents who had been lured into vice; they had gone in with their eyes wide open. Ward was undoubtedly a pimp, but without the demand he would not have been tempted to supply. He was a vain social creep, but he was made to appear the architect of all that happened. Fleet Street had some sympathy for him, for there was a general feeling among reporters that he was being made the scapegoat. The monkey was to be punished for the organ grinder.

A succession of prostitutes took the oath, some identified by just an initial. One of them was treated as a hostile witness by Mr Mervyn Griffith-Jones prosecuting, when she said she had lied at the committal proceedings. She said she had been scared, and that some of the statements she was said to have made were invented by the police.

Mandy looked sweetly innocent and could not understand

all the fuss. 'He [Ward] doesn't deserve to go to jail. You might as well arrest every bachelor in London,' she said from the witness box. And she caused quite a flutter in the reserved seats when she said she had been to bed with Douglas Fairbanks and Lord Astor. She also claimed that Lord Astor had contributed towards the rent of the flat she shared with Christine.

At times, Mr Griffith-Jones was unconsciously amusing with some of his questions which teetered on the brink of pomposity. When a young woman gave evidence that she was paid for whipping men, he asked, 'What is the market rate?' She replied as if she was a factory hand being asked about piece work. 'One pound a stroke.' As usual, a crop of new jokes went the round of the Fleet Street bars. One was a parody of the talking clock: when you dialled Tim a voice replied, 'At the third stroke it will be three pounds.'

Ward made no attempt to hide the fact that he had the morals of an alley cat. 'I like sleeping with attractive girls', and 'I am a thoroughly immoral man', were two of his replies. But he claimed that some of the women, including Christine Keeler, had committed perjury in their evidence.

During the course of the trial a conviction against Aloysius 'Lucky' Gordon – who had been jailed for three years for assaulting Miss Keeler – was quashed by the Court of Criminal Appeal. In view of this, Ward's allegations did not seem too far-fetched.

When Mr Justice Marshall addressed the jury, he described Ward as an abandoned man, but not in the sense that Ward described himself: he had been abandoned by the friends who could have come forward to support his case.

The next day Ward was found guilty of living on the immoral earnings of Keeler and Rice-Davies. Tom Mangold knew that Ward was resigned to being found guilty, because he had been invited to his Chelsea flat where the osteopath had said to him, 'My lawyers say there is little hope left. Tomorrow I'm going to be nailed at the Old Bailey. It's not a pleasant thought. I don't think I am going to be able to do time for these offences. It's not prison that worries me. It's taking the blame, being the victim of a witch hunt – that's what hurts.' And he added, 'This has been a political revenge trial. Someone had to be sacrificed, and that was me.' Tom shared that view and reported what Ward had told him.

Ward was never sentenced because he took an overdose and was rushed to St Stephen's Hospital in Fulham. There he died after being in a coma for a long time.

The story did not end there, however. Public confidence in the conduct of people in public life had received such a bruising that Lord Denning, Master of the Rolls, was asked to make an independent inquiry into the Profumo Affair, in order to put the foundering ship of state on a more even keel.

There was a general feeling at the time that the Press had hounded Mr Profumo out of office, and he got a lot more sympathy than he deserved. It *was* a sad ending to a brilliant political career, for he retired completely from public service and devoted his life to working for the Toynbee Hall in the East End of London. But I personally know that, as far as the *Express* was concerned, there was no witch hunt for prominent people. During the months of investigative journalism we built up an enormous dossier of stories which had all been thoroughly checked and owed nothing to gossip. But Lord Beaverbrook did not use any of it. Once the question of security was ruled out he lost interest.

Lord Denning interviewed a hundred and sixty witnesses after appealing for anyone to come forward who might have information which would assist him in his task. I recall one woman, a Hyde Park prostitute, who called at the *Express* seeking advice as to whether or not the information she had would be of help. She related a story of a Minister, now dead, which showed a depth of depravity that could have been exploited if it had ever reached Russian ears. I accompanied her to see Lord Denning, where she duly repeated her story. But he saw nothing dangerous in it. When he finally produced his 55,000-word report, some described it as a *tour de force*; others compared it to a third-rate novel. He wrote of Ward, 'He was the provider of popsies for rich people.'

No matter what anyone thought of the style, the important thing was that it cleared all Ministers of immorality. Chapman Pincher was later to describe it as 'One of the most misleading documents ever foisted on the public.' His observation was not a criticism of Lord Denning but of some witnesses, notably Sir Roger Hollis, Director-General of MI5, who he was convinced deliberately misled Lord Denning.

My own view was that the report had provided what Parliament most desired: it assured the public that there was no need to worry about the lax morals of those who controlled our destiny. Not a breath of scandal could be attached to any of them. But I was not alone in thinking that it was rather odd that, throughout months of intensive inquiries, we had never encountered anyone capable of telling the truth. If not a whitewash, the report had a greyish pallor.

When Christine was jailed for nine months for committing perjury at the trail of 'Lucky' Gordon, the West Indian who was jailed for assaulting her, it was felt that the curtain had finally been rung down.

For me, however, it ended in 1965, when I was working on what became known as 'The Nude Murders', when six London prostitutes were killed within the space of a few miles of Shepherds Bush. One of them I had last seen when she gave evidence at the Ward trial. She had plummeted a long way since then. It was a particularly sordid end for a girl who had figured in a trial about sex in high places.

25

PINK CHRYSANTHEMUMS

I only saw George Blake once and that was in the dock at the Old Bailey, where he sat bearded and impassive when he was sentenced to a record forty-two years for spying for the Russians. Apart from being the most damaging of the traitors – he was said to have done more harm than the Krogers, Lonsdale and Vassall put together – he was certainly the most loathsome. He betrayed a country that had welcomed him, granted him honours, and given him opportunities that would not have been available in the land to which he eventually defected.

He was born of Dutch-Egyptian parents, served in the Royal Navy during the war, and was on Montgomery's staff when Germany surrendered. He then joined the Foreign Office, which was merely a cover for his work with MI6. He was captured in Korea where he was Vice-Consul in Seoul, and after his release was sent to Berlin where he worked for the Secret Service. At the time of his arrest he was attending a course in Arabic at the Foreign Office School near Beirut. He was already fluent in Russian, having taken a course at Downing College, Cambridge. He seemed devoted to his wife Gillian and their children, and on their wedding certificate he was described as a Government Official FO, the same employment as Gillian's father.

Most of his trial was heard in camera in order to conceal the extensive damage he had done to the country, but I had a pretty shrewd idea of it as I had been detailed to build up a background dossier, and was detached from all other work and allowed to follow any lead I thought promising. I was appalled at the little amount of checking that seemed to have been done before he was admitted into such a sensitive sphere of work. His word, which proved pretty worthless, seemed to have been accepted as gospel.

I started at a small village near Arnhem – the Dutch town where the Paras had carved an imperishable niche in the annals of military valour – where Blake had lived and from which he escaped from the Germans by cycling to Spain, before going on to England and joining the Navy. He claimed that his work for the Resistance had made his departure imperative. I was accompanied by Freddie Girling, who had joined the *Express* after the *Chronicle* folded, and was one of the most experienced photographers in The Street. By a sheer stroke of luck we were able to obtain a great deal of information about Blake which immediately aroused suspicion. Much of it seemed contradictory to what he had told the authorities on his arrival in England.

In Amsterdam Freddie had tripped down a flight of steps in the hotel and badly cut his head; typically he had brushed it aside as nothing more than a slight graze. But when we arrived at our destination it was still bleeding profusely, and I insisted on taking him to a doctor. As he was being stitched up I casually asked the doctor if he could put us in touch with the person who had led the Resistance in the area. He said I was talking to him. When I explained the purpose of our visit he took us to the town hall where the Mayor opened up the wartime files. Far from being a local hero, Blake – I can't recall the name under which he was known – was suspected of being linked with collaborators, and his sudden departure for Spain did not appear to have been motivated by the reasons he gave.

Meanwhile, other reporters were chasing different leads, especially regarding his internment in Korea. Fellow captives recalled that he was repeatedly beaten and had established something of a reputation for never having revealed anything to his interrogators. But the reporters gained the impression, which turned out to be correct, that his heroism was a cover, and that he was already a convert to Communism.

On information provided by Chapman Pincher, I then travelled to Berlin where I met Brigitte Eitner, whose husband was awaiting trial for treason for spying for the

Russians. Horst Eitner was in fact a double agent, and also worked for Blake, who was working for the British Secret Service. It turned out that Blake was also working for the Russians.

Eitner, it transpired, had actually tipped off British Intelligence that there was a spy in their organisation six months before Blake's arrest. The long gap was due to the fact that Eitner only knew him as Max de Fries.

Frau Eitner was able to supply me with a lot of information that further convinced me of the ineptitude, deliberate or otherwise, of our Security Services, and I found myself listening to a story that would have been farcical had not so much been at stake. At one of their meetings, Eitner was trying to photograph Blake and also tape their conversation, while Blake was trying to photograph him with a concealed camera. Both were doing it for the Russians.

Brigitte Eitner was only able to identify Blake and de Fries as the same person when her husband showed her a picture of Blake which had appeared in a newspaper when he was arrested. Until then she had thought he was a Dutchman working for the British and that he was a bachelor – a 'monk', not at all interested in women. He was certainly spartan in his life style, for he did not smoke and seldom drank.

'He did not trouble much to hide that he was an Intelligence Officer. One day he would go to great lengths to meet my husband secretly in the suburbs, and next day seemed to discard caution by meeting him in a café that was a well-known haunt of agents,' she told me. When they spoke she had to leave the room. 'Once they had a row when he asked my husband for a list of all the agents he knew.'

How such a man could have avoided suspicion for so long seemed incredible to a layman such as me.

But there was nothing even remotely amusing about the destruction he caused. He had tipped off the Russians about an Anglo-American project to tunnel into East Berlin in order to intercept Red Army signals and telephone conversations. The result was that the British and Americans spent vast sums of money for phoney information fed to them by the Soviets.

That was only part of his treachery, though: in addition to supplying the Russians with every item of secret information that came into his possession, he also betrayed at least forty agents for the West, many of whom were executed.

I always met Brigitte Eitner in a park near my hotel because she would not say a word if there was the slightest chance of being overheard. At our last meeting she asked me to drop her off at a police headquarters, explaining that she had to report regularly while her husband was awaiting trial, and that anything she said was *sub judice*. I caught the next plane back to London and wrote my story in the office under a Berlin date-line.

Soon afterwards, Pincher wrote a *Daily Express* front-page splash, which was topped by a long row of featureless men drawn by an office artist. Each one, he said, represented an agent who had been betrayed by Blake. It was a first-rate story, which caused some angry muttering, as every effort had been made to play down the extent of Blake's treachery.

Throughout my inquiries I had tried desperately hard to track down Blake's wife but without success as she was being kept well away from the Press. I also tried to find his mother, Catherine Blake. When I finally did, it was by another stroke of good fortune which I dared not reveal to the office. How could I when I had received the following letter from Keith Howard?

> Dear Alf,
>   A word of thanks for the tremendous job which you did on the Blake background. All too often weeks or months of work can be hidden behind a few facts on this sort of job, but I hope you appreciate that in this case we had by far the best story of any paper – and a great deal of the credit goes to you.

During the story, I was enjoying an off-duty pint of beer in The Railway, my local in Radlett, when I was surprised by the unexpected appearance of Tom Tullett, and Hugh Saker of the *Daily Mirror*. A most formidable team. As we bought our rounds the conversation went something like this:

Tom: How did you get onto it?

Me: I had a tip off. (I could not tell Tom that I hadn't the foggiest idea what he was talking about. But I knew it had to be something big to bring him to Radlett where nothing ever happened.)

Hugh: Shall we follow your car?

Me: No. It's too well known in the village. I'll come in yours.

We drove up a steep hill, over the railway bridge and along the drive of a big house adjoining Porters Park Golf Club. It was a house I knew as it was owned by Lachlan Rose of Rose's Lime Juice. Tom knocked on the door, and when the housekeeper opened it he said, 'Mrs Blake?' I had been looking for her for months, and all that time she was less than a mile from my home. It wasn't until long after that I had the nerve to tell Tom that I hadn't known. I didn't get anything from her, though.

When Blake was jailed I was confident that that would be the last I or anyone else would ever hear of him. By the time he was released I would have either retired or be harping or stoking. But just five years later I was standing below the high gaunt wall of Wormwood Scrubs Prison looking at the spot where he had clambered over.

That such a top-security prisoner could have escaped, with such apparent ease after serving so little of his record sentence, was hard to believe. Again, Percy and I worked in harness, and as we pieced together the story it seemed that a section of Russian Intelligence, known as the 'Illegal Apparatus', had been responsible, simply to demonstrate to Russian agents that even when detected they could rest assured that they would not be forgotten.

Certainly, it looked as if he had been 'sprung' as a prestige gesture, because so many clues were left behind. The nylon ladder with which he scaled the wall was made of a material not used in the prison workshops; the same applied to the plastic-covered knitting needles which had been used to reinforce the rungs. For some time a pot of pink chrysanthemums had rested at the foot of the wall where he clambered over. It was obviously a marker for the pick-up car. But it was untraceable, having been bought from one of a chain of florists which sold hundreds of similar plants. Somehow that theatrical flavour left a taste of something suspicious.

From prison contacts we soon found out that Blake, normally a loner, had gone out of his way that day to talk to fellow prisoners and warders to establish his presence shortly before he broke out. He was in the central hall at 5.30 p.m., which gave him ninety minutes during the recreation period before another check was made

Even more mysterious was that the bars on the landing window from which he escaped had been broken and not sawn through, yet no tool or implement was found which could have done the job.

It began to look as if no great effort had been made to stop Blake escaping, which led to a natural suspicion that some kind of deal had been made.

During my inquiries I met a convicted murderer who had been released but had known Blake in prison. He too was amazed that Blake had been able to escape with such ease; and he was sure that he had not been assisted by any fellow prisoners, for no matter what crimes they had committed they would not have lifted a finger to help a traitor.

Blake eventually turned up in Moscow, where he was soon sharing a flat with an Irishman, Sean Bourke, who claimed that he had engineered the escape.

Meanwhile, I had been keeping a close watch on his mother, and when she disclosed that she had received a letter from him, I thought it would not be long before she joined her son to whom she was utterly devoted. While there was no reason at all why she should not visit him, I knew it would make a good story, so I asked the manager of my local newsagent to tip me off as soon as she cancelled her regular order. One morning he telephoned my wife, and said she had done that and had also bought some paperbacks. For some inexplicable reason, however, I had been sent to Margate, where Blake's sister worked as a nurse – a rather pointless assignment as she had refused to talk to the *Express* after Pincher's disclosures – and it was late that night when I got the news. Harry Dempster and I drove at great speed to Harwich to try to catch the ferry to the Hook of Holland, which we suspected was the route she would take. But we missed her, and the next we heard was of the Moscow reunion.

I am still puzzled at the decision to send me to Margate when I was sitting on a much better story, but then there were a lot of things about the Blake story that did not make much sense ...

From the moment the story first broke, I had tried hard to trace Blake's wife Gillian, but she was kept well out of sight by the authorities. It was not until March 1967 that I caught my first glimpse of her in a divorce court, when she was granted a decree nisi on the grounds that treasonable conduct amounted to cruelty; originally Blake himself had sought a divorce on the grounds of her adultery with an agricultural scientist, but this was dropped when he escaped.

Gillian Blake left with the man she intended to marry, escorted by Special Branch officers, through a little-used corridor known as 'the chicken run'. The court had been told that she was now living under an assumed name so that her children could start a new life. Knowing the name of the man she planned to marry and his occupation, however, it was not difficult to find his place of work and where he lived. Within a few days I met Mrs Blake, and although I did not get an interview we at least obtained a picture, and it was not hard to write a good story around that. But before I got back to the office, a solicitor's letter had arrived warning the paper not to use the story.

Such letters were not unusual, though, and I sat down and had begun typing my piece when Percy came up and said, 'Better drop that, Alf. Elwyn Jones wants to see you at the Yard.' I gave him a short one-word reply that suggested that Mr Jones would have to wait. 'I don't think so,' said Percy. 'He's head of the Special Branch.'

Twenty minutes later I was ushered into his office at Scotland Yard, and immediately knew that he did not want me for a social chat. A colleague sat in one corner with a notebook on his lap, and Mr Jones was far from affable. He wanted to know the source of the information which had led me to Mrs Blake, and by the tone of his voice I suspected that he thought I had some special contact.

I relaxed as the note-taker's pencil poised over his book. I had absolutely nothing to worry about. I had found her whereabouts by simple common sense. I explained that

although she had assumed a different surname, she had an
unusual second Christian name, and when I went through the
local electoral register I discovered a woman who had similar
Christian names. It seemed too much of a coincidence that
there could be two women in the area sharing the same
names. From then on, I explained, it was simply a question of
keeping the house under observation until she emerged.

Mr Jones was suitably impressed and his hostility
disappeared, and we adjourned to the bar at the Yard known
as the Tank Room, where he bought me a couple of drinks.
'You ought to work for us,' he said, and I was suitably
flattered, but he made it clear there would be no story.

I did not really mind because I shared the view that she was
entitled to find a fresh life. But I had spent months trying to
find her and all I had to show for my efforts was a note from
Keith:

> Although we were unable to make use of the information, I
> would like to say how much I appreciated your dedication
> to the task of finding Mrs Blake. We certainly would still
> be looking if it hadn't been for your persistent and tireless
> efforts.

One was grateful for that kind of note, because so often
months of work ended up on the spike, and people outside
the office tended to think you had been put out to grass as
your name had not appeared in the paper. That was the side of
journalism the public never heard about.

Gillian Blake was totally unaware of her husband's double
life, and I hope she found the peace and anonymity she
sought for herself and her children.

26

MEMORY LANE

When I was a cub reporter my idea of a splendid night out was a meal in a pie and eel shop off the Edgware Road, where I always ordered saveloys, mash and gravy – purely, I suspect, to hear the none-too-mellifluous voice of the owner bellowing to the cook: 'Two Zeppelins in a cloud, and make it rainy.' This would be followed by a visit to the Metropolitan Theatre nearby, where I was guaranteed a free seat. The front hall manager always wore a top hat, white tie and tails, and when he wasn't busy would reminisce about the Good Old Days, when Charlie Chaplin, Marie Lloyd, Little Tich and Vesta Tilley appeared there.

I used to ensconce myself in the glass-walled bar overlooking the stage. It was all gas and gilt, and the brass tags on the counter and walls showed the prices that existed in Edwardian times, and every act was signalled by an illuminated number which appeared on either side of the proscenium. The opening turn was seldom worth watching; it simply enabled latecomers to take their seats without missing much, and the same applied to the act immediately before the interval.

Later I reflected that it resembled my own career in Fleet Street – big headlines followed by down-column paragraphs – and, like the theatre manager, revealed a weakness for nostalgia. It may not have been cakes and ale all the time and there were occasions when the message of the old man who paraded up and down with a 'Prepare To Meet Thy Doom' placard, really seemed prophetic.

It was a feeling shared by most newspapermen. One morning I walked into the Big Room to hear the Editor having a heated exchange with the man who did the horoscope. It seemed odd to me that the Editor, who hammered into us the importance of hard facts, should be so concerned about what the stars foretold. The conversation went something like this:

'Just what have you got against me?'

'Nothing, sir.'

'Then why is my horoscope always so bloody depressing? I'm scared to get out of bed because the day promises to be nothing but a series of disasters.'

The conversation went on in that vein until the bewildered star-gazer asked the Editor when his birthday was. When he was told he relaxed visibly. 'I wasn't getting at you, sir. It just happens to be my wife's birthday.'

From then on the Editor could get up, confident in the knowledge that a happy and rewarding day lay ahead. But life is not an endless summer of cloudless skies, and we all knew that. There is always a bump at the end of the toboggan run. As I so often found out.

For several years I covered Wimbledon fortnight, and enjoyed it so much I used to volunteer for the job. I seldom wrote about the actual tennis – that was left to the experts. My job was to mix with the players and spectators and dig out off-beat stories.

On the first day of the tournament a squad of detectives would arrive to watch out for the 'bustle punchers', the kinky men who used to haunt the outside courts and pester young women and schoolgirls. The name derived from Edwardian days when men would attach a piece of mirror to their shoes so that they could lift the hem of ladies' skirts and get a glimpse of ankle. Somehow the name stuck.

The stories we wrote gave no inkling that such a delightful game as tennis had this murky side to it. They were the days of Georgeous Gussie and her frilly panties; when play was halted on the Centre Court when a man removed his shirt, and the only people who swore were the reporters. Players did not abuse each other, or the referee. We had to rely on less dramatic material, such as a lineswoman who fell asleep, having had a sherry too many.

One afternoon before play was due to start, Terry Fincher

and I were making our way into the All England Club when we spotted a policeman barring admittance to Lady Churchill, whom he had not recognised. Terry took several pictures and we had a front-page show which must have taken the poor man years to live down. Another time I saw Bing Crosby trying to buy a ticket from a tout, and loaned him a Press pass. He rewarded me with a splendid interview.

When John Newcombe won the men's singles, Princess Marina asked him what he was going to do that night and he said, 'Get drunk.' You could take pleasure in chronicling such trivial events. Players in those days were sportsmen and gentlemen, but then a new breed appeared on the scene, who substituted foul mouths for wit, and tantrums for tenacity. I lost interest in Wimbledon.

I have always loved cricket, and often when I was on a late shift spent the afternoon at Lord's, where you could doze off knowing you would not miss much. So when John Young, the Night News Editor, and an afficionado and member of the MCC, said there was an interesting story he wanted me to cover at Lord's, and as England were playing Australia, I jumped at the opportunity. There was a man, he told me, who always occupied the same seat below the scoreboard near the now demolished Tavern. He had never been known to miss a match, but he intrigued members because, throughout the day, at exactly the same times, he would get up and disappear for several minutes. It wasn't to the bar, and it wasn't to the gents.

I duly turned up on the first day and spotted the man immediately. Was it true that he never missed a game at the home of cricket? No, it was not true. He normally supported Surrey.

Where did he nip off to? To telephone his bookmaker.

I phoned John at the end of the day and said the man hadn't turned up. He was even more interested.

I sat through the next day and repeated my story. I would have liked to sit through the entire game, but that I thought would be chancing my arm. However, I did manage day three, and at the end told John the truth.

'Never mind, my dear boy, it could have made a good story.'

I covered the triumphant homecoming of Bobby Moore's West Ham when they won the Cup Final, and 25,000 fans jammed five miles of bunting-festooned streets around the ground, and there was not a bloody nose at the end of it. I did a similar story when Arsenal were victorious, and the photographs that covered the front page depicted just happy jubilant fans. Yet, not too long afterwards, I was reporting the Home Secretary, James Callaghan, promising stern measures to stamp out soccer hooliganism. What had happened to the people on the terraces?

The saddest aspect of my career was when I had to witness the downfall of people who had become personal friends. But I was always uplifted by the incurable optimism of some who accepted failure, but never conceded defeat.

One was the Oscar-winning film producer Herbert Wilcox, who was married to Anna Neagle. Twenty-one years ago I met him after he had left the Bankruptcy Court, said to have amassed debts of £112,317. The man who made *Spring in Park Lane* was now living in a £4-a-week flat at the seaside. Many of his films had been enormous box office successes. *Spring in Park Lane* made a profit of £500,000, *Victoria the Great* £300,000, *Odette* £400,000. Now he was being asked to hand over his four Oscars to his creditors – they were valued at £80 each. Nevertheless his parting words were: 'But I'll make a comeback.'

Money was money then, and I remember filling half a page in the *Express* with a story of the first football pools half-millionaire. 'Half a million crispy oncers,' I wrote, 'you could die of old age just thumbing and fingering your way through that mountain of lolly.'

Today it would make a down-column paragraph.

One of the most remarkable stories I covered was about a young Welsh chap who had gone to Australia, and become homesick for the valleys. So he persuaded three friends to pack him into a crate and send him by air COD from Australia. They crammed him into the wooden crate, along with his suitcase, a pint of water, five biscuits, a pillow, torch, and a hammer with which to force his way out when he arrived at Heathrow. But the plan misfired, and he spent ninety-six hours in the crate which nearly became his coffin. Instead of flying to London, the aircraft went to Los Angeles, where he ended up in the freight shed and spent sixteen hours upside down. He was only rescued when the beam of his torch was spotted through a crack.

But it had taught him a valuable lesson: 'Never travel in a crate marked "Fragile This Side Up". You spend hours standing on your head.'

From the safety of the Press benches, I had seen hundreds of people standing in the dock; but I never envisaged the day when I would be one of them. It happened at Lewes Assizes when I was covering a horse-doping trial. Several people had been charged, but I was solely interested in one member of the ring, a beautiful Belgian woman who had posed as a wealthy buyer and visited stables in order to spy out the land.

Posing as a solicitor's clerk, I went to the cells to sign her up for an exclusive story, but when I emerged from the cell a bell started ringing and I found myself being bundled into line with the accused people. Despite my protests I was not allowed to leave, and I found myself standing in the dock with them. I could see the judge and clerk silently counting, and realising there was one too many. I tried to clamber out, but was pushed back. Then I found a waist-high door and managed to slip out. I headed for the hotel opposite and ordered a nerve-calming drink. Suddenly I heard a voice call out 'You!' and I turned and saw the detective in charge of the case beckoning me with a forefinger. 'Who? Me?' I asked rather pointlessly, as I was the only other person there. 'Yes, you,' he said with that spine-chilling coolness that policemen somehow acquire.

We sat down, and he told me that I had a bit of explaining to do, such as what I was doing in the dock. I explained that, although it looked bad, I had gone to the cells purely to ask the woman if, in the event of her acquittal, she would let me have her exclusive story. At no time had we discussed the case, or what had been said in court. That would have been highly improper. Burning a hole in my pocket was the story I had already written and which she had signed.

'I'll tell it to the judge,' he said in a voice that implied he did not fancy my chances. But I heard no more about it. The story was never used.

The last big trial I covered was what came to be known as 'The Jersey Monster Case', and although headlines tend to exaggerate, this was one occasion when it was an understatement.

Over a period of eleven years, the Channel Island tax haven and holiday resort had been terrorised by a sex pervert who abducted and assaulted women, boys and girls. I went there on a number of occasions to report some fresh attack, but despite the most intensive investigation no arrest was made.

Then late one night a stolen car jumped a red light and a 70-mile-an-hour chase developed as police tried to catch it. When the car crashed and the driver ran away, he was brought down with a Rugby tackle by a young constable. The fleeing man was Edward Paisnel, a forty-six-year-old father of three. He was wearing wristbands – one black, the other white – studded with nails, and a padded coat with more nails protruding from the shoulders and lapels. They were designed to make any pursuer let go, but Rugby players fortunately go for the legs. In his car they found a rubber mask, a woman's black wig, and sashcords. The long search for the Monster was over. His explanation for the odd attire was that he was going to a sex orgy where people did not wish to be recognised. The police then went to his home, where they found a secret room with a shrine, altar and chalice, books on black magic, and more nail-studded clothing.

At his trial he was accused of a series of sex offences against women and children, covering the eleven-year period. He pleaded not guilty, but painstaking police work over the years had not been in vain. Anonymous letters he had sent to the police boasting of his crimes were identified by his stepdaughter. And some of his victims were able to recall the strange attire their assailant had worn. In addition, he was vain enough to have kept a tape-recording of one of his attacks and his victim recognised his voice. He was sentenced to thirty years' imprisonment.

Paisnel was a strange man. Outwardly he loved children, who called him Uncle Ted, but secretly he believed he was descended from the fifteenth-century Baron Gilles de Rais, who kidnapped and murdered children for pleasure, and is thought to be an original of Bluebeard. He also dabbled in

witchcraft, and had a raven outside his house which neighbours thought was a pet, but which to him was the symbol of
death.

The court gave us permission to publish a photograph of his
terrifying clothing, and a picture of the macabre clothing filled
half the front page of the *Express*. Letters flooded in, protesting
at the use of such a horrifying picture – but how else could we
have brought home to our readers the full extent of the man's
evil?

Immediately after the verdict, I hired a lobster boat to take
me out to the barren reef off Jersey known as the Ecrehous, to
break the news to Alphonse le Gastleois, who had been there as
a self-exiled hermit for eleven years. He had gone there when it
was rumoured he was the No. 1 suspect. During an earlier visit
he had told me, 'I thought if I came here and the sex attacks
continued I would automatically clear myself.'

A detective also went out to tell him he was cleared, but he
had no wish to leave. 'I want to be left in peace,' he said.

In the loneliness of the windswept rocks, he had proclaimed
himself King of the Ecrehous. 'I have proved beyond all
question that this is now my property after establishing squat-
ters' rights. I am the law, the police, I am everything.'

He was a man at peace with himself and life.

It had been one of the most exhausting stories I had ever
covered. Apart from the actual case, the Press corps were
invited to numerous parties on an island renowned for its
hospitality and duty-free drink. The police, who had become
personal friends, gave a farewell party the night before we were
due to leave.

We could not wait to get away and resume a life of some
normality, but as we packed our cases the sound of sirens filled
the street outside our hotel – the police had arrived to drive us
to the airport. And when we arrived there a thick fog had
descended and there was no flying. The bar was opened ...

Not long after that story, I took part in another farewell
party – my own.

While I was writing this book I paid a visit to the *Daily Express*
to check some cuttings. I walked from Farringdon Station, and
past Edgar Wallace's plaque, relieved to find it still there, for it

was one of the few things I could connect with my own days in Fleet Street.

In the *Express* Big Room, there was hardly a face I recognised – most of my old colleagues had gone in the latest exodus of voluntary redundancies. Household names had departed, irrespective of talent; so many heads had to go. Just numbers. Some went to other papers, others wiped their feet clean of The Street.

There was no one I knew in the new Poppinjay, which replaced the old Poppins. The same applied to The Bell, and Punch. The Press Club was shuttered and bolted. In one afternoon Fleet Street's history had been obliterated by the auctioneer's hammer. The priceless collection of journalistic memorabilia had been split up and sold to the highest bidder. The Murdoch papers had gone to Wapping, and the *Telegraph* and *Mail* newspapers were due to leave Fleet Street. The exodus had begun. And it is still going on.

My mind went back to the night the *News Chronicle* died. A television reporter, who had once worked in Fleet Street, hit upon the idea of doing a documentary about its dying hours. With police permission, he had part of Fleet Street barricaded off against traffic, and when the cameras focused on him he began his funeral oration: 'Tonight Fleet Street is a sad place ... ' He dried up, and started again with the same result. 'Sod it!' he exclaimed and did it again, and again. A police inspector reminded him that the time was rapidly approaching when he would have to take the barriers away. This time the reporter got it right, but was interrupted by the sound of toppling barriers. Three sozzled reporters from the dead newspaper hugged him and said, 'Come on, join us for a drink.'

Today I cannot imagine television bothering to attend another wake if a newspaper died. Neither can I visualise real tears being shed.

I am not being maudlin, or yearning for a non-recoverable past. I left it with no regrets. But I remember old men who looked back with affection on their days in the mud-clogged trenches of Flanders. It was the camaraderie they missed. Some may consider it strange that that took precedence over the carnage, but memory plays tricks with all of us. And this is how the years have affected my memory when it comes to Fleet Street. Failures? Disappointments? Frustrations? Ruthless bosses? Never! They are figments of my imagination. Watches do stop, and sometimes there is a reluctance to wind them up and catch up with the time.

INDEX